THE LITERARY GUIDE TO THE UNITED STATES

THE
LITERARY GUIDE
TO THE
UNITED STATES

Stewart Benedict
Consultant Editor

Facts On File
119 West 57th Street, New York, N.Y. 10019

THE LITERARY GUIDE TO THE UNITED STATES

Consultant Editor
Stewart Benedict

First published in the United States
in 1981 by **Facts On File, Inc.**

Copyright ©1981 by **Quarto Marketing Ltd.**

Library of Congress Cataloging in Publication Data
Main entry under title:
Literary guide to the United States.

1. Literary landmarks—United States. 2. United States—Description
and travel—1960–   . 3. American literature—History and criticism.
4. Authors, American—Biography. I. Benedict, Stewart H. II. Facts on File, Inc.,
New York.
PS141.L5   810'.9 [B]   80-26823
ISBN 0-87196-304-3

10 9 8 7 6 5 4 3 2 1

The Literary Guide to the United States
was produced and prepared by Quarto Marketing Ltd.
212 Fifth Avenue, New York, New York 10010

Editor: Gene Santoro
Copy Editor: Marie D'Amico
Designer: Elizabeth Fox
Design Assistant: Jack Donaghy

Typesetting by BPE Graphics
Printed and bound in the United States
by Maple-Vail Group

CONTENTS

NOTES ON CONTRIBUTORS

INTRODUCTION

I
NEW YORK & ENVIRONS/1

*Sleepy Hollow & Manahatta: Irving, Cooper, Melville,
Whitman... Elegant Fifth Avenue... the lower East Side slums...
Greenwich Village bohemians; politics & art... The Harlem
Renaissance... The Wits of the Algonquin Round Table... Changing
Scene... The Beats... Newark, Philadelphia, Pittsburgh & Baltimore*

II
NEW ENGLAND/51

*The Puritan Imagination... Maine: E.A. Robinson & Harriet Beecher
Stowe... Robert Frost & New Hampshire... Hawthorne & Melville...
Emily Dickinson...Cambridge... The Transcendentalists...Salem...
John Greenleaf Whittier...Concord...Boston...
Provincetown... The Hartford Wits...Wallace Stevens*

III
THE MIDWEST/87

*The Indians & Discovery Narratives... The Frontier Civilized:
Frances Trollope & Harriet Martineau... Hamlin Garland & Populism...
The Chicago Robin's Egg Renaissance: Dreiser, Dell, Sandburg...
The Depression & the documentary... The Contemporary Midwest*

IV
THE SOUTH & BORDER STATES/129

*The Fundamental Themes...The Dismal Swamp...Cultured
Charleston... The Scars of Georgia: McCullers, O'Connor, Caldwell,
Chandler Harris...Florida's Writers...Mississippi Myths:
Faulkner, Welty, Wright...New Orleans...The Fugitive Poets*

V
THE MOUNTAIN STATES & SOUTHWEST/159

*Ned Buntline & Buffalo Bill...The Virginian... Zane Grey...
Taos: Mable Dodge meets D.H. Lawrence...Death Comes
For the Archbishop...Texas & Oklahoma: Edna Ferber,
Woody Guthrie, Larry McMurty...A.B. Guthrie &
Vardis Fisher...Sam Clemens...The Ox-Bow Incident...
Oscar Wilde in the mining camps...James Michener*

VI
CALIFORNIA & THE FAR WEST/193

*The Yankees Arrive: Dana, Harte, Twain...Life Amongst the Modocs...
The Landscape Envisioned...King, Muir, & Austin...
Frank Norris & Jack London...The Coastal Poets...The Valley:
Steinbeck & Saroyan...Hollywood...Watching the
Detectives: Hammett, Chandler, MacDonald...
The San Francisco Renaissance...Didion, Kesey, & LeGuin*

BIBLIOGRAPHY/234

SUGGESTED FURTHER READING/239

INDEX/242

SOME NOTES ON THE CONTRIBUTORS

NEW YORK. Stewart Benedict.
Stewart Benedict received his M.A. from Johns Hopkins University, and did further graduate work at New York University. He has written *A Teacher's Guide to Drama* and *A Teacher's Guide to Poetry*, and has also published literary and scholarly articles in *South Atlantic Quarterly, Claremont Quarterly*, and *Papers of the Michigan Academy of Sciences, Arts and Letters*. His field is comparative literature and his special interest is drama.

NEW ENGLAND. Eugene and Patricia Flinn.
Eugene Flinn holds the doctorate from St. John's University; his dissertation was called *Ambrose Bierce and the Journalization of the American Short Story*. He has taught American literature and worked in public relations. Patricia Flinn holds the doctorate in drama from New York University, and has taught American literature at Stevens Institute of Technology and Montclair State College.

THE MIDWEST. Jon Spayde.
Jon Spayde was born in Iowa City, Iowa. After studying modern and classical Japanese in Illinois, Wisconsin, Indiana, and Minnesota, he enrolled in Harvard College. On his graduation he lived in Minneapolis for a year, worked as an actor and writer in Cambridge, Massachusetts, and did his graduate study at Stanford University. He has written on Japanese and American popular culture for *Tabloid* and *In These Times*.

THE SOUTH & BORDER STATES. Butler Brewton.
Butler Brewton received his B.A. from Benedict College in his native state of South Carolina, and the doctorate from Rutgers University. His dissertation was titled *Richard Wright's Thematic Treatment of Women in Native Son, Uncle Tom's Children, and Black Boy*. His poetry has been published in *Blacklash* and *Rustlings*, and he was a contributor to the *Modern Century Encyclopedia*.

THE MOUNTAIN STATES & SOUTHWEST. Curtis Casewit.
Curtis Casewit born and educated in Europe, has taught creative writing at the Denver campus of Colorado University since 1964 and has served as a lecturer at Colorado Women's College. He has written 25 books, among them *Sagas of the Sierras* and *The Studio Book of Colorado*, along with hundreds of magazine and newspaper articles. Researcher Ben Daviss is a nationally known magazine and travel writer. He is now at work on a series of historical books about Colorado and the West.

CALIFORNIA & THE FAR WEST. Bill Logan.
Bill Logan has a B.A. from Columbia University and an M.A. in comparative literature from Stanford University. He has lived in the Mojave Desert, the Ojai Valley, and the San Francisco Bay area. He has translated the works of Federico Garcia Lorca and Pedro Calderon de la Barca.

INTRODUCTION

America has always occupied a special place in the world's imagination. Christopher Columbus sailed into it only after he imagined it to be the Far East of fabled riches; and he died before he was corrected by the facts. A similar misconception led to the misnaming of the American natives; the name Indians stuck anyway. Even later, for the waves of immigrants who abandoned homes and ways of life to go there, the United States was open territory, a place where the imagination could stretch hopeful and unrestricted.

And so it has been also for the writers who have lived and worked there. Each of them presents in his or her work an aspect of American life; yet each vision is unique and necessarily only a fragment, like the shards of a broken mirror whose every reflection seems complete in itself but is only a part of a larger picture. As a result, it seems that American writers must go to great lengths to claim a special validity for their visions, however fragmentary. "A nation," wrote Mark Twain, "is only an individual multiplied"; and as this most American writer knew, the special nature of America can be found in its emphasis on the individual and the particular. This emphasis finds at least part of its cause in the diversity of cultural heritages that have come to call the United States home. This diversity, and the individual's relationship to it, combine to produce a kind of cultural confusion that may well be singularly American: there is no easily identifiable or "official" culture that the individual can automatically feel a part of (or, on the other hand, reject); there is no really consistent cultural framework. In literary terms, this means that each American writer must in effect imagine his or her own intellectual genealogy virtually from scratch. This dilemma sets American literature apart from European literature, whose writers seem more able to draw confidently on long established traditions and languages. For example: French writers have a recognizable and distinctive cultural heritage encompassing Montaigne and Foucault; even the most contemporary English writer operates within the language shaped by Chaucer, Shakespeare, or Dickens. On the other hand, when American writers envision something called "America," they must recreate a single image—and a language for that image—from the spectrum of cultural, racial, and geographical styles that is America.

This sense of incompleteness and arbitrariness regarding an American cultural identity results in a pressure to redefine the individual with respect to place. It is axiomatic that Americans are a people "on the move," that they uproot themselves more frequently than other peoples whose ties to the places of their origins are stronger, more durable, more woven into the particular texture of their own individual histories: "The land was ours before we were the land's" is how Robert Frost put it. One consequence of this need to locate oneself in some sort of context is that feeling of improvisation that runs through much of American literature, that sense of daring some unknown frontier whose real boundaries can only be imagined. "America is a poem in our eyes; its ample geography dazzles the imagination, and it will not wait long for meters." So wrote Ralph Waldo Emerson, who early on in American literary history set out with so much apparent authority on a punningly verbal journey through a cunningly imagined landscape. Like the other writers treated in this book, Emerson was too clever a craftsman not to realize that even so vast an imagined landscape must be firmly planted somehow in a particular place.

It should be clear by now that to grasp an American writer's sense of place is no easy task; and yet the effort is essential to a fuller understanding and enjoyment of American literature. This, in part, is the motivation behind *The Literary Guide to the United States*.

Like the authors they discuss, the six contributors to the *Literary Guide* have inevitably had to make their own selections—which authors to include, which quotations to use—in order to tell their own versions of the many stories that could be literary America. Since the theme of this book is generous in scope (like the land itself), those stories vary widely from chapter to chapter. Some focus more on the physical place; others have used history and geography to construct chronicles of their region's literature. In this they accurately reflect the variety of both the land and its literature, and guide the reader to both in a way that informs and delights, amuses and instructs.

NEW YORK & ENVIRONS

STEWART BENEDICT

IN ITS BEGINNINGS, NEW YORK'S literary imagination reflected the classic tension between urban and rural ways of life. The majority of the Founding Fathers, Jefferson most prominently, regarded cities as moral sewers, open sinkholes in which every type of vice, corruption, and sin mixed and multiplied in a dangerous sludge. The true American, said Jefferson, was the stalwart and sturdy yeoman farmer with his self-sufficient bit of land: he had just enough property to confer on him a true sense of social responsibility, but not enough to cause his sense of the value of labor to grow slack.

The Dutch patroons who settled on vast estates over the rich Hudson River Valley would hardly qualify as yeoman farmers, but they looked back with incurable nostalgia to those early settlements around Manahatta; a fondness reflected in the work of the first American writer to secure an international reputation, who sets some of his most enduring creations not at the infant metropolis at the river's mouth but further north in the rich valley, in a mythic and pastoral past that is gently satirized:

> In the bosom of one of those spacious coves which indent
> the eastern shore of the Hudson, at that broad expansion
> of the river denominated by the ancient Dutch navigators
> the Tappan Zee...there lies a small market-town by the
> name of Tarry Town....Not far from this village, perhaps
> about two miles, there is a little valley...among high hills,
> which is one of the quietest places in the world....From
> the listless repose of the place...this sequestered glen has
> long been known by the name of Sleepy Hollow.

This valley was the home of Washington Irving, creator of the hapless Ichabod Crane. Irving's prestige in the region was enormous; the name of a nearby town, Deerman, was changed to Irvington in 1854. But despite the close relationship between Irving's most famous work and the place he lived, it had really been his home only after 1836, for he was a native of New York City.

The metropolis where he was born numbered about 30,000 people (the size of Minot, North Dakota today), and almost all of them lived at the tip of Manhattan, south of the modern Chambers Street. Just to the north were the broken remains of the palisades erected against the Indians in earlier years. In the area now bounded by White, Leonard, Lafayette, and Mulberry Streets was the Collect, a pond surrounded by swampland, an ideal breeding-spot for the mosquitoes who brought periodic epidemics of yellow fever. The outlet for the Collect was a stream that meandered along the line of the modern Canal Street.

If Irving's more famous creations people the Hudson Valley, his first efforts—and indeed, his whole satirical bent—were clearly formed by a sophisticated urban sensibility. Pastoral myths are, after all, the classic form in which urban writers imagine rural life—stylized, simple, nostalgic, free of the problems that clog urban life.

He first came to public attention as an author with the "Letters of Jonathan Oldstyle, Gent.," published in 1802–3 in the *Morning Chronicle*, a pro-Aaron Burr newspaper edited by Irving's brother Peter. In these short pieces, the conservative young writer satirized New York society of his time, with special attention to the theater, which he had attended and loved since childhood.

Irving went to Europe from 1804 to 1806 and on his return was admitted to the bar, although he evidently never practiced. In 1807–8 he, his brother William, and his brother-in-law J.K. Paulding published *Salmagundi; or, The Whim-Whams and Opinions of Launcelot Langstaff, Esq., and Others.* One satire, Selection XII, deals with residential snobbery:

> Broadway....great difference in the gentility of streets....
> a man who resides in Pearl-street, or Chatham-row, derives
> no kind of dignity from his domicil, but place him in a
> certain part of Broadway....any where between the Bat-
> tery and Wall-street, and he straightway becomes entitled
> to figure in the beaumonde.

Directly after *Salmagundi* was published, Irving began work on the book that made his reputation, *History of New York*, a satirical study allegedly written by the Dutch-American scholar Diedrich Knickerbocker. On the surface, it discusses the years when the city was under Dutch control, but in fact it was intended as a critique of Jeffersonian democracy.

Irving's most distinguished contemporary, James Fenimore Cooper, launched his literary career in the town of Scarsdale. The *Leather Stocking Tales* allowed Cooper's imagination to explore the edge of rural life, the quintessentially American myth of the frontier, just as that frontier was extending farther west and that way of life was vanishing.

Born in New Jersey, Cooper was taken as an infant to the family estate in Cooperstown, the city now best known, rather ironically, as the home of baseball's Hall of Fame. Here his father, Judge William Cooper—no yeoman farmer he—owned 750,000 acres on the shore of Otsego Lake. The family estate appears in his 1823 Leather-Stocking Tale, *The Pioneers*, under the name of Templeton, where the region is described this way:

> Near the center of the State of New York lies an extensive district of country whose surface is a succession of... mountains and valleys. It is among these hills that the Delaware takes its rise; and flowing from the limpid lakes and thousand springs of this region, the numerous sources of the Susquehanna meander through the valleys, until, uniting their streams, they form one of the proudest rivers of the United States.... Beautiful and thriving villages are found interspersed along the margins of the small lakes, or situated at those points of the streams which are favorable for manufacturing; and neat and comfortable farms, with every indication of wealth about them, are scattered profusely through the vales, and even to the mountain tops.

One night, while he was reading a novel to his wife, he asserted that he could write a better one. She challenged him to do just that, and the result was his first book, *Precaution*, a work that most critics agree could not have been a vast improvement over the novel which prompted it.

The next year, however, he published *The Spy*, which made his reputation. It is a tale of the American Revolution set in Westchester County. (Major John Andre, who negotiated with Benedict Arnold, was captured, tried, and executed in Westchester, and, in fact, the tree from which he was hanged also figures in Irving's story of Ichabod Crane.) Cooper used Westchester again in his 1845 novel *Satanstoe*, the first work in the trilogy called the Littlepage Manuscripts.

> There is a tradition... which says that the Father of Lies, on a particular occasion when he was violently expelled from certain roistering taverns in the New Netherlands, made his exit by this well-known dangerous pass (Hell Gate),... leaving behind him... all the whirlpools and rocks that render navigation so difficult in that celebrated strait.

In his later years, Cooper authored a series of books from *A Letter to His Countrymen* (1834) to *Home as Found* (1838), that brought him years of trouble and litigation, for in them he defended the ideal of an aristocracy and attacked by name some of those who disagreed with him. Cooper was a devotee of the American system and had even written a trilogy while abroad that upheld democratic liberalism. But, as one critic put it, "his dignified agrarian republicanism had little in common with the coonskin democracy of Andrew Jackson," and he found egalitarianism not at all to his liking.

Although he won most of the lawsuits brought against him, he alienated a large segment of the press in the process and became what one writer has called "the most popular author and the most unpopular man in the United States." Perhaps because of that, he withdrew to the family estate in 1839, where he wrote steadily until his death in 1851.

A writer who spent many of his most productive years in New York was Edgar Allan Poe, whose life provides a sharp contrast to the opulence which characterized Cooper's. Poe lived briefly in the city in 1831, after his dismissal from West Point, and published *Poems by Edgar A. Poe*. He returned for another short stay in 1837-8. After a period in Philadelphia he was back in Manhattan once more in 1844 with his wife; they were later joined by his mother-in-law. When he got back to New York for what were to be some of the most tragic years of his life, he was optimistic. In a letter to his mother-in-law dated April 7, 1844, he wrote:

> I went up Greenwich Street and soon found a boarding-house [at No. 130]. It is just before you get to Cedar Street on the West side.... It has brown stone steps with a porch with brown pillars. "Morrison" is the name on the door.... The house is old and looks buggy....
>
> Last night, for supper we had the nicest tea you ever drank...tea cakes...a great dish of elegant ham, and 2 of cold veal...No fear of starving here. For breakfast we had excellent-flavored coffee....I never sat down to a more plentiful or nicer breakfast....Sis [his wife] is delighted, and we are both in excellent spirits. She has coughed hardly any and had no night sweat.
>
> We have now got $4 and a half left. Tomorrow I am going to try & borrow $3—so that I may have a fortnight to go upon. I feel in excellent spirits & haven't drunk a drop—so that I hope to get out of trouble.

For about a year he was a literary critic of the *New York Mirror*, where he created a furor by accusing Longfellow of plagiarism. While he was editor of the *Broadway Journal*, he and his family were living in a cottage in the Bronx, now moved from its original location and placed at 2640 Grand

Concourse. They were so destitute that his mother-in-law was forced to beg food money from the neighbors in the isolated rural community; his wife died of tuberculosis during the winter. Yet the artist's creative urge continued, and during this trying period he wrote "Annabel Lee," "Ulalume," and "The Bells." He left New York for Richmond, Virginia in 1849.

A native who established a major reputation and then faded from public notice was Herman Melville, born at 6 Pearl Street, near State Street, in 1819. In 1847, married and returned from his travels to Manhattan, he lived at 103 Fourth Avenue in Greenwich Village, where he produced *Mardi*, *Redburn*, and *White-Jacket*, and foreshadowed some of the political and social views that later inhabitants of that section of town would also hold. As he wrote to his cousin:

> It appears that I used in my letter to you the expression "people of leisure." If I did, it was a faulty expression—as applied in that case. I doubtless meant people the disposition of whose time is not subject to another.... Whoever is not in the possession of leisure can hardly be said to possess independence. They talk of the *dignity of work*. Bosh. True Work is the *necessity* of poor humanity's

Dockworkers in a typical scene from the mid-19th century: it would have been a familiar sight to Melville.
Harper's Weekly

Walt Whitman in 1887, confined by ill health to Camden.
New York Public Library

earthly condition. The dignity is in leisure. Besides, 99 hundreths of all the *work* done in the world is either foolish and unnecessary, or harmful and wicked.

In 1863 Melville was appointed a deputy inspector at the New York customhouse, living at 104 West 26th Street and often working on the docks at the foot of Gansevoort Street. In 1891 he died in obscurity.

Born on Long Island, on State Route 110 in Huntington Station, Walt Whitman taught at Smithtown, Woodbury, and Whitestone. He lived in Brooklyn for a time in 1839 and moved to Manhattan in 1841 to work for the *Aurora and Union*, and lived at 12 Centre Street. Like many newspapermen of the time, he shifted from paper to paper, finally becoming editor of the *Brooklyn Eagle* from 1846 to 1848 and later of the *Brooklyn Times* and the *Brooklyn Freeman*. While serving in this latter capacity, he lived at 106 Myrtle Avenue.

Whitman's imagination sought to reconcile the irreconcilable, to fuse in his verse an America that was rapidly becoming more and more polarized—by slavery, by disparities in wealth, by increasing industrialization and urbanization—so that what he foresaw as a shining future could be realized. The imagery of "Manahatta" reflects this attempt to unify a multiplicity of diverse fragments, as Whitman seeks to reconcile nature and that very unnatural creature, man, and his unnatural creations, epitomized by the city:

I was asking for something specific and perfect for my
city,
Whereupon lo! upsprang the aboriginal name.

Now I see what there is in a name, a word, liquid, sane,
unruly, musical, self-sufficient,
I see that the word of my city is that word from of old,
Because I see that word nested in nests of water-bays,
superb,
Rich, hemm'd thick all around with sailships and
steamships, an island sixteen miles long,
solid-founded,
Numberless crowded streets, high growths of iron,
slender, strong, light, splendidly uprising toward clear
skies,
Tides swift and ample, well-loved by me, toward
sundown,
The flowing sea-currents, the little islands, larger
adjoining islands, the heights, the villas.
The countless masts, the white shore-steamers, the
lighters, the ferry-boats, the black sea-steamers
well-model'd,
The down-town streets, the jobbers' houses of business,
the houses of business of the ship-merchants and
money-brokers, the river-streets....

From a far different background, one of inherited wealth and gentility,
Henry James was born at 21 Washington Place in Greenwich Village in
1843. The city into which he was born had about half a million residents
and was quickly spreading northward, with some citizens building homes
even to the north of the city reservoir, located at the corner of Fifth Avenue
and 42nd Street where the main branch of the public library now stands.
Since the southern tip of Manhattan was increasingly being filled by banks,
department stores, and other businesses, residents in that part of the city
were being forced out.

In 1847, after a trip to Europe and a brief move to Albany, the James
family returned to Manhattan and bought a house at 58 West 14th Street,
on the northern edge of the Village. The world of the child Henry and his
older brother William was pretty well circumscribed by those geographical
—and social—limits. Nor did they associate with everybody even in that
fashionable part of the city. The unfolding of the city into larger and larger
spaces and the increasing complexity of urban life find a mirror in James's
complicated—some might call it tortuous—prose. An older Henry James,
living in Europe, looked back at his childhood world in *A Small Boy and
Others*:

*In 1848 New York was still a small town dominated by church spires: its famous
skyscraper skyline was yet to come.*
Museum of the City of New York

> I see a small and compact and ingenuous society, screened
> in somehow conveniently from north and west, but open
> wide to the east and comparatively to the south and,
> though perpetually moving up Broadway, none the less
> constantly and delightfully walking down it. Broadway
> was the feature and the artery, the joy and the adventure of
> one's childhood, and it stretched, and prodigiously, from
> Union Square to Barnum's great American Museum by
> City Hall.

Urban space, congested and tight, has always demanded open space as
compensation, a place to unwind and relax; but the end of the 19th century
in America saw a dramatic redefinition of exactly what those places would
be like. In place of the paved piazzas of Renaissance Italian cities or the
broad boulevards and vast *places* of rebuilt Paris, both typically urban
features in Europe, the village green or common, a simple affair of grass and
walkways, furnished the kernel around which the typical American city
grew. As the country became urbanized and industrialized, rural landscapes became scarcer and more romanticized. So it was that New York
hired architects at the end of the 19th century (among them Frederick Law
Olmstead, who designed Central Park and Prospect Park) to create elaborately sculpted pastoral settings designed to be dropped into the midst of
the thickening urban landscape. James was especially fond of Washington
Square, and in his 1881 novel of that name interrupted his narrative for this
excursus:

I know not whether it is owing to the tenderness of early associations, but this portion of New York appears to many persons the most delectable. It has a kind of established repose which is not of frequent occurrence in other quarters of the long, shrill city; it has a riper, richer, more honorable look than any of the upper ramifications of the great longitudinal thoroughfare—the look of having had something of a social history....

Yet he did not find it without blemishes, as this comparison with Union Square (at 14th Street) shows:

We seemed to have come up from a world of quieter harmonies, the world of Washington Square and thereabouts, so decent in its dignity, so instinctively unpretentious.... The ancient name of the Parade-ground still hung about the central space, and the ancient wooden palings, then so generally accounted proper for central spaces... affected even my innocent childhood as rustic and mean. Union Square, at the top of the Avenue...was encased, more smartly, in iron rails and further adorned with a fountain and an aged amateur looking constable.

Thus New York City provided material for the novelist even though he had little contact with it after 1855, when his family went to Europe. Whenever he did return for one of his infrequent visits, he stayed at 21 East 11th Street with Edith Wharton's sister-in-law.

Edith Wharton was herself the product of a background very similar to James's; she was the daughter of a family with wealth and social position, related to several of the city's first families. Her first long novel, *The Valley of Decision,* was published in 1902, and her reputation grew in 1905 with *The House of Mirth,* in which she wrote about the world where she had grown up, a world where "persons...lived in an atmosphere of faint implications and pale delicacies" and had "always lived well, dressed expensively, and done little else."

She describes one aspect of their social activity in this brief passage:

The holidays had gone by and the season was beginning. Fifth Avenue had become a nightly torrent of carriages surging upward to the fashionable quarters of the Park, where illuminated windows and outspread awnings betokened the usual routine of hospitality. Other tributary currents crossed the main stream, bearing their freight to the theaters, restaurants or opera; and Mrs. Peniston [the heroine's guardian], from the secluded watch-tower of her upper window, could tell to a nicety just when the chronic volume of sound was increased by the influx setting toward a...ball, or when the multiplication of wheels meant merely that the opera was over, or that there was a big supper at Sherry's.

Mrs. Wharton moved to France in 1907, but returned to the society of her formative years in her Pulitzer Prize-winning novel *The Age of Innocence* in 1920. There can be found a jarring juxtaposition; the old family homes in University Place and lower Fifth Avenue:

These were of the purest 1830, with a grim harmony of cabbage-rose-garlanded carpets, rose-wood consoles, round-arched fireplaces with black marble mantels, and immense glazed bookcases of mahogany....

and an apartment in an area beyond the pale taken by one of the more unconventional characters:

The peeling stucco house with a giant wisteria throttling its feeble cast-iron balcony...far down West Twenty-third Street....
It was certainly a strange quarter...Small dress-makers, bird-stuffers and "people who wrote" were...neighbors.

STRANGE QUARTER INDEED; but while the privileged few were promenading down Fifth Avenue and cultivating everything that was refined, there were whole sections of Manhattan to the far east and west where the city's poor struggled to stay alive. These "greenhorns," as the recently arrived immigrants were called, tumbled into and redefined urban American, especially New York, life—first the Irish, then the Germans, the Jews, and finally the Italians. Between 1881 and 1900, most of the nine million immigrants arriving in the United States landed in New York and many settled there. The lower East Side, that section of the city east of Third Avenue and south of 14th Street, housed—if you could call it that—a large number of these latest dreamers of the American dream. Huddled in overcrowded tenements, they earned money by doing piecework for the garment trade, buying and selling rags and junk, or running fruit and vegetable stands and other small retail businesses from pushcarts that almost became a trademark of the area. The urban landscape became denser and denser, more European, for the immigrant poor—Jefferson would have been horrified at both their numbers and their lack of property—while the rich built their brownstones farther uptown and retreated to the created wilderness of Central Park for entertainment and relaxation.

In his 1872 study, *The Dangerous Classes of New York*, Charles Loring Brace quotes a visitor of the Children's Aid Society:

> In a dark cellar filled with smoke, there sleep, all in one room, with no kind of partition dividing them, two men with their wives, a girl of thirteen or fourteen, two men and a large boy of about seventeen years of age, a mother with two more boys, one about ten years old and one large boy of fifteen; another woman with two boys, nine and eleven years of age—in all, fourteen persons.

Brace reports on his own research:

> On the eastern side of the city, in the neighborhood of Fortieth Street, is a village of squatters, which enjoys the title of "Dutch Hill." The inhabitants are not, however, "Dutch," but mainly poor Irish, who have taken temporary possession of unused sites on a hill, and have erected shanties which serve at once for pig-pens, hen-coops, bed-rooms, and living-rooms....the filth and wretchedness in which they sometimes live are beyond description.

Jacob Riis had emigrated from his native Copenhagen with the goal of becoming a carpenter, but the America of 1870 that he found was deep in the grip of depression. Homeless, hungry, jobless, Riis tramped around New York for three years until he finally got a job with a New York news association. In 1877 he became a police reporter for the *New York Tribune*, Horace Greeley's crusading paper, and the Associated Press Bureau; and as a result he spent a great deal of time at police headquarters on Mulberry Street, then the center of the lower East Side slums. From the time of the first waves of immigration in the early 19th century, landlords had overbuilt the lower East Side, sub-dividing tenement houses into increasingly small and illegal cubicles, and had herded the successive shiploads of Irish, German, Jewish, and Italian immigrants into tiny, airless, lightless, and unsanitary apartments where the rents were too high for individual families. This described a typical situation:

> "In a room not thirteen feet either way slept twelve men and women, two or three in bunks set in a sort of alcove, the rest on the floor."

Riis's hardhitting articles for the *Tribune* were crucial in causing the appointment in 1884 of the Tenement House Commission, which led to the abolition of rear tenements, the redesign of living quarters, and the opening of playgrounds. (In honor of Riis's commitment to the creation of playgrounds and parks throughout the city, Riis Park in Brooklyn was named after him.)

How the Other Half Lives was published in 1890, to a broad and responsive audience that included the young Theodore Roosevelt, who, as New York City police commissioner, shut down the police lodging houses where the young immigrant Riis and thousands like him had had to spend terrible and crowded nights. Not that Riis's own crusade was free from blindness—some, at least, of the prejudices of his time were his own, as the following excerpt indicates:

> Like the Chinese, the Italian is a born gambler. His soul is in the game from the moment the cards are on the table, and very frequently his knife is in it too before the game is ended. No Sunday has passed in New York since "the Bend" became a suburb of Naples without one or more of these murderous affrays coming to the notice of the police.

But more than the text, passionate, committed, and laden with irrefutable facts as it was, the photographs that Riis learned to take dramatized vividly, graphically, desperately, the plight of the slumdwellers. Pictures, the journalist was quick to realize, were worth countless words to a deaf world; and so he bought a camera and lugged it around on his nighttime prowlings.

This was the New York that fostered a school of writing devoted to realism under the tutelage of William Dean Howells, and later developed into the political phenomenon called muckraking. These writers (most of whom lived around Gramercy Park—by a historical irony, the only park within New York City to remain locked behind beautiful wrought-iron gates for which only the wealthy local residents have keys) were interested in depicting the deprivations and poverty of the folk squeezed into lightless nooks around town, rather than the Fifth Avenue promenades. Nor were all the new urban poor immigrants from abroad: many of them, like the writers who wrote about them, were drawn to New York by hopes of success or fame or money.

Howells, famous for *The Rise of Silas Lapham,* had felt his realistic fiction pulled increasingly toward a socialistic viewpoint because of his reactions to the Haymarket Riot convictions, the influence of Tolstoy's Christian radicalism, and his reading of social reformers like Henry George. From his editor's chair at *Harper's Monthly* and his cultural position as preeminent American man of letters, he championed such writers as Mark Twain, Hamlin Garland, Frank Norris, and Stephen Crane.

Crane converted the ragged world of the non-rich into pungent fiction. Born in New Jersey into a family of writers (his father was a Methodist minister who published religious tracts; his mother was the daughter of a clergyman who edited the *Christian Advocate* and the *Methodist Quarterly Review*; his brothers Jonathan and Wilbur became journalists, as did he himself) Crane used his journalist's eye to record what he saw.

After attending Lafayette College and Syracuse University, he went to New York, where he did some reporting for the *Herald* and the *Tribune*, while living at various spots on the lower East Side. There he wrote and published privately under a pseudonym his first book, *Maggie: A Girl of the Streets*, which depicts the tragedy of a girl who becomes a prostitute and then commits suicide. He sent a copy to Hamlin Garland, who suggested that he send one to Howells as well. Howells read it, loved it, befriended Crane, and promoted the book because of its zealous, even painful, realism. Here, for example, is how Crane describes Maggie's home:

> Eventually they [Maggie's brother and father] entered a dark region where, from a careening building, a dozen gruesome doorways gave up loads of babies to the street and the gutter. A wind of early autumn raised yellow dust from cobbles and swirled it against a hundred windows. Long streamers of garments fluttered from fire-escapes. In all unhandy places there were buckets, brooms, rags and bottles.... A thousand odours of cooking food came forth to the street. The building quivered and creaked from the weight of humanity stamping about in its bowels.

Despite Howells's boosting, *Maggie* was too realistic for its time and was a resounding failure. It was reissued, however, after Crane achieved success with his more idealized *The Red Badge of Courage* two years later.

By the turn of the century when William Sydney Porter—his famous pseudonym is O. Henry—was living in Gramercy Park, New York had swollen into the city of *The Four Million*, as he called his first collection of stories. His fatalism, his sense of whimsy and irony, his surprise endings, all mark his voice as urban and sophisticated in ways that the following excerpt demonstrates:

> Silent, grim, colossal, the big city has ever stood against its revilers. They call it hard as iron; they say that no pulse of pity beats in its bosom; they compare its streets with lonely forests and deserts of lava. But beneath the hard crust of the lobster is found a delectable and luscious food. Perhaps a different simile would have been wiser. Still, nobody should take offense. We would call no one a lobster without good and sufficient claws.

Whimsical, fatalistic, and sophisticated as he was, Porter also had, like Crane, an acute vision of the daily life of the not-rich: the opposite of a

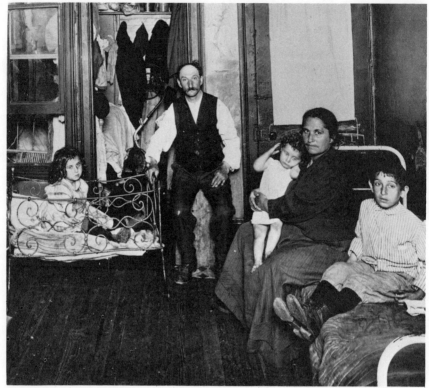

*One of Jacob Riis's most famous photographs, showing all too vividly a typical tenement
living situation.*
Museum of the City of New York

Jamesian concern, just as Porter's short jabbing sentences and vignette-like
stories were the opposite of the carefully cadenced and elaborated intrica-
cies of James's sentences and narratives. His interests lay almost entirely in
"strange quarters"; perhaps partly because of his own rather unfair convic-
tion and subsequent imprisonment on charges of embezzling when he was
young.

> The Blue Light Drugstore is downtown between the
> Bowery and First Avenue, where the distance between the
> two streets is the shortest. The Blue Light does not
> consider that pharmacy is a thing of bric-a-brac, scent and
> ice-cream soda. If you ask it for a pain-killer it will not give
> you a bonbon.
> The Blue Light scorns the labor-saving arts of modern
> pharmacy. It macerates its opium and percolates its own
> laudanum and paregoric.... The store is on a corner about
> which coveys of ragged-plumed, hilarious children play

and become candidates for the cough drops and soothing syrups that wait for them inside.

In the 1880s and 1890s, the lower East Side of Manhattan was largely Jewish, and no one wrote about it more vividly than Abraham Cahan. Born in Russia in 1860, he came to this country in 1882 and 14 years later wrote his first novel, *Yekl, A Tale of the New York Ghetto.* In this passage he describes a walk his hero, Jake, is taking to Suffolk Street:

> He had to pick and nudge his way through dense swarms of bedraggled half-naked humanity; past garbage barrels rearing their overflowing contents in sickening piles, and lining the streets in malicious suggestion of rows of trees; underneath tiers and tiers of fire escapes, barricaded and festooned with mattresses, pillows, and feather-beds not yet gathered in for the night. The pent-in sultry atmosphere was laden with nausea and pierced with a discordant and, as it were, plaintive buzz....

The following year he founded the *Jewish Daily Forward,* which became America's most successful Yiddish newspaper.

A masterpiece of American literature, neglected until Alfred Kazin helped rescue it from obscurity, is *Call It Sleep* by Henry Roth. Roth's lower East Side may have expanded further north and may be two or three decades later than Cahan's, but the similarities are striking. Here his young hero's family comes to Manhattan:

> It was a new and violent world.... Here in 9th Street it wasn't the sun that swamped one as one left the doorway, it was sound—an avalanche of sound. There were countless children, there were countless baby carriages, there were countless mothers.... On Avenue D horse-cars clattered and banged. Avenue D was thronged with beer wagons, garbage carts and coal trucks.... Beyond Avenue D, at the end of a stunted, ruined block that began with shacks and smithies and seltzer bottling works and ended in a junk heap, was the East River on which many boat horns sounded.

This, of course, was the New York landscape familiar to "those huddled masses, yearning to breathe free"—not the small and self-contained world of lower Fifth Avenue, summers in Newport, and frequent jaunts to Europe.

THE VERY DENSITY OF NEW YORK'S LANDSCAPE, the juxtaposition of so many varied cultures and languages and dreams, produced misery to be sure, but a deep vitality and energy as well, one which drew its strength from the adversity and diversity that were its bases. Movement, color, smells, sound, ideas—life was rich in intensity if poor in almost everything else. Writing in New York meant feeling your imagination fired on the thick heat generated by its life. "The city," wrote Lincoln Steffens, "is human nature posing nude"—and by the city he did not mean the world north of Washington Square. As police reporter for the *New York Post*, Steffens haunted the Bowery, the lower East Side, the Greenwich Village tenements; and so it was inevitable that he would meet Jacob Riis. Thus it was during the 1890s that the Danish immigrant showed the young immigrant from California that a reporter should not only report what happened, but make it happen as well. Riis could point to what he had wrought—the changes in housing laws, the creation of parks and play-grounds, the complete revamping of the city's water supply system when water contaminated by sewage threatened some two million people with cholera.

Steffens sought to convert Riis's sense of sympathy into a method of political and social investigation, and thus to place investigative reporting on a more scientific plane. Steffens seemed able to approach the slum-dwellers less as an outsider than Riis, which is especially odd since Riis had actually lived the life of the slum poor, while Steffens came from a well-to-do California family that could afford, among other things, to finance for him an extended time of study in German and English universities. Compare this segment to Riis's on Little Italy to see the difference:

> You may make a detour, too, through Mulberry Street and
> see the great stalwart laborers of Italy lying half awake,
> bathing in the sunlight on benches, stoops, and on the
> sidewalks. And they are not mere loafers. They are men
> who work in season. When they have nothing to do they
> do nothing calmly and pleasantly. Their women gossip on
> their haunches in the alleys and on the curbs, while the
> children creep about in the gutters or play out under the
> horses' hooves. This also is not work and neither is it
> misery. It is only not your idea of living.

It was during the period at the turn of the century, while he was an editor, along with Ida Tarbell and Roy Stannard Baker, on *McClure's Magazine*, that Steffens perfected the writing technique its critics dubbed muckrak-ing. This "scientific method" of Steffens's seems to have really been more of a moral stance that fused a kind of Christian activism, inspired by Tolstoy and Henry George, among others; a brand of utopian anarchism evolved from the long discussions Steffens had with Abraham Cahan, whose own writings about the lower East Side were informed by Marx, Bakunin, and Kropotkin; and an inordinate and dangerous admiration for the "strong man" who could, in times of stress, simply bypass the laws that inadvertently or not allowed graft and corruption to rot the American system—an admiration that ultimately led Steffens to support, in turn, both Lenin and Mussolini.

If his own commitment to change was to remain largely morally based and politically ambiguous, Steffens was still in the early 1900s the epicenter of an earthquake in political and social writing and reporting. He wrote and made things happen: elections were decided, laws were enacted, power blocs shifted position because of his work. So it was that he attracted the best and the brightest of the younger intellectuals and writers he met, and led most of them to New York.

> Of all the ambitions of the Great Unpublished, the one that is strongest, the most abiding, is the ambition to get to New York. For these, New York is the *point de depart,* the pedestal, the niche, the indispensable vantage ground.

So wrote Frank Norris, a writer usually more closely associated with San Francisco than with New York; but he felt the dual lure of Steffens at *McClure's* and of the bohemia that was rapidly sprouting at the southern end of Washington Square, directly across from the Whartons and Jameses on its north. By the time Norris arrived at 61 Washington Square South in 1898, Greenwich Village was well on its way to becoming New York's Left Bank or Latin Quarter. The Little Africa that had occupied most of the Village during the 19th century was replaced by a Little Italy, as the old houses gave way to tenements full of railroad flats and the elegant brick edifices fronting the park were broken up into rooming houses for the young artists, writers, and political activists who quickly discovered that the drop in local real estate values brought plentiful and cheap housing onto the market.

Thanks to Mabel Dodge, the no-man's-land of Washington Square was frequently crossed—though in ways that ultimately satisfied no one. Steffens had suggested to Mrs. Dodge, a wealthy and bored socialite perpetually in search of stimulation, that she "Have Evenings," as he capitalized it; and so one of New York's most famous salons began. Freud and Jung—both only then introduced to America—Marx and Bakunin were discussed and debated by people with addresses on both sides of the Square. Steffens brought his protégés Walter Lippmann and John Reed; Margaret Sanger and Emma Goldman discussed sex and anarchy; Big Bill Haywood of the Industrial Workers of the World performed several times for a mixed audience of society people, artists, and would-be radicals.

John Reed soon became a star of these Evenings in his own right, and eventually he moved from that platform to a more important place in both political history and political writing. He lived at 42 Washington Square South, where the NYU law building now stands, with a group of fellow Harvard alumni. Harvard was where he, Lippmann, T.S. Eliot, Conrad

Aiken, and Heywood Broun had been drawn into political and social awareness by their contact with Lincoln Steffens during one of Charles Eliot Norton's seminars. Reed quickly followed Steffens to New York and was immediately immersed in bohemian life, which inspired a long poem, more indicative of his enthusiasm than of his poetic abilities, "The Day in Bohemia: Or Life Among the Artists in Manhattan's Quartier Latin," published in 1913.

> In the winter the water is frigid,
> In summer the water is hot;
> And we're forming a club for controlling the tub
> For there's only one bath to the lot.
> You shave in unlathering Croton,
> If there's water at all, which is rare—
> But the life isn't bad for a talented lad
> At Forty-Two Washington Square!

Needless to say, this was not the piece of writing that would bring immortal fame to John Reed. Through Steffens and Mabel Dodge's salon Reed came into contact with some of the best-paying magazines uptown, and was soon selling material to *Century, Saturday Evening Post, Collier's,* and the *Metropolitan.* But at the same time he was working for them, he was becoming more deeply involved with the radical thought clustering south of the Square. One such cluster formed around Greenwich Village's Liberal Club, a group of self-proclaimed radical intellectuals who once refused membership to Emma Goldman. Many of these later found an outlet for publication in *The Masses.* Under editor Max Eastman, with Floyd Dell and John Reed on the staff, the magazine pursued its motto (Fun, Truth, Beauty, Realism, Peace, Feminism, and Revolution) with a committed if playful vigor.

It happened that one night in 1913 found Reed at the apartment of Big Bill Haywood, also near Washington Square, a night when the famous IWW leader spoke about the strike of the textile workers in Paterson, New Jersey. Haywood was forceful and vehement in describing this especially bitter labor struggle that was so important to the IWW and that was being largely ignored by the press. Also present was Mabel Dodge, who, swayed as his listeners usually were by the dual force of his personality and presentation, urged Haywood to put on a pageant in New York dramatizing the plight of the strikers. She suggested Madison Square Garden, then at 26th Street and Madison Avenue, as the place to hold it. Infected by her enthusiasm, Reed volunteered to write the script, and, characteristically, the next morning he set out for Paterson, where he was immediately arrested for the vicious and subversive crime of standing with some strikers. Taken before a court recorder, he endeared himself to the literary community by giving his occupation as "poet." His sentence was 20 days in jail, but his influential friends were able to get him out of his cell, jammed with strikers, after only five days.

The arrest had a profound effect on Reed. Harvard had molded him as a conservative, bohemian life in the Village had developed liberal sympathies, but jail left him permanently radicalized. Immediately after his release he hastened home to write the story "War in Paterson," and then began rehearsals for the pageant, which he was now directing as well as writing. Reed was brutally honest in his appraisal of the situation:

> There's war in Paterson, New Jersey. But it's a curious kind of war. All the violence is the work of one side—the mill owners. Their servants, the police, club unresisting men and women and ride down law-abiding crowds on horseback. Their paid mercenaries, the armed detectives, shoot and kill innocent people. Their newspapers...publish incendiary and crime-inciting appeals to mob violence against the strike leaders.... They control absolutely the police, the press, the courts.

The spectacle boasted a cast of 2,000—most of them strikers—and entranced its audience of 15,000 so completely that Reed's reputation was made, both as a writer and as a radical. Soon afterward Reed and Mrs. Dodge left for Europe, where they became lovers. Back in the U.S., Reed moved into Mrs. Dodge's Fifth Avenue apartment.

It wasn't long until he received an offer from *Metropolitan* magazine to go to the Mexican border and cover the exploits of Pancho Villa, and he hastened to join Villa's army in Mexico, where he reported the uprising from a rather romantic point of view. When war broke out in Europe, he hurried there. In France he found the soldiers apathetic and fatalistic and rapidly learned that the stories of atrocities by the Hun were fabrications. He became an adamant advocate of American non-involvement. In 1917 he made his famous journey to Russia to cover the revolution. He returned to America in early 1918 to stand trial with Eastman, Dell, and others from the editorial staff of *The Masses.* In keeping with its socialist viewpoint, the magazine had taken a position against the war and held it even when most other "radical" intellectuals, from John Dewey to Walter Lippmann to Lincoln Steffens himself, had shifted to believing that some sort of action against militaristic Germany was necessary. In late 1917 the Department of Justice banned *The Masses* and then suppressed it under the Sedition Act. While he stood trial, Reed wrote the official version of the Bolshevik revolution, *Ten Days that Shook the World,* for which Lenin himself wrote the foreword. After his acquittal, he returned to Moscow, where he died, some claim of neglect, in a hospital in 1920. His importance to the cause, at least posthumously, was such that he became the only non-Russian to be buried in the huge mausoleum on Red Square.

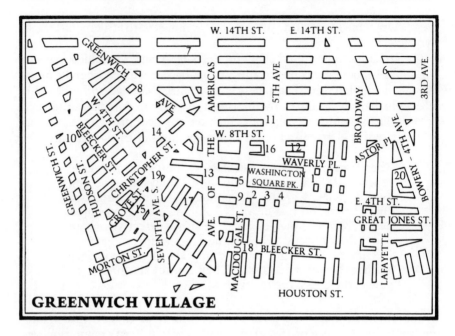

GREENWICH VILLAGE

1   *Henry James*
    21 Washington Pl.

2   *Frank Norris*
    61 Washington Sq. S.

3   *John Reed*
    Lincoln Steffens
    Eugene O'Neill
    42 Washington Sq. S.

4   *Edith Wharton*
    7 Washington Sq. S.

5   *Polly's Restaurant*
    137 MacDougal St.
    Liberal Club located upstairs
    Frequented by Dreiser, Sinclair,
    Lindsay, Steffens, Lewis, Anderson,
    Untermeyer, Eastman, Reed.

6   *Herman Melville*
    103 Fourth Ave.

7   *The Liberator*
    138 W. 13 St.

8   *The Masses*
    91 Greenwich Ave.

9   *Provincetown Playhouse*
    139 MacDougal St.

10 *White Horse Tavern*
    Hudson and W. 11 Sts.
    Hangout for Dylan Thomas, Norman
    Mailer, and others

11 *Mark Twain*
    21 Fifth Ave.

12 *John Dos Passos*
    Washington Mews Behind #3
    Washington Sq. N.

13 *Hell Hole Bar*
    6 Ave. and W. 4 St.
    Eugene O'Neill

14 *Theodore Dreiser*
    165 W. 10 St.

15 *Hart Crane*
    45 Grove St.

16 *Mabel Dodge's literary salon*
    5th Ave.

17 *Caffè Cino*
    31 Cornelia St.
    Site of Beat poetry readings

18 *San Remo*
    Bleecker and MacDougal Sts.
    Popular with the Beats, James Agee,
    W. Styron

19 *Circle-in-the-Square*
    5 Sheridan Sq.

20 *New York Shakespeare*
    Festival/Public Theatre
    Lafayette St.

ANOTHER BOHEMIAN BEGAN HER JOURNEY TO FAME and Greenwich Village by losing a poetry contest. An anthology called *The Lyric Year* anounced a prize of $500 for the best contribution and, although the prize was awarded to St. Louis poet Orrick Johns for a work of social consciousness called "Second Avenue," everyone found "Renascence" by Edna St. Vincent Millay the best poem in the collection even though it had won no prize at all. In fact, winner Johns was so convinced of the superiority of the Millay poem that he did not attend the award banquet.

Only nineteen when "Renascence" was published, Edna St. Vincent Millay came from a poor and broken home in Maine. But a high-ranking official of the New York YWCA, impressed with her talent, undertook to raise the money to send her to college. In the spring of 1917 the poet was graduated from Vassar, determined to go to New York and become an actress. That fall she took up residence at 139 Waverly Place and began her quest for a stage career, living principally on bread.

Although she was considered physically attractive and had a low-pitched, resonant voice, Broadway didn't pay any attention. Her failure there sent her back to poetry, and she began the collection that was to appear in 1920 as *A Few Figs from Thistles.*

Undiscouraged by her apparent inability to break in on Broadway, Edna and her sister Norma both began working with the Provincetown Players on MacDougal Street. Soon she had completed a one-act play, *The Princess Marries the Page*, which was staged in 1918. The following year she wrote another one-act play, her finest dramatic work, *Aria da Capo*, which she directed and which starred sister Norma.

A Few Figs from Thistles scored an immediate success; what one critic has called its "conspicuously cynical flippancy" was very much in the mood of its time. Subjective in tone, it nevertheless contained a few poems describing the New York scene, among them "MacDougal Street" ("The women squatting on the steps were slovenly and fat/And everywhere I stepped there was a baby or a cat").

No spiritualized esthete, Millay was quickly caught up in the sexual freedom that swept the artists' sections of Greenwich Village at the turn of the decade. She was notoriously fickle and went through a string of lovers, among whom have been numbered critic Edmund Wilson, novelist Floyd Dell, and poets John Peale Bishop and Arthur Davison Ficke.

The Provincetown Players for whom Millay wrote and directed were a group of Greenwich Village residents who summered on Cape Cod, none of them theater professionals. The leader was George Cram "Jig" Cook, a novelist and critic, married to the short-story writer Susan Glaspell. Others included John Reed, poet Harry Kemp, and novelist Mary Heaton Vorst. Their venture into theater reads almost like a B-picture scenario out of Hollywood, where the unknowns suggest, "Let's put on a play!"

The group started in Massachusetts in 1915 in a bungalow and staged two one-act plays. Opening night was so successful that the budding company moved to a wharf owned by Mary Vorst to continue its run and even presented a second double bill.

The following year when they began a more intensive search for new material, Eugene O'Neill was one of the potential sources sent to them. He arrived with *Bound East for Cardiff*, which was turned over to someone else to read when the author refused, typically, to read it himself. The play dazzled its first audience.

It was Reed who suggested that the work begun in Provincetown be carried to New York during the 1916–17 season, and Cook who seized on the suggestion and raised a total of $240 to rent a theatre there. Such a relatively minute amount of production capital necessarily restricted his search to the Village rather than the expensive theatres uptown, and he soon found a remodeled house at 139 MacDougal Street to serve as the company's home base.

At the end of the summer, O'Neill also moved back to the city, spending much of his time at the saloon on the corner of Sixth Avenue and West Fourth Street variously called the Hell Hole, the Bucket of Blood, and the Tub of Blood. In its earlier days this tavern had been a hangout for members of the notorious Hudson Dusters gang, and their successors still gathered there, pushed into a back room by the crush of bohemians at the bar. These street people rather than the Village's bohemians and intellectuals, were the ones whom O'Neill found the most congenial and with whom he spent most of his time.

He observed them and their surroundings with a careful scrutiny, as the following scene description from *The Iceman Cometh* shows:

> The right wall of the back room is a dirty black curtain which separates it from the bar.... In the middle of the rear wall is a door opening on a hallway. In the corner, built out into the room, is the toilet with a sign "This is it" on the door.... Two windows, so glazed with grime one cannot see through them, are in the left wall, looking out on a backyard. The walls and ceilings once were white, but it was a long time ago, and they are now so splotched, peeled, stained, and dusty that their color can best be described as dirty. The floor, with iron spittoons placed here and there, is covered with sawdust.

The Provincetown's first year in New York brought successful productions of *Bound East for Cardiff*, *Before Breakfast*, and *The Long Voyage Home* by O'Neill and short works by Glaspell, Floyd Dell, Michael Gold, and Rita Wellman. Dell's *Angel Inside* starred the multi-talented Edna St. Vincent Millay.

In 1918–19 the Provincetown produced *The Moon of the Caribbees* and continued to attract larger audiences, more and more of them coming from uptown and the suburbs. This was precisely the type of success that the amateurs who had organized the company were not looking for and did not want. They saw themselves revolting against the Broadway theater that attracted these same patrons and battling instead for theater as art; so when the cash registers began to jingle and the drawers to fill, the fear naturally arose in them that they had lost their fight.

Their fears were aggravated both by O'Neill's continuing sophistication as a stage craftsman and by his growth as a talent who could say something significant in such a way as to attract a wide theatergoing audience. For his part, O'Neill began to feel constricted by the production capability and the theoretical posture of the Provincetown, so much so that he took his first major full-length play, *Beyond the Horizon*, to Broadway for production.

The same year (1920) the playwright won the Pulitzer Prize for *Beyond the Horizon*, his long one-act play *The Emperor Jones* brought the Provincetown its greatest triumph: the morning after it opened, the queue at the ticket window was blocks long. The play was quickly moved to Broadway, however, as was the full-length *Diff'rent*, which opened later that same year. The 1920–21 season at the Provincetown was climaxed by *The Hairy Ape*, but this, too, was shunted uptown posthaste. That was the end for Cook, who pulled out of the company and went to live in Greece.

WHILE O'NEILL, MILLAY, AND REED WERE THRIVING in the bohemia around Washington Square, farther east a young writer named Theodore Dreiser was trying to break into print. He arrived in New York in 1894 as an aspiring newspaper reporter, but the best job he could find was for the *New York World* at space rates: his first day netted him a whopping $1.86. He took a room on East Fourth Street just off the Bowery where, unaware that the rooming-house doubled as a meeting-place for prostitutes and their customers, he spent this time studying the uptown magazines and trying to write fiction that would sell to that market. Inevitably, the building was raided and he was sent on his way.

He then shifted to hack writing, and was turning out articles for popular magazines with such success that he was soon earning an enviable $100 a week. At the same time, he was devouring the realistic writings of Balzac, and soon he was working on *Sister Carrie*, which he based on the experiences of his sister Emma.

By a bit of luck, Frank Norris, whose *McTeague* Doubleday, Page had published the year before, had become an editor for the company, and it was to him that the manuscript of *Carrie* went. He read it, loved it, and urged partner Walter Hines Page to publish it (Frank Doubleday was in Europe).

Page, caught up by Norris's enthusiasm, signed an agreement to do so. Then Doubleday and his wife returned from Europe and set in motion one of the great *causes celebres* in American literary history.

Doubleday was no prude, nor was his wife—both were, in fact, ardent admirers of Zola—but he was a churchgoer and, perhaps more significantly, a former book salesman. He read *Carrie* and objected to it on two grounds: it was dirty and it would not sell. When his wife read it and agreed, Doubleday vetoed the book.

Page wrote to Dreiser asking to be released from the agreement, but Dreiser insisted on publication. Page next asked the author's permission to arrange publication with any one of five other reputable publishers. Dreiser refused.

In later years Dreiser was given to saying that his first novel was suppressed, but that was simply not the case. While only 1,000 copies were bound, Norris appointed himself a drumbeater for the book and sent out a phenomenal 127 copies to reviewers, each accompanied by a personal letter. The results of this herculean effort were minimal. *Carrie* was in fact widely reviewed, but those who did not find it immoral thought it pessimistic and depressing. If the critics were not ready for it, the public

A bread line in the Bowery at the turn of the century. The old Bowery elevated was torn down in 1942.
Museum of the City of New York

was even less so: it sold a mere 456 copies and Dreiser was crushed. He had envisioned the book as a combination of what he had learned both from Balzac and from his stint at newspaper reporting—like so many of the other realists and muckrakers writing in the Village, Dreiser drew on his own experiences to support his moral stance. It was New York's vastness and diversity that engaged his imagination as a reporter in such a way as to enable him to begin—like Riis, Steffens, and their followers—to draw political and social conclusions, and to create new types of fiction from the welter of phenomena to which he was daily exposed. Witness this section from *The Color of a Great City*:

> The thing that interested me then as now about New York—as indeed about any great city, but more definitely New York because it was and is so preponderantly large— was the sharp, and at the same time immense, contrast it showed between the dull and the shrewd, the strong and the weak, the rich and the poor, the wise and the ignorant. This, perhaps, was more by reason of numbers and opportunity than anything else, for of course humanity is much the same everywhere. But the number from which to choose was so great here that the strong, or those who ultimately dominated, were so very strong, and the weak so very, very weak—and so very, very many.

In 1914 Dreiser had settled at 165 West 10th Street in the Village with his mistress of the moment, Kirah Markham; here he met many of the bohemians, but did not really fit in well with them perhaps because he perceived their socialism as a genteel entertainment, a far cry from the deeply felt commitment that later led him to join the Communist Party. He and Markham began a series of Sunday soirees which they soon abandoned because they found the conversation too noisy. But when *The Genius* fell afoul of the literary censors, Villagers rallied to his support and he in turn became more sympathetic to their points of view.

Younger than these bohemian writers, but equally committed to the "realistic" exploration of everyday life, were Hart Crane and John Dos Passos. Both writers lived in the Village during the 1920s, and both sought to structure their works into overarching visions of New York as the epitome of modern American life: urban, industrial, uncentered, unfocused.

In his *Manhattan Transfer*, Dos Passos traces the jumbled and fragmentary lives of a variety of characters as they wend their occasionally converging ways through the tangle of urban New York. Here, a recent arrival in the city stops an inhabitant to ask for directions that are not only physical but metaphysical:

"How do I get to Broadway?...I want to get to the center of things."
"Walk east a block and turn down Broadway and you'll find the center of things if you walk far enough."

As the book unfolds, mirroring the complexity of the city it describes, he finds that there is no real or possible center, only an urban labyrinth that holds in its byways a multiplicity of populations, races, and for that matter Freudian surprises:

> Big snake appears on Fifth Avenue....Ladies screamed and ran in all directions this morning at eleven-thirty when a big snake crawled out of crack in the masonry of the retaining wall of the reservoir at Fifth Avenue and Forty-second Street and started to cross the sidewalk....

Hart Crane also rejected the constrictions imposed on his imagination by the outmoded conventions of Fifth Avenue's literary past:

> We have come a long way from the pattern-making preoccupations of a Henry James when we can welcome a statement from an artist with as bold a contrasting simplicity as the answer that Sherwood Anderson once gave me an analysis I had attempted of one of his short stories. "I am in truth mighty little interested in any discussions of art or life, or what a man's place in the scheme of things may be. It has to be done, I suppose, but after all there is the *fact* of life. Its story wants telling and singing. That's what I want—the tale and the song of it."

In his own way, this is exactly what Hart Crane attempted in his vast and panoramic poem "The Bridge." Sometimes he does it by juxtaposing celebrated pieces of New York's literary past with the daily realities of its present:

> And Rip forgot the office hours,
>   and he forgot the pay;
> Van Winkle sweeps a tenement
>   way down on Avenue A,—
> And Rip was slowly made aware
>   that he, Van Winkle, was not here
> nor there. He woke and swore he'd seen Broadway
>   a Catskill daisy chain in May—

The intense pessimism Crane felt about the chaos of the modern world, especially manifest in New York, led ultimately to his suicide in the Gulf of Mexico, where he walked off the stern of the steamer "Orizaba" on April 27, 1932.

HARLEM HAS NOT ALWAYS BEEN A COLLECTION OF DECAYING TENEMENTS in which blacks live cut off from the wealth of the white world. When the first blacks moved into Harlem, it was a fashionable residential area, largely white. The economic boom that followed the panic and bust of 1897 generated overbuilding; and more and more landlords found themselves stuck with empty apartment houses. A resourceful black realtor, Phillip Payton, suggested to several landlords in the Harlem area that he could find them tenants from among the better-off blacks who wanted to escape the then-slums of Greenwich Village. Soon Payton and other realtors were buying buildings for themselves, tossing out the white tenants, raising the rents, and renting to upwardly-mobile blacks. Harlem's beautiful new housing and wide, well-lit streets were certain to draw the black elite; and only 20 years later, Harlem was black from 130th to 145th Streets, from Madison Avenue on the east to Seventh Avenue on the west.

In those years great changes were taking place in black America, changes that would lead to the explosion of talent called the Harlem Renaissance. In 1895 the president of Tuskegee Institute in Alabama, Booker T. Washington, delivered a speech at the Cotton States Exposition in Atlanta in which he stated that blacks were not primarily interested in political participation, social equality, or higher education. This speech made Washington an influential figure among whites, but understandably provoked the most violent opposition among blacks. However, considered in the context of 1895, this conciliatory speech may not seem quite as sycophantic as it appears almost a hundred years later: after all, only 32 years had passed since Lincoln's Emancipation Proclamation, and Washington himself had been born a slave.

The blacks opposed to Washington found a leader in William Edward Burghardt Du Bois, author of the influential work *The Souls of Black Folk*. Du Bois led a meeting of militant blacks in Buffalo on July 11-13, 1905 to start the Niagara Movement and oppose Washington's philosophy of accommodation.

Du Bois soon began to feel, however, that blacks could not improve their situation without help from the whites. In May of 1910, he was instrumental in establishing the National Association for the Advancement of Colored People, a biracial organization which included blacks like Walter White and William Monroe Trotter, the militant editor of the *Boston Guardian* and whites like Jane Addams of Chicago's Hull House, Columbia professor John Dewey, and the novelist William Dean Howells. Almost at once the NAACP decided to sponsor a monthly publication, *The Crisis,* and Du Bois was named editor and moved to New York.

More directly involved in the beginnings of the Harlem Renaissance was James Weldon Johnson, widely known for his 1912 novel *The Autobiography of an Ex-Colored Man.* A song he and his brother had written in 1900, "Lift Every Voice and Sing," was considered by many as the black national anthem.

What inspired the Harlem Renaissance? First, it was the rise of a generation of college-educated blacks. Only 50 years after emancipation, this was the first generation to have the advantage of higher education in any great number. Then, too, like whites, blacks were drawn to New York as the literary, publishing and show-business Mecca. Finally, there was the presence of money in Harlem: if black workers did not have top jobs, at least they had jobs, and white money flowed into the area through the jazz clubs, through bootlegging, and through prostitution.

When did the Harlem Renaissance actually begin? Some date it from 1919, when, in response to a race riot, Claude McKay wrote:

> If we must die—let it not be like hogs
> Hunted and penned in an inglorious spot,
> While round us bark the mad and hungry dogs,
> Making their mock at our accursed lot.

But whether he started it or not, McKay was the first major figure to herald this literary awakening, and his fiction and poetry captured Harlem's heart in a way no other writer's did. For example: Seventh Avenue was known as Harlem's Broadway during the week and its Fifth Avenue on Sunday. In *Home to Harlem,* McKay describes it on a weekday:

> The lovely trees of Seventh Avenue were a vivid flame-green. Children, lightly clad, skipped on the pavement. Light open coats prevailed and the smooth bare throats of brown girls were a token as charming as the first pussy-willows. Far and high over all, the sky was a grand blue benediction, and beneath it the wonderful air of New York tasted like fine dry champagne.

And then again on a Sunday or holiday:

> The broad pavements of Seventh Avenue were colorful with promenaders. Brown babies in white carriages pushed by little black brothers wearing nice sailor suits. All the various and varying pigmentation of the human race were assembled there: dim brown, clear brown, rich

brown, chestnut, copper, yellow, near-white, mahogany, and gleaming anthracite. Charming brown matrons, proud yellow matrons, dark nursemaids pulled a zigzag course by their restive little charges....

And the elegant strutters in faultless spats; West Indians carrying canes and wearing trousers of a different pattern from their coats and vests, drawing sharp comments from their Afro-Yank rivals.

If he depicted the rivalry between the men from the Caribbean and the native-born blacks, McKay was only too aware of the confrontations between blacks and whites. Another section of *Home to Harlem* reads:

They had walked down Madison Avenue, turned on One Hundred and Thirtieth Street, passing the solid gray grim mass of the whites' Presbyterian church, and were under the timidly whispering trees of the decorously silent and distinguished Block Beautiful.... The whites had not evacuated that block yet.... The Block Beautiful was worth a struggle. With its charming green lawns and quaint white-fronted houses, it preserved the most Arcadian atmosphere in all New York.

But he also saw blacks and whites mixing and mingling in Harlem nightclubs:

The lights in the basements had been dimmed and the reveling dancers cast grotesque shadows on the tapestried walls. Color lines had been completely eradicated. Whites and blacks clung passionately together as if trying to effect a permanent merger. Liquor, jazz, music, and close physical contact had achieved what decades of propaganda had advocated with little success.

Of course, the presence of many whites in the area was prompted only by thrill-seeking. Prohibition went into effect in 1920, and Harlem was only too glad to provide places where both blacks and whites could spend freely to drink illicit liquor. This expansion of Harlem's economy provided a widening fiscal base for the upsurge of artistic and cultural activities that marked the Roaring Twenties; the liquor that flowed so freely and illegally north of 125th Street watered, as it were, the aspirations of countless black artists, fertilized their options with the influx of white downtown wealth, and led them to blossom in the Harlem Renaissance. But the proliferation of speakeasies was accompanied by an upsurge in prostitution. McKay saw that clearly, as the title poem of *Harlem Shadows* shows:

I hear the halting footsteps of a lass
In Negro Harlem when the night lets fall
It veil. I see the shapes of girls who pass
To bend and barter at desire's call.
Ah, little dark girls who in slippered feet
Go prowling through the night from street to street.

Ah, stern harsh world, that in the wretched way
Of poverty, dishonor and disgrace,
Has pushed the timid little feet of clay,
The sacred brown feet of my fallen race!
Ah, heart of me, the weary, weary feet
In Harlem wandering from street to street.

McKay was not, however, a voice that spoke only of Harlem. Some of his poetry, like Whitman's, gave an impression of the city as a whole, although it was unlike Whitman's in its gritty reality:

The Dawn! The Dawn! The crimson-tinted comes
Out of the low still skies, over the hills,
Manhattan's roofs and spires and cheerless domes!
The Dawn! My spirit to its spirit thrills.
Almost the mighty city is asleep,
No pushing crowd, no tramping, tramping feet.
But here and there a few cars groaning creep
Along, above and underneath the street,
Bearing their strangely-ghostly burdens by,
The women and the men of garish nights,
Their eyes wine-weakened and their clothes awry,
Grotesques beneath the strong electric lights.
The shadows wane. The Dawn comes to New York.
And I go darkly-rebel to my work.

McKay was hired as an associate editor by *The Masses* and its more radical successor, *The Liberator*, and thus fell in with editor Max Eastman, Floyd Dell, and John Reed—all Marxist bohemians from Greenwich Village far to the south, whose politics bridged both geography and color. Although *The Masses* and *The Liberator* were not magazines aimed only at black readers, it was *The Liberator* that published "If We Must Die." Like many other figures of the Harlem Renaissance, McKay was active as a writer through the 1930s and then faded away.

As more young black writers found their voices, more publications were begun to carry their words to an appreciative and growing black audience. In 1917, A. Philip Randolph, head of the Brotherhood of Sleeping Car Porters, and Chandler Owen established *The Messenger*, and in 1923 the Urban League founded *Opportunity*. With Charles Johnson as its editor and Eric Walrond as its business manager, *Opportunity* was unusually sympathetic to young black writers. Jessie Fauset was the literary editor of *The Crisis* from 1919–1920, and published her first novel, *There Is Confusion*, during that same period. At that time she lived at 1947 Seventh Avenue, and her soirees there were famous.

Such gatherings are an inevitable by-product of literary life, as is the competition among hosts and hostesses. If Fauset's parties were the most prestigious among literary Harlemites, those of A'Leilia Walker Robinson were far better known. The daughter of C.J. Walker, who had invented a hair-straightening process and risen from poverty to affluence, Mrs. Robinson's mansion at 104 West 136th Street, now the site of the Countee Cullen branch of the New York Public Library, was then the site of continuous partying. There black and white writers, politicians, publishing tycoons, and show business personalities gathered to exchange gossip, to drink, and to wheel and deal.

Many young blacks were naturally drawn to the city to work on the growing number of magazines, and one of the most talented was Wallace Thurman, who arraived in 1925. He worked as managing editor of *The Messenger*, then as a reader for the publishing house of Macaulay, and coauthored *Harlem*, the first successful black play on Broadway. When he first arrived in the city, he lived at 267 West 137th Street, where Langston

Street life was and is an important ingredient of life in Harlem.
Schomberg Collection

Hughes, Zora Neale Hurston, and Gwendolyn Bennett had also stayed. Years later in his novel *Infants of the Spring*, Thurman skewered the black writers who had lived in that house before or while he did, derisively titling it "Niggerati Manor" and suggesting that most of the residents were insignificant figures.

The archetypal artist of the Harlem Renaissance, however, was Countee Cullen with his rather self-conscious artistic sensibilities, his Francophilia, his non-militant view on injustices to blacks, and his attendance of all the fashionable black literary salons.

The young Cullen was a bookish boy, concerned about keeping up high grades in school and often seen carrying a pad and pencil to jot down impressions as they came to him. He did not have long to wait for recognition of his writing talent. His first book, *Color*, was published in 1925, when he was only twenty-two.

In 1926, M.A. in hand, he became an assistant editor of *Opportunity* with the chance to write a literary column, and began to move actively in Harlem literary circles; he was often at A'Leilia Robinson's parties. The following year he published his second and third verse collections, *Copper Sun* and *Ballad of the Brown Girl*; edited an anthology of black poets, *Caroling Dusk*; and won a Guggenheim fellowship for study in Europe.

On April 9, 1928, the social event of the decade in Harlem took place when Yolande Du Bois, daughter of W. E. B. Du Bois, and Countee Cullen were married in an elaborate ceremony at his father's church. There were 1,300 guests in the church and thousands outside; the church was filled with canaries in gilded cages; 16 bridesmaids came from Baltimore; all the ushers were poets and writers, among them Langston Hughes and Arna Bontemps.

In spite of this hopeful beginning, they were divorced within two years, during which time they saw little of each other. Cullen spent a good part of those years in Europe studying and writing. His fourth volume of poetry, *The Black Christ*, written while Cullen was in Paris, was published in 1929. When Cullen finally returned permanently to America in the mid-1930s he began teaching French at a Harlem school. From then on, his writing was diminished sharply in both quality and quantity.

If Cullen was the archetypal figure of the Harlem Renaissance, Langston Hughes was certainly its most productive and enduring talent and one of its most colorful personalities. Born in Joplin, Missouri, in 1902, he moved often during his childhood. Before he was twelve he had lived in Mexico City, Topeka, Colorado Springs, Kansas City, Buffalo, and Charlestown, Indiana. His parents separated and he went to live with his mother in Cleveland, where he graduated from high school in 1920. He then left for Mexico to join his father, who felt that he should go to college. So young Hughes enrolled at Columbia and arrived in New York in the fall of 1920, but soon found that he did not enjoy attending college. With thirteen dollars in his pocket, he broke with his father and set off on his own, working first for a truck-farmer on Staten Island and then as a delivery man for a florist's shop, and writing poetry in his spare time. In 1921 he published his first poem, "The Negro Speaks of Rivers," which received wide critical attention.

He signed on as a mess-boy aboard a ship that touched at the Canary Islands, the Azores, and West Africa, and, since he thought life at sea congenial, became a sailor on the New York-to-Europe run. The highlight of his career as a seaman came in 1924, when he found himself stranded in Paris with seven dollars. Fortunately, he was able to get a job as a doorman at the Grand Duc restaurant, and even moved up to second cook and then waiter. He met an Italian family who invited him to spend some time with them at Lago di Garda; after his stay there he journeyed to Venice and Genoa, where his passport was stolen, forcing him to live as a sort of beachcomber. Eventually he made his way back to the States by way of Spain.

He joined the literary life of Harlem and worked actively at his poetry. In 1926 his first collection, *The Weary Blues*, was published and he became a student at Lincoln University in Pennsylvania, where he was to remain for the next three years, commuting to Harlem on weekends.

In *The Weary Blues*, Hughes established many of the themes that were to dominate his poetry for the next four decades. He was particularly interested in jazz and its rhythms, and so found himself drawn to Harlem nightlife. The title poem from that book is characteristic:

> Droning a drowsy syncopated tune,
> Rocking back and forth to a mellow croon,
> I heard a Negro play.
> Down on Lenox Avenue the other night
> By the pale dull pallor of an old gas light
> He did a lazy sway....
> He did a lazy sway....
> To the tune o' those Weary Blues.
> With his ebony hands on each ivory key
> He made that poor piano moan with melody
> O Blues!
> Swaying to and fro on his rickety stool
> He played that sad raggy tune like a musical fool.
> Sweet Blues!
> Coming from a black man's soul.
> O Blues!

Among the musicians Hughes saw in the Harlem clubs were many of jazz's most important figures. Duke Ellington with his Washingtonians; Fats Waller; Bessie Smith; Ma Rainey; Louis Armstrong; Cab Calloway with

The sumptuous interior of famed Connie's Inn, a nightclub popular with whites and blacks alike during the heyday of the Harlem Renaissance.
New York Public Library

his Missourians; Billie Holiday; all the greats played Harlem. Many of the clubs where they performed were distinguished by nothing but the talent of these performers who drew people from all over the city, whites as well as blacks.

Hughes captured the spirit of these cabarets in "Harlem Club":

> Sleek black boys in a cabaret.
> Jazz-band, jazz-band,—
> Play, plAY, PLAY!
> Tomorrow.... who knows?
> Dance today!

Hughes's poetry reveals an intimate knowledge of the ambiguities and ironies of black urban life; from "Lenox Avenue: MIDNIGHT":

> The broken heart of love,
> The weary, weary heart of pain,—
> > Overtones,
> > Undertones,
> To the rumble of street cars,
> To the swish of rain.

Lenox Avenue,
Honey.
Midnight,
And the gods are laughing at us.

Just as a date for the start of the Harlem Renaissance cannot be fixed exactly, it is impossible to say when or why it ended. Many critics feel that its vitality was sapped by the effects of the 1929 crash on Harlem's always fragile economy; others feel that the Depression shifted the concerns of black· writers—and, for that matter, those of their white counterparts— from artistic matters to questions of economic and social justice. The literary torch was passed then to a more militant group of writers, chief among them Richard Wright, who built a new literature on the foundations laid during the Renaissance.

FARTHER SOUTH, A CONSTELLATION OF VERBAL STARS was clustering around the Great White Way and its theater. At the center of this small galaxy, already known for the pyrotechnics of his biting tongue, was Alexander Woollcott who had come to New York in 1909 and, after a brief spell as a bank teller, had gotten a job as a *Times* reporter.

At that time New York as it exists today was taking shape, with skyscrapers emerging as its characteristic feature. The first skyscraper was the Tower Building at 50 Broadway, completed in 1889. Within the next 10 years, once the N.Y. Building Law in 1892 made its first provisions concerning construction of skeletal steel frames, the race to build was on— the Havemeyer, the Manhattan Life Insurance Company, American Surety, Commercial Cable, St. Paul, and Park Row skyscrapers all went up before the turn of the century, and were followed by the Flatiron Building in 1902, the Times Tower in 1904, the Singer Tower (612 feet high) in 1908, and the Woolworth Building (792 feet) in 1913. This, then, was the Manhattan— bursting with energy and exploding up to the skies, hustling and bustling with theater, art, and culture—in which the young Woollcott worked.

Woollcott did not especially enjoy reporting, so he became a rewrite man, and finally found his niche when he was appointed drama critic in 1914, the position from which he revolutionized theater criticism in New York. Up to then, it had been understood that a producer who took an ad for his play in a given newspaper could expect a glowing review. Woollcott trod gently at first, acquiring such a reputation for benevolence that fellow newsman Walter Winchell observed, "He always praises the first production of each season, being reluctant to stone the first cast."

At the time the Shubert brothers were the most active producers on Broadway, and they were ruthless in barring reviewers who had any adverse criticisms of their plays. Among those expelled was Winchell, who commented, "A certain columnist has been barred from all Shubert openings. Now he can wait three days and go to their closings."

As Woollcott grew into his job and became more and more objective, he, too, found himself in trouble with the Shuberts. Notified that he was persona non grata in their theaters, he asked the *Times* to back him up. To its credit the paper did so: any tickets sent with a proviso barring Woollcott from using them were returned, all the Shubert advertising—a lucrative account—was tossed out of the theater pages. Eventually the Shuberts capitulated, and the principle of critical independence was established in the New York theater.

It was in 1919 that theatrical press agent John Peter Toohey took Woollcott to lunch at the Hotel Algonquin, 59 West 44th Street, where the luncheon regulars already included Woollcott's warbuddy Franklin P. Adams (F.P.A.), humorist and critic Robert Benchley, and newsman Heywood Broun. Woollcott returned for lunch several times, always delivering monologues of some length about his wartime experiences. It wasn't long before the others at the Algonquin decided to put an end to these apparently interminable reminiscences by arranging a noontime banquet ostensibly to honor him, the Welcome Home to Woollcott from the Wars Luncheon. It was at this affair that Toohey suggested they meet every day.

Thus from a moment of typical irony was born the group that came to be called the Round Table, the Algonquin Wits, or the Vicious Circle. In addition to Woollcott, F.P.A., Benchley, Broun, and Toohey, it widened to include Laurence Stallings, later to coauthor *What Price Glory?*; musicologist Deems Taylor; Art Samuels, the editor of *Harper's Bazaar;* Bill Murray, music critic of the *Brooklyn Eagle;* producer Brock Pemberton and his brother; Robert E. Sherwood, later a prize-winning dramatist and speechwriter for President Franklin Roosevelt; theatrical press agent Herman Mankiewicz; magazine writer Dorothy Parker; drama editor and playwright George S. Kaufman and his wife Beatrice; novelist Edna Ferber; actresses Peggy Wood and Margalo Gillmore; *New York Times* reporter Hane Grant; and magazine illustrator Neysa McMein.

Most of these were talented and ambitious young people with a dedication to excellence and a deadly eye for the insincere and pretentious. Like the theater that most of them were so closely involved with, the self-proclaimed wits had a wide self-dramatizing streak that wove its way through their quotable quotes—indeed, it could apparently be said that no one at the Algonquin ever spoke without casting a careful look beyond the Round Table toward their larger audience and, hopefully, immortality. F.P.A., whose humor column, "The Conning Tower," printed contributions from readers, was the best known, and he helped several others at the Round Table break into print by featuring their jokes and quips. A relatively benign wit, he could draw the rapier. One of his friends started to conclude on over-long anecdote by remarking, "Well, to make a long story short—" "Too late," said F.P.A. On another occasion a colleague summed up a devastating assessment of a mutual acquaintance by saying, "After all, he's his own worst enemy." "Not while I'm around," F.P.A. shot back.

Among those particularly indebted to F.P.A. was George S. Kaufman, who had worked in the *Tribune* drama department under Broun and switched to the *Times*, where he later became drama editor. At the start of his career, F.P.A. had gotten him a job at the *Washington Times*, a job he lost because of the publisher's anti-Semitism. By 1919, Kaufman already had one play to his credit (if credit is the word), the unfortunately titled and ill-fated *Someone in the House*. The poor reviews and public apathy prompted more than one wag to note that there was no one in the house. Since the play ran during the great influenza epidemic of 1918, when public health officials urged people to avoid crowds, Kaufman suggested that theatergoers who wanted to do just that buy tickets for his play.

The caricatured habitués of the Round Table. Clockwise in the foreground: Robert Sherwood, Dorothy Parker, Robert Benchley, Alexander Woollcott, Heywood Broun, Marc Connelly, Franklin P. Adams, Edna Ferber, George Kaufman; in the rear, Lynn Fontanne, Alfred Lunt, Frank Crowninshield, and Frank Case.
Al Hirshfeld

Obviously, in such company quick wit was highly valued, and no one acquitted herself better at the Round Table than Dorothy Parker. The daughter of a Scottish mother and a Jewish father, Parker was born on West 72nd Street in Manhattan and grew up in comfortable economic circumstances, although an unhappy child terrified of her father. In 1919, when the Round Table was taking shape, Benchley was hired as *Vanity Fair's* managing editor and Sherwood as its drama editor; Mrs. Parker took over as a drama critic, and a devastating one she was. Always succinct, she wrote that *House Beautiful* "is the play lousy." She observed that one actress "ran the whole gamut of emotions from A to B," and of another said, "In the last act she is strangled by one of her admirers. For me, the murder came too late."

Her career as an aisle-sitter did not last too long. The following year she reviewed Billie Burke most negatively: "She plays her lighter scenes as if she were giving an imitation of Eva Tanguay." Unfortunately for Parker, Miss Burke's husband was Florenz Ziegfeld, and he used his influence to get the reviewer fired. Both Benchley and Sherwood resigned in support of Parker and critical candor.

Benchley and Parker took an office in the Metropolitan Opera House building at 39th Street and offered their services as freelance writers. They were not conspicuously successful, and when Benchley soon took a job at *Life,* Parker was left alone in the office. She found the isolation difficult to take, but quickly hit on a way to combat it: on a piece of cardboard tacked to her door, she lettered the single word "men."

Dorothy Parker's remarks to and about other women were particularly quoted. One crack that has been retold for almost six decades runs, "If all the girls at a Yale prom were laid end to end, I wouldn't be surprised." Of one acquaintance she said, "That woman speaks 18 languages and can't say 'No' in any of them." Of another, who broke her leg while in London: "I bet she broke it sliding down a barrister." Of a third, who was described to her as outspoken: "By whom?"

Nor did she spare herself. Separated, then divorced, from Edwin Parker, she had a series of lovers and was always on the lookout for men. Asked if she had enjoyed a cocktail party, she replied, "Did I! One more drink and I'd have been under the host." Shown a new apartment, she turned it down: "It's much too big. All I need is room enough to lay a hat and a few friends."

In 1921, Kaufman began a long and fruitful collaboration with Marc Connelly, a sometime Round Table member, to write *Dulcy,* a play based on a character in F.P.A.'s column. Connelly was a kind and gentle man, but dangerous to tamper with. On one occasion, an acquaintance ran his hand over the playwright's bald head and said, "That feels just like my wife's behind." Connelly repeated the gesture and returned, "By God, you're right."

Meanwhile the Round Table members were becoming more close-knit and, because so many of them worked in the media and wrote about their friends, better known. They began to save their witticisms for use at the Algonquin, and their bon mots circulated quickly all around New York.

Naturally enough, the accusation spread that the Algonquin wits were engaged in a steady round of you-scratch-my-back-I'll-scratch-yours, promoting their own members and ignoring outsiders. The second half, at least, of this charge was patently untrue, for Woollcott was actively beating the drums for both Fitzgerald and Hemingway. Nevertheless in her 1923 novel *Black Oxen* Gertrude Alberton, who lunched at the Algonquin but not in the charmed circle, excoriated "The Sophisticates": "...the cleverest of them—and those who were so excitedly sure of their cleverness that for the moment they convinced others as well as themselves—foregathered daily....They appraised, debated, rejected, finally placed the seal of their august approval upon a favored few."

Also in 1923, Dorothy Parker found herself pregnant by her lover of the moment and, after much soul-searching, decided to have an abortion. She summed it up with a bit of self-criticism: "It serves me right for putting all my eggs in one bastard." But as with other members of the circle, she used flippancy to mask deep feelings, and did not take the abortion as lightly as her words suggest: a short time later she attempted suicide by slashing her wrists. In the hospital she pointed out a bell to visitors: "That bell is supposed to summon the night nurse, so I ring it whenever I want an hour of uninterrupted privacy." A little more than a year later she tried suicide again, this time with sleeping pills, prompting her good friend Benchley to advise her: "You want to go easy on this suicide stuff. First thing you know you'll ruin your health."

But soon after her first attempt, Parker was back in circulation, her wit, at least, still in good form. When told that her dog had mange, she muttered, "I suppose he got it from a lamp post." And when her pet lost a fight with another dog from the neighborhood the neighbor charged, "Well, he started it." "And I have no doubt he was carrying a revolver," retorted Parker icily.

Benchley, who had been *Life's* theater critic since 1920, was rapidly building a reputation as an important humorist in his own right, with a variety of books including *Of All Things, Love Conquers All,* and *Pluck and Luck.* After arriving home with some friends one rainy evening, he urged, "Let's get out of these wet clothes and into a dry martini." Stepping out of the Algonquin, he saw a uniformed man at the door. "Please get us a taxi," he asked. "I'm sorry," said the uniformed man, "but I'm a rear admiral in the United States Navy." "In that case," Benchley said, "please get us a battleship." On the subject of his growing success, he wrote, "It took me 15 years to discover that I had no talent for writing, but I couldn't give it up because by that time I was too famous."

The *New Yorker* was born on February 21, 1925 under the editorship of Harold Ross, who, in Woollcott's phrase, looked like "a dishonest Abe Lincoln." Within the Algonquin Circle he was known as a puritan, and according to one of the members, "He's very uninhibited that way." To his friend F.P.A. he confessed, "I never struck a woman but once." "And even then unfavorably, I'll be bound," F.P.A. answered. Using a gimmick for which he later apologized, Ross listed on his staff Broun, Connelly, Ferber, Kaufman, Alice Duer Miller, Parker, Stallings, and Woollcott, among others. Perhaps it was the glitter of these names or perhaps it was the general excellence of the magazine, but it soon caught on and gave Round Table members yet another outlet.

With the passage of time, Woollcott was becoming more and more the autocrat of the luncheon table, driving Edna Ferber to call him "that New Jersey Nero who mistakes his pinafore for a toga." As his position became more assured, Woollcott's exchanges with his friends, always incisive, sometimes went beyond the bounds of good humor. Fortunately his friends were tolerant. At one lunch, he called Kaufman a "Christ-killer." Kaufman rose in mock anger and addressed the table: "This is the last time that I will tolerate any slur upon my religion at this table. I am now walking out of this dining room and out of this hotel. And I hope that Mrs. Parker will walk out with me—half way."

Although his Washington experience with anti-Semitism had been bitter enough for him to repeat the story often in later years, Kaufman could obviously laugh at his ethnic background. He started one story, "Once upon a time there were two Jews—and *now* look." On another occasion he was in the company of someone who was boasting about his ancestry and tracing it back to the Crusades. "I had an ancestor who went on the Crusades," Kaufman said. "As a spy, of course."

As the decade progressed, more and more of the wits became better and better known. Kaufman teamed with Connelly to write *Beggar on Horseback* and with Edna Ferber to write *The Royal Family.* Parker's first book of poetry, *Enough Rope,* was a smash hit and had eight printings. Sherwood scored successes with *The Road to Rome, The Love Nest,* and *The Queen's Husband.* Woollcott published *Mr. Dickens Goes to the Play, Enchanted Aisles, The Story of Irving Berlin,* and *Going to Pieces.*

In 1927, Dorothy Parker turned Ross's deception into fact by joining the staff of the *New Yorker* as a book reviewer, under the name "Constant Reader." She was every bit as devastating in dealing with the written word as she had been with the spoken one. Of one book she observed, "This is not a novel to be tossed aside lightly. It should be thrown with great force." Of another, "This book's author is a writer for the ages—for the ages of four to eight." Finally, she was all but overcome by the whimsy in one novel by A. A. Milne, and was moved to confess, "Tonstant Weader fwowed up."

When the crash came in 1929, the beginning of the end of the Round Table was already in sight. Many of the members were hard hit by the stock market's collapse although, odd as it may seem, they were still able to earn large sums for their writing. Nor was their wit impaired by the Depression.

Woollcott, for example, defined a stockbroker as "a man who can run your fortune into a shoestring."

Although he was often out of town on the lecture circuit, Woollcott still made his headquarters in New York, and was still much in evidence at the *New Yorker*, where one of his fits of pique caused illustrator Rea Irvin to describe him as "a butterfly in heat." Stallings and Mankiewicz both went to Hollywood, where they were followed by Dorothy Parker and her new husband, Alan Campbell, who as a team commanded the almost incredible salary of $5,200 a week from 1933 to 1938. F.P.A., Ross, Kaufman, Benchley, Sherwood, Broun, and Edna Ferber all moved out of New York, some to Connecticut and some to Bucks County, Pennsylvania.

WORLD WAR II DISPERSED NEW YORK WRITERS all over the world and, when that conflict was over, many did not return. One factor that tended to drive authors out, then as now, was the rising cost of housing, which was one of the reasons John Cheever was forced to abandon the city.

> It was a wonderful life and it didn't seem that it would ever end. In the winter there were those days with a smart polish on the air and the buildings, and then there were the first south winds of spring with their exciting and unclean odors of backyards and all the women shoppers walking east at dusk, carrying bunches of apple blossoms and lilac....I don't suppose there was a day, an hour, when the middle class got their marching orders, but toward the end of the 1940s the middle class began to move...the rich of the city were getting richer and the friable middle ground where we stood was vanishing.

But there were those who stayed, most of them natives whose dedication both to the city and to the literary life so dependent on its rich and diverse resources was too profound for them to conceive of living elsewhere. One such was Marcia Davenport, whose 1947 novel *East Side, West Side* delved into neighborhood life, principally on the East Side. Her heroine Jessie Bourne makes some choice observations about that posh and desirable residential area:

> Riding down Park Avenue in a filthy, raddled taxicab on her way to dinner, Jessie looked at the great imposing sweep of the avenue in the dusk. For many reasons she disliked the street, but as a sight it was undeniably beautiful. She sat watching the two dense streams of traffic slide past the grass-plots under which the New York Central trains make themselves heard just enough to

bring to mind the vast vague westward space from which they come, where the people like to tell one another that New York is not America.

Another writer raised in New York who has remained in the city is Norman Mailer. Brought up in Brooklyn, Mailer attended Harvard and made an auspicious literary debut in 1948 with *The Naked and the Dead,* widely acclaimed as the best American novel about World War II. Using a device borrowed from John Dos Passos's trilogy *U.S.A.,* he flashed back over the lives of the men in the platoon whose progress he follows throughout the book. One of them is Joey Goldstein, a boy born on the lower East Side of Manhattan:

> The candy store is small and dirty as are all the stores on the cobblestoned street. When it drizzles the cobblestones wash bare and gleaming on top, and the manhole covers puff forth their shapeless gouts of mist. The night fogs cloak the muggings, the gangs who wander raucously through the darkness, the prostitutes, and the lovers mating in the dark bedrooms with the sweating stained wallpaper of brown. The walls of the street fester in summer, are clammy in winter; there is an aged odor in this part of the city, a compact of food scraps, of shredded dung balls in the cracks of the cobblestones, of tar, smoke, the sour damp scent of the city people, and the smell of coal stoves and gas stoves in the cold-water flats. All of them blend and lose identity.

From 1953 to 1963 Mailer was an editor at *Dissent,* and in 1956 he was a co-founder of the *Village Voice,* which soon became one of the city's most influential weekly newspapers as it espoused New Journalism, a technique that allowed aggressive reporters to write with a personal point of view— something the larger establishment papers wouldn't permit.

In the mid-1950s, especially in his 1957 essay "The White Negro," Mailer articulated the philosophy of Hip, which he opposed to the *Weltanschauung* of the Square. His detractors charged that hipsterism was merely a carbon copy of the beat philosophy developed in the 1950s by such writers as Jack Kerouac and Allen Ginsberg. Essentially, Mailer saw Hip as a kind of American existentialism. In his thinking, the Negro in the United States has two simple alternatives: "to live a life of constant humility or ever-threatening danger," and the hipster had absorbed the existentialist premises of the Negro and so might be thought a "white Negro." In pursuit of his goal, which is to move forward into growth rather than backward into death, the hipster divorces himself from society, encourages the psychopath in himself, and abdicates all conventional moral responsibility. The hipster differs from the beatnik however: he is proletarian rather than bourgeois; he looks for action instead of sitting, like the beatnik, in the coffeehouse; and he finds his act of violence to be murder even as the beatnik discovers his in suicide.

Mailer's essay drew fire from black novelist and essayist James Baldwin, who argued that Mailer had oversimplified the situation of American blacks and was, in any event, not well qualified to write on the subject since he is white.

Mailer has had a prodigious talent for staying in the news apart from his literary career. In June of 1960 he hailed a police car as a taxi in Provincetown, Massachusetts, because he saw a light on top the car; taken to the police station, he fought with the officers and had his head split open in the battle. In November of that same year, he was arrested in Birdland, a Broadway nightclub, when he argued about a check. A week later, he stabbed his wife after a party in their apartment, but she refused to press charges.

The East Village has been a prime literary location since the turn of the century, and during the 1950s it found itself back in the cultural spotlight once again. Even as the off-Broadway forces were developing their repertories at LaMama and St. Marks, the Beats were declaiming in dark cramped bars. Despite Mailer's characterizations of them, they had an immediate and reverberating effect on broad areas of American culture.

The groundwork for the Beat movement was laid, however, not on the lower East Side but in the Columbia University area of the Upper West Side in 1945 when the undergraduate enfant terrible Allen Ginsberg met former football player Jack Kerouac, who was a Columbia dropout. Another of Kerouac's associates was William Burroughs, the black sheep of the office machine family, then a heroin addict. The fourth prominent figure among the Beats was Gregory Corso, whom Ginsberg met in a Greenwich Village bar in 1950, after Corso had just finished a prison sentence. Even in its origins, then, the Beat movement took up an outlaw position.

The name "Beat" probably comes from the word common among jazz musicians in the 1930s and 1940s, meaning tired or low in spirit. According to John Clellon Holmes, Kerouac said the Beat movement was the outgrowth of "a weariness with all the forms, all the conventions of the world." It was rabidly anti-academic, rejecting prescribed literary formulas, and equally determined to shock the middle class, which it did through its constant involvement with drugs and homosexuality. Ginsberg's particular inspiration was New Jersey poet William Carlos Williams, an artist he saw to be in direct descent from Walt Whitman.

The Beats moved in and out of New York, traveling around the country like Kerouac or shuttling between Manhattan and the West Coast like Ginsberg and his lover Peter Orlovsky. But when they were in Gotham, most of them gravitated to the Lower East Side.

The Beats used one another as figures in their works, sometimes by name, sometimes under pseudonyms. In the first Beat novel, *Go*, by Holmes, Ginsberg appears as David Stofsky and Kerouac as Gene Pasternak. In Kerouac's *On the Road* Ginsberg's ex-lover Neal Cassady appears as Dean Moriarity and in the same author's *The Subterraneans*, Yuri Gligoric is Gregory Corso. Poet Frank O'Hara, more in the literary mainstream than the other Beats, presents a whole cast of characters in his "Adieu to Norman, Bon Jour to Joan and Jean-Paul":

> ....
> and Allen is back talking about god a lot
> and Peter is back not talking very much
> and Joe has a cold and is not coming to Kenneth's
> although he is coming to lunch with Norman
> I suspect he is making a distinction
> well, who isn't....

In 1951 Ginsberg moved to 206 East Seventh Street, where he lived until he went to San Francisco two years later. It was in the California city that he came to wide notice with his long Whitmanesque poem "Howl," in which he attacked American cities, but principally New York, as embodiments of all that the Beats hated about American life:

> What sphinx of cement and aluminum bashed open
>   their skulls and ate up their brains and imagination?
> Moloch! Solitude! Filth! Ugliness! Ashcans and
>   unobtainable dollars! Children screaming under the
>   stairways! Boys sobbing in armies! Old men weeping
>   in the parks!
> Moloch! Moloch! Nightmare of Moloch! Moloch the
>   loveless! Mental Moloch! Moloch the heavy judger of
>   men!
> Moloch the incomprehensible prison! Moloch the
>   crossbone soulless jailhouse and Congress of sorrows!
>   Moloch whose buildings are judgement! Moloch the
>   vast stone of war! Moloch the stunned governments!
> Moloch whose mind is pure machinery! Moloch whose
>   blood is running money! Moloch whose fingers are
>   ten armies! Moloch whose breast is a cannibal
>   dynamo! Moloch whose ear is a smoking tomb!
> Moloch whose eyes are a thousand blind windows!
>   Moloch whose skyscrapers stand in the long streets
>   like endless Jehovahs! Moloch whose factories dream
>   and croak in the fog! Moloch whose smokestacks
>   and antennae crown the cities!

It is, of course, rather ironic that the Beats should focus so vehement an attack on city life, since they themselves—their poetry readings, their posing, even their access to the drugs and sexuality that they thought so threatening to the straight world—were made possible only by the levels of sophistication that a dense urban environment offers. In that way, the Beats were reenacting the very traditional opposition in American literature between urban life and pastoral dreams.

Ginsberg returned to New York with Orlovsky in 1959 and took up residence at 170 East Second Street. By this time, the Beat movement was in full swing and had attracted such figures as O'Hara, Tuli Kupferberg, Seymour Krim, LeRoi Jones (now Imamu Baraka) and Hubert Selby.

Ginsberg's new location inspired the poem "I beg you come back & be cheerful," published in 1963 in *Reality Sandwiches:*

> Tonite I got hi in the window of my apartment
>   chair at 3 : AM
> gazing at Blue incandescent torches
>   bright-lit street below
> clotted shadows loomin on a new laid pave
> —as last week Medieval rabbiz
>   plodded thru the brown raw
>   dirt turned over—sticks
>   & cans
>   and tired ladies sitting on spanish
> garbage pails in the deadly heat

The Beat movement was essentially a movement of young people, largely auto-didacts and, interestingly, without the elements of left radicalism that had characterized so many youthful literary uprisings in the past. By the mid-1960s, Kerouac and Ginsberg were in their forties and Burroughs over fifty; and the generation coming to the fore was passionately committed to the social activism that was diametrically opposed to the philosophy of the Beats, with their rather romantic interest in the accumulation of personal experience. The result was that the Beats were simply left in the dust as the crowd moved on.

A PART OF GREATER NEW YORK'S HARBOR is shaped by Newark Bay, on which lies New Jersey's largest city, a center of banking and industry. Born there in 1933, novelist Philip Roth won acclaim and a National Book Award for his first work of fiction, *Goodbye, Columbus* (1959). Much of the book takes place in Newark and the posh suburb of Short Hills. Ten years later, when Roth published his best-known work, *Portnoy's Complaint*, it was something of a succes de scandale, for in it protagonist Alexander Portnoy discusses in almost clinical detail the compulsive masturbation that characterized his adolescence. Since Portnoy was born in 1933 and, like Roth, grew up in the Weequahic section of Newark, many critics took the book to be simple and straightforward autobiography. This prompted Jacqueline Susann to remark that, while she would like very much to meet Roth, she wouldn't care to shake his hand.

It is near Newark that Willa Cather's memorable short story "Paul's Case" reaches its climax when young Paul carries out his decision to end his life:

> When Paul arrived at Newark, he got off the train and took another cab, directing the driver to follow the Pennsylvania tracks out of the town. The snow lay heavy on the roadways and had drifted deep in the open fields. Only here and there the dead grass or dried weed stalks projected, singularly black, above it.
>
> Once well into the country, Paul dismissed the carriage and walked, floundering along the tracks.... When he reached a little hillside, where the tracks ran through a cut some twenty feet below him, he stopped and sat down.

A few miles north of Newark is the suburb of Rutherford, the home of physician, poet and playwright William Carlos Williams. Williams's most ambitious work is *Paterson*, an intricate five-part poem with long prose quotations about the industrial city near his home. The poet begins by envisioning the city as a partially mythic man, then describes the famous falls in the Passaic River which provided the hydroelectric power to make the city a manufacturing giant in the 19th and early 20th centuries:

> From above, higher than the spires, higher even than the office towers, from oozy fields abandoned to grey beds of dead grass, black sumac, withered weed-stalks, mud and thickets cluttered with dead leaves—the river comes pouring in above the city and crashes from the edge of the gorge in a recoil of spray and rainbow mists—

After writing of the community's modern history and calling it "the city of cheap hotels and private entrances," he turns the clock back to colonial times for contrast:

> In the early days of Paterson, the breathing spot of the village was the triangle square bounded by Park Street (now lower Main St.) and Bank Street. Not including the Falls it was the prettiest spot in town. Well shaded by trees with a common in the center where the country circus pitched its tents.

Young Ben Franklin with his loaves of bread on his arrival in Philadelphia.
New York Public Library

Directly across the Delaware River from Camden is Philadelphia, the capital of the United States from 1790 to 1800 and one of its first intellectual and cultural centers. One who helped make it so was Benjamin Franklin, who arrived there in 1723 at age seventeen. Indeed, the scene of his arrival in his adopted city, as related in his *Autobiography*, is one of the most famous passages in American literature:

> Then I walked up the street, gazing about till near the market-house I met a boy with bread. I had made many a meal on bread, and, inquiring where he got it, I went immediately to the baker's he directed me to in Second-street, and ask'd for a biskit, intending such as we had in Boston; but they, it seems, were not made in Philadelphia. Then I asked for a three-penny loaf, and was told they had none such. So not considering or knowing the difference of money, and the greater cheapness nor the names of his

bread, I bad him give me three-penny worth of any sort. He gave me, accordingly, three great puffy rolls. I was surpriz'd at the quantity, but took it, and, having no room in my pockets, walk'd off with a roll under each arm, and eating the other. Thus I went up Market-street as far as Fourth-street, passing by the door of Mr. Read, my future wife's father; when she, standing at the door, saw me, and thought I made, as I certainly did, a most awkward, ridiculous appearance. Then I turned and went down Chestnut-street and part of Walnut-street, eating my roll all the way, and, coming round, found myself again at Market-street wharf, near the boat I came in....

From this decidedly inauspicious beginning, Franklin went on to become Philadelphia's foremost citizen—statesman, diplomat, scientist, philosopher, publisher, worker for civic betterment. And of course he continued to write throughout his long life.

In 1729 he bought a newspaper from Samuel Keimer, the owner of the printing shop where he had worked. It became the *Pennsylvania Gazette*, one of the most widely read and respected periodicals in the colony. In 1732, he founded the *Philadelphia Zeitung*, the first foreign-language paper in America and also a success.

That same year he began *Poor Richard's Almanack*, whose fame has endured to the present day, although in part for the wrong reasons. Franklin borrowed a great many aphorisms from earlier English writers, maxims like "A penny saved is a penny got" and "Early to bed and early to rise makes a man healthy, wealthy and wise," but so successful was his borrowing that their original writers have been forgotten in the United States: any schoolchild would say Ben Franklin wrote them.

Later there came papers in the physical sciences, pamphlets on politics, essays on such varied subjects as choosing a mistress and dealing with the gout, and, of course, the *Autobiography*, begun in 1771 but never completed. Finally, there was an ever-widening and enormous stream of correspondence flowing almost to the moment of his death in 1790.

Eastern Pennsylvania in general serves as the locale for many of the novels and stories of John O'Hara. Figuring frequently in them is the fictional town of Gibbsville, which some critics identify with Pottsville, the author's birthplace. *The Farmer's Hotel* takes place near Allentown and Bethlehem, while, in a prefatory note to *A Rage to Live* O'Hara writes that "Fort Penn" on the "Nesquehela River" both is and is not Harrisburg on the Susquehanna. Another native of eastern Pennsylvania is John Updike, who was born in Shillington, a suburb of Reading. Several of his novels, including *Rabbit, Run, The Centaur* and *Rabbit Redux*, are set in his home state.

At the end of this block of the alley he [Rabbit Angstrom] turns up a street, Wilbur Street in the town of Mt. Judge, suburb of the city of Brewer, fifth largest city in Pennsylvania [Scranton]. Running uphill. Past a block of big homes, small fortresses of cement and brick inset with doorways of stained and beveled glass and windows of potted plants; and then half the way up another block, which holds a development built all at once in the thirties. The frame homes climb the hill like a single staircase. The space of six feet or so that each double house rises above its neighbor contains two wan windows...and is covered with composition shingling varying in color from bruise to dung. The fronts are scabby clapboards once white. There are a dozen three-story homes, and each has two doors. The seventh door is his.

At the far western end of the state is Pittsburgh, the nation's steel manufacturing center, where Theodore Dreiser spent a number of months as a newspaper reporter in 1894. Although he was there for a relatively short time, he developed a great affection for the city, perhaps because it appealed to his own proletarian roots. In *A Book About Myself* he tells the story of his arrival there and describes the most memorable impression he carried away:

The whole [Monongahela] river for a mile or more was suddenly lit to a rosy glow, a glow which...came from the tops of some forty or fifty stacks belching a deep orange-red flame. At the same time an enormous pounding and crackling came from somewhere, as though titans were at work on subterranean anvils.

Fifteen months before Dreiser's arrival, the Pittsburgh suburb of Homestead had been the scene of the great confrontation between the Carnegie Steel Company and the Amalgamated Steel Workers, when the corporate giant tried to break the power of the union. The newsman saw an unhappy town filling up with foreign workers imported to take the places of those ousted during and after the strike. He recorded this reaction:

Along the river sprawled for a quarter of a mile or more the huge low length of the furnaces, great black bottle-like affairs with rows of stacks and long low sheds or buildings paralleling them, sheds from which came a continuous hammering and sputtering and glow of red fire. The whole was shrouded by a pall of gray smoke, even in the bright sunlight.

Many miles to the southeast, where the Patapsco River empties into Chesapeake Bay, is Baltimore, where lived H.L. Mencken, one of the most influential tastemakers in American history. A few years after his birth, his father, a well-to-do cigar manufacturer, bought a house at 1524 Hollins Street, and it was there that the Sage of Baltimore grew up and lived most of his life. Here, in *Happy Days 1880–1892*, he recalls his childhood:

> The Hollins street neighborhood, in the eighties, was still almost rural, for there were plenty of vacant lots nearby, and the open country began only a few blocks away. Across the street from our house was the wide green of Union Square, with a fishpond, a cast-iron Greek temple housing a drinking-fountain, and a little brick office and tool-house for the square-keeper.... A block to the west-ward...was the vast, mysterious compound of the House of the Good Shepherd, with...a high stone wall shutting it in from the world.

Mencken carved out a successful career as a newspaperman and quickly rose to a position of leadership in that field: he was the editor of the *Evening Herald* within six years after starting as a reporter. His first love, however, was the writing of magazine articles and essays, and he became literary critic of the *Smart Set* in 1908 and then co-edited that important journal with George Jean Nathan from 1914 to 1923. The following year Mencken and Nathan founded *The American Mercury*. Mencken stayed with it until 1933 and helped make it one of the most respected periodicals in the country, fighting for the recognition of writers like Anderson, Lewis, and Dreiser, blasting the American "booboisie," lambasting the denizens of the "Bible Belt," and stirring up the South by referring to it in one of his more benevolent moments as the Sahara of the beaux arts. He also gained recognition as a scholar for his multi-volume work *The American Language*, presenting the then-revolutionary thesis that American English and British English were, in fact, two quite separate languages, and should be recognized as such. Of course, Mencken also claimed for his native tongue a greater suppleness, variety, and inventiveness.

Mencken was a prolific writer, active almost until he died in 1956, specializing in nostalgic autobiographical pieces. His influence began to wane in the 1930s, when his Germanophile elitism caused him to alienate large sections of his public, but in his heyday both his candidly-labeled prejudices and his less strongly held opinions (which were apparently numbered near infinity) were always guaranteed an audience in the intelligentsia.

NEW ENGLAND

EUGENE & PATRICIA FLINN

BACK AT THE BEGINNINGS OF the New England imagination stand the Puritans; and their viewpoints focus the preoccupations of many of the best-known writers from that section of the United States. The Puritans left the Old World for the New in order to found "the city on a hill," as they called it—a place where the elect of God could dwell and prosper in righteousness. As Perry Miller, preeminent historian of Puritan thought, writes: "New England was not an allegiance, it was a laboratory." The setting for that laboratory could not have been what they expected. The nature that they found in New England was far from gentle, though it can paint beautiful scenes: winters there lend themselves easily to nostalgic or picturesque reproduction, but the difficulty of surviving them still poses a real threat to the inhabitants. It is easy to imagine, then, the horror, fear, and loathing that such brutal winters and bleak landscapes must have struck into the unprepared if upright souls of those first Puritan settlers. Unprepared, that is, for the rigors and demands of that strange New England climate: without the help of the friendly Indians who surrounded their struggling community, the colonists would have starved that very first winter. Little wonder, then, that many New England writers, under the sway of the Puritan ethic as they were, would come to consider nature an uncomfortable presence to be locked outside the provident walls of the theocratic civilization they were building.

Thus, unlike writers in the Far West, for example, who delight in the totally alien aspects of nature, its very unpredictability and inhumanity, New England writers tend to see nature as a concrete manifestation of moral judgments. For a writer like Hawthorne—who, with Melville, epitomizes one aspect of that tendency—nature repeatedly emerges as a symbol of the moral lawlessness that begins at the edge of the Puritan

Winslow Homer's rendition of Thanksgiving shows the feast of plenty that the holiday,
which commemorates the early difficulties of the Puritans, evolved into.
New York Public Library

town. Over and over, Hawthorne portrays his own ambiguous reactions to
the deep-seated prejudices behind the Puritan law that shapes the New
England consciousness by turning his characters out of town and loose in
the murky forests. (Melville, in *Moby Dick*, turns his loose upon the vast
and threatening deep.) There they are forced to draw their own
conclusions, make their own judgments, take their own actions without
the strictures of Puritan morality to guide or support them. As Hawthorne
wrote in *Young Goodman Brown:*

> At one extremity of an open space, hemmed in by the dark
> wall of the forest, arose a rock, bearing some rude, natural
> resemblance either to an altar or a pulpit, and surrounded
> by four blazing pines, their tops aflame, their stems
> untouched, like candles at an evening meeting. The mass
> of foliage that had overgrown the summit of the rock was
> all on fire, blazing high into the night and fitfully
> illuminating the whole field. Each pendent twig and leafy
> festoon was in a blaze. As the red light arose and fell, a
> numerous congregation alternately shone forth, then
> disappeared in shadow, and again grew, as it were, out of

the darkness, peopling the heart of the solitary woods at
once.

Another verse of the hymn arose, a slow and mournful
strain, such as the pious love, but joined to words which
hinted at far more. Unfathomable to mere mortals is the
lore of fiends. Verse after verse was sung; and still the
chorus of the desert swelled between like the deepest tone
of a mighty organ; and with the final peal of that dreadful
anthem there came a sound, as if the roaring wind, the
rushing streams, the howling beasts, and every other voice
of the unconcerted wilderness were mingling and according with the voice of guilty man in homage to the prince of
all. The four blazing pines threw up a loftier flame, and
obscurely discovered shapes and visages of horror on the
smoke wreaths above the impious assembly. At the same
moment the fire on the rock shot redly forth and formed a
glowing arch above its base.

Melville is even more explicit in *Moby Dick* about the metaphysical
thrust of his concern with nature:

Let the most absent-minded of men be plunged in his
deepest reveries—stand that man on his legs, set his feet a-
going, and he will infallibly lead you to water, if water
there be in all that region. Should you ever be athirst in the
great American desert, try this experiment, if your caravan
happen to be supplied with a metaphysical professor. Yes,
as every one knows, meditation and water are wedded for
ever.

But here is an artist. He desires to paint you the
dreamiest, shadiest, quietest, most enchanting bit of
romantic landscape in all the valley of the Saco. What is
the chief element he employs? There stand his trees, each
with a hollow trunk, as if a hermit and a crucifix were
within; and here sleeps his meadow, and there sleep his
cattle; and up from yonder cottage goes a sleepy smoke.
Deep into distant woodlands winds a mazy way, reaching
to overlapping spurs of mountains bathed in their hill-side
blue. But though the picture lies thus tranced, and though
this pine-tree shakes down its sighs like leaves upon this
shepherd's head, yet all were vain, unless the shepherd's
eye were fixed upon the magic stream before him. Go visit
the Prairies in June, when for scores on scores of miles you
wade knee-deep among Tiger-lilies—what is the one
charm wanting?—Water—there is not a drop of water
there! Were Niagara but a cataract of sand, would you
travel your thousand miles to see it? Why did the poor
poet of Tennessee, upon suddenly receiving two handfuls

of silver, deliberate whether to buy him a coat, which he sadly needed, or invest his money in a pedestrian trip to Rockaway Beach? Why is almost every robust healthy boy with a robust healthy soul in him, at some time or other crazy to go to sea? Why upon your first voyage as a passenger, did you yourself feel such a mystical vibration, when first told that you and your ship were now out of sight of land? Why did the old Persians hold the sea holy? Why did the Greeks give it a separate deity, and own brother of Jove? Surely all this is not without meaning. And still deeper the meaning of that story of Narcissus, who because he could not grasp the tormenting, mild image he saw in the fountain, plunged into it and was drowned. But that same image, we ourselves see in all rivers and oceans. It is the image of the ungraspable phantom of life; and this is the key to it all.

The other aspect of this New England tendency to moralize nature manifests itself most clearly in the writings of Ralph Waldo Emerson, Henry David Thoreau, and their fellow transcendentalists. Here the desire to understand nature theologically is transmuted: these writers revolt (Unitarianism was their rallying point) against their Puritan heritage and envision the world through the lenses of Swedenborgianism, German Idealism, and Buddhism. Nature for them becomes a repository of moral potential, the vehicle by which people may strive to understand and realize the profundity of their own powers and the fullness of their beings. The order of nature is a divinely inspired gift that is intended to function as a kind of macrocosmic mirror in which the individual can be interpreted and evaluated, and then act. But there is also a kind of wonder called forth by its elegant harmony, as one of the memorable passages from Thoreau's *Walden* shows:

Time is but the stream I go a-fishing in. I drink at it; but while I drink I see the sandy bottom and detect how shallow it is. Its thin current slides away, but eternity remains. I would drink deeper; fish in the sky, whose bottom is pebbly with stars. I cannot count one. I know not the first letter of the alphabet. I have always been regretting that I was not as wise as the day I was born. The intellect is a cleaver; it discerns and rifts its way into the secret of things. I do not wish to be any more busy with my hands than is necessary. My head is hands and feet. I feel all my best faculties concentrated in it. My instinct tells me that my head is an organ for burrowing, as some creatures use their snout and fore paws, and with it I would mine and burrow my way through these hills. I

think that the richest vein is somewhere hereabouts; so by
the divining-rod and thin rising vapors I judge; and here I
will begin to mine.

Not all New England writers are as overt in their intentions as
Hawthorne or Thoreau, but the echoes reverberate once the reader learns
to listen to each writer's variation on the basic themes.

BAR HARBOR AND MT. DESERT ISLAND, among Maine's most beautiful
vacation spots, are where the poet Elinor Wylie spent her summers. Here
one day when the sea was singing and her imagination was running high
she wrote "Atavism," which captures the haunting presence of the Indians
in the Maine forests:

There, when the frost makes all the birches burn
Yellow as cow-lilacs, and the pale sky shines
Like a polished shell between black spruce and pines
Some strange thing tracks us....

Across Penobscot Bay is Camden, the girlhood town of Edna St. Vincent
Millay. There "amid the green piles groaning under the windy wooden
piers" the young poet drank in the tangy ocean air and composed her lyrics.
When she was just nineteen, she wrote the poem that changed her life,
"Renascence."

Her poetry was described by Van Wyck Brooks as "full of the odours and
flavours of New England, bayberry, hay, clover, seaweed, sorrel and the salt
smell of the ocean...." Although she lived for some time in New York and
Europe, she tried always to return home to Maine with her husband for the
summer. Eventually they bought a desolate retreat in Cosco Bay, off the
Maine coast, which she lovingly called Ragged Island and which she
afterwards immortalized in a poem by that name that mined a
transcendentalist vein:

There, there where those black spruces crowd
    To the edge of the precipitous cliff,
Above your boat, under the eastern wall of the Island;
    And no wave breaks;
There, thought unbraids itself, and the mind becomes
    single.

Perhaps no town in Maine has been written about so much as Gardiner,
30 miles to the west of Camden. Edwin Arlington Robinson described the
small port town that he called Tilbury Town on the banks of the Kennebec
in "The Dead Village":

Now there is nothing but the ghosts of things,—
No life, no love, no children, and no men;
And over the forgotten place there clings
The strange and unrememberable light
That is in dreams. The music faded, and then
God frowned, and shut the village from his sight.

Robinson's Gardiner is a Puritan New England version of Edgar Lee Masters's Lewiston, Illinois, the small town he called "Spoon River" in his famous work in which more than 200 of the dead of the little village tell what their lives were really like from the perspectives of their grave sites. In his work, however, Robinson does the speaking himself, describing persons such as the town miser, Aaron Stark, whose only amusement came when he observed people feeling sorry for him

And oftentimes there crept into his ears
A sound of alien pity, touched with tears,—
And then (and only then) did Aaron laugh.

Charles Carville with "melancholy face" and "insufficient eyes" did not fare much better.

He never was a fellow that said much,
And half of what he did say was not heard
By many of us: we were out of touch
With all his whims and all his theories
Till he was dead...

Cliff Klingenhagen, according to Robinson, was happy in the Gardiner-Tilbury Town surroundings drinking wormwood when he could have had wine, perhaps remembering, with Mithridates, that by taking a bit of the poison of life each day, one can usually manage to live a little longer.

Not so Richard Cory, who despite the wealth that his neighbors perceived to be "everything/To make us wish we were in his place," on a "calm summer night/Went home and put a bullet through his head."

That most of the people of Gardiner were unable to see the world through another person's eyes is indeed Robinson's theme. Consider Bewick Finzer: like Robinson's own father, a wealthy man who lost his fortune.

Poor Finzer, with his dreams and schemes
    Fares hard now in the race,
With heart and eye that have a task
    When he looks in the face
Of one who might so easily
    Have been in Finzer's place.

With "nothing but the ghost of things" to haunt them, Robinson's fellow townspeople became the object of his fascinated genius. Certainly the young poet must have observed many a sad old soul like Eben Flood standing alone on a god-forsaken hermitage with only his bottle of whiskey to keep him company.

> The road was his with not a native near;
> And Eben, having leisure, said aloud,
> For no man else in Tilbury Town to hear:
>
> "Well, Mr. Flood, we have the harvest moon
> Again, and we may not have many more;
> The bird is on the wing, the poet says,
> And you and I have said it here before.
> Drink to the bird." He raised up to the light
> The jug that he had gone so far to fill,
> And answered huskily: "Well, Mr. Flood,
> Since you propose it, I believe I will."
>
> Alone, as if enduring to the end
> A valiant armor of scarred hopes outworn,
> He stood there in the middle of the road
> Like Roland's ghost winding a silent horn.
> Below him, in the town among the trees,
> Where friends of other days had honored him,
> A phantom salutation of the dead
> Rang thinly till old Eben's eyes were dim.

Robinson's skillful touch makes men like Flood seem poignant, haunting human beings with dignity and substance. Reuben Bright the butcher, for example, shook with grief and fright and cried like "a great baby half the night" when he was told his wife must die. Symbolically, after he buried his wife and paid the singers and sexton, he tore down his slaughterhouse as well.

Robinson's poetry paints the disappointed and disenchanted, the shrewd and the sorry, the men and women worn down by the frustrations of life in a frosty land where the expectations are limited.

Harriet Beecher Stowe moved to Brunswick, Maine after her husband, Calvin, a professor of biblical literature, was offered a position at Bowdoin. The Stowes settled into a colonial house on Federal Street that had been the residence of Longfellow when he was an undergraduate.

One day, while she was in a church near her home, she conceived Uncle Tom's death and, to the consternation of the preacher, rushed out in the middle of the sermon to write the scene. After she read it to her children, who seemed to enjoy it, Mrs. Stowe continued to write and in a few weeks completed the novel. By the time of the Civil War, sales had reached a phenomenal three million and Mrs. Stowe became a very wealthy woman.

Her next important work, *The Pearl of Orr's Island*, an account of her New England childhood, later inspired Sarah Orne Jewett to write about her own girlhood in Maine.

Farther to the south lies South Berwick, where Sarah Orne Jewett was born in 1849. She claimed that the white picket fence surrounding her house was her earliest memory, and enjoyed telling friends how she used to climb it and watch with fascination the townspeople visiting the village shops that stood right outside her wide green world. Later these same folk would people the pages of her most memorable works, *Deephaven* and *A Country of Pointed Firs*.

When she was not in her own yard, she could be found next door in her grandfather's house, a wonderful haven for an imaginative, inquisitive child. A prosperous owner and builder of ships, this salty former sea captain constructed an elegant colonial home with exquisite taste and furnished it with exotic bric-a-brac from all over the world. On cold wintry days she would snuggle up before the wide brick fireplace and listen to his sea stories and tales of far-off ports, no doubt hearing about odd details and strange characters that would return in her own writings.

As a young girl, Jewett's favorite pastimes were wandering along the Piscataqua River and investigating the many empty old houses that dotted the area or driving about the countryside with her doctor-father while he made his house calls. A former Bowdoin College professor, Dr. Jewett influenced his daughter greatly. *A Country of Pointed Firs* is in fact based on her experiences while traveling through the country with her father. While they drove from fishermen's houses near the sea to inland farms, he talked endlessly about the books that stocked their library and about the lives of his patients. Sometimes while Jewett waited for him, she would be invited inside a house and given cider and spice cakes, which she ate as the patient's worried family confided in her. She found stories everywhere. She mined the countryside and began keeping sketches of daily occurrences and scenes. Jewett observed with a poet's careful eye the lonely woods, the long dark forests of spruce trees and the weatherbeaten houses whose gardens were overgrown with weeds. Her first novel, *Deephaven*, published when she was just twenty-eight, was the result of these ramblings. The crusty talk of Captain Lant and Captain Sands are proof of her talent for capturing the New Englander's nasal twang and speech cadence. Her descriptions of Dunnet Landing, Green Island, and the sea in *A Country of Pointed Firs* are paintings wrought with words. In later years, Jewett would state that she simply followed her father's advice and wrote things exactly as she saw them.

PORTSMOUTH, NEW HAMPSHIRE, just across the border from southern Maine, was the home of Thomas Bailey Aldrich, author of the famous surprise-ending short story, "Marjorie Daw," about a patient who falls in love with the lady of the title, who...but that would spoil the surprise. Scenes from Aldrich's novel *The Story of a Bad Boy* were set in Portsmouth. Like Twain's *Tom Sawyer, Bad Boy* captures the spirit of a mischevious young lad growing up in a small American town. A master stylist, Aldrich filled his works with adventure, compassion and humor, catching the details of everyday life in the southern part of his native state, as he does here in a description of an old-fashioned Fourth of July celebration he remembered from his youth.

> Great were the bustle and confusion on the square. By the way, I don't know why they called this large open space a Square, unless because it was an oval—an oval formed by the confluence of half a dozen streets, now thronged by crowds of smartly dressed townspeople and country folks; for Rivermouth on the Fourth was the centre of attraction to the inhabitants of the neighboring villages.

> On one side of the square were twenty or thirty booths arranged in a semi-circle, gay with little flags and seductive with lemonade, ginger-beer, and seed cakes. Many of the adjacent houses made a pretty display of bunting, and across each of the streets opening on the Square was an arch and evergreen, blossoming all over with patriotic mottoes and paper roses.

Farther to the west is Derry, where Robert Frost, New England's most famous poet, had his farm. Lionel Trilling shocked admirers of the poet when he pointed out at Frost's eightieth birthday party that the octogenarian was a "terrifying poet." He tried to quell the protests by explaining that he was seeking to change the image of a quaint, Currier-and-Ives Frost, and to have him recognized as a writer of profundity and paradox—a quality that suffused his life as well.

He was a New England poet in language, philosophy, style, and subject matter; yet he was born in San Francisco. He was revered as quintessentially American; yet he first became established as a poet while living in England, where "The Road Not Taken," was written in 1914. Frost was a poet of autumn and winter, and just as these two seasons suggest the onset of death, so was Frost's poetry more on the somber than the happy side.

Frost saw the advantage of commenting on our highly industrialized society from the point of view of rural New Hampshire villages. Thus he was like Sherwood Anderson viewing the nation from Winesburg, Ohio, or of Faulkner seeing the universe through his mythical Yoknapatawpha County, Mississippi. Frost's New England has been called mythical, and it was—in the same sense that Yoknapatawpha was.

Frost never tired of acknowledging his debt to Emerson and Thoreau, especially to Emerson's *Essays* and Thoreau's *Walden*. He declared that Emerson's *Nature*, written in 1836, provided him with the argument that nature is symbolically diffused with spiritual facts. And through all of his poetry, whether it be the quiet majesty of a winter's night when a man stopped his horse and buggy to watch a woods fill up with snow or the road that "made all the difference" Frost's images have primarily been ones he culled from his beloved New Hampshire and Vermont.

NOT AS MANY WRITERS WERE BORN IN VERMONT as in neighboring New England states, but many writers from around the world have chosen to adopt it as home. Authors as diverse as Bernard Malamud, Rudyard Kipling, and Pearl Buck, lured by the verdant foliage and gentle hills, settled in the Green Mountain State.

Toward the picturesquely named town of Camel's Hump lies the village of Hinesburg, hometown of contemporary writer Lisa Alther, whose first novel, *Kinflicks*, was partially set in the fictitious Stark's Bog, Vermont, inspired by nearby Starksboro.

> Although Stark's Bog township actually included the bog and the surrounding hills and farms, the town proper consisted of one road, which came from St. Johnsbury and led to a border crossing into Quebec. Where the road passed through town, it was lined with a feed store, a hardware store, a hotel where hunters stayed in the fall, an IGA grocery store, a gun shop, a taxidermy parlor, a funeral home, a farm equipment franchise, and a snow machine showroom called Sno Cat City. All these were housed in buildings from the early 1800s with colonial cornices and returns and doorways, which were pleasing in their simplicity. Pleasing to everyone but the Stark Boggers, who were sick to death of them....

AT THE NORTHWESTERN BORDER OF MASSACHUSETTS are the breathtakingly beautiful Berkshires, the mountains enjoyed by many of America's best-known writers, among them Jonathan Edwards, Nathaniel Hawthorne, Herman Melville, William Cullen Bryant, Henry James, and Edith Wharton. One of the Berkshire's most tranquil settings, Tanglewood, the Mecca of music and nature lovers the world over, was in fact named by Hawthorne, who spent two happy summers there. His *Tanglewood Tales*, set in these idyllic woods, helped to make the name stick.

It was in May of 1850 that Hawthorne, anxious to free himself from his numbing job as a surveyor at the Custom House in Salem, took his wife and two children and escaped to the Berkshires. There they rented a cottage from a Boston banker. Although Hawthorne did not really like this cottage—he said it was ugly—they lived there until November, 1851, taking walks through the woods and over the hills, and occasionally riding into the nearby towns of Lenox, Lee, and Stockbridge.

But Hawthorne did not take a vacation from his profession as writer. When he was in town, he talked to the people, savoring their speech and tucking their colorful twists of language away in his notebooks. He was captivated as well by the beauty of the surrounding countryside and watched with delight the changing hues of Monument Mountain as the sun colored it through the passing day. The sheer abundance of his observations spilled over into his fiction and was transformed into the characters, settings, and events of his *Tanglewood Tales* and *A Wonder Book for Boys and Girls.*

"Ethan Brand," his well-known story of a solitary old lime-kiln keeper who goes in search of the unpardonable sin, takes place at Mount Greylock in the Berkshires. His descriptions of Brand's kiln are taken from observations of the ones he found scattered around the hills of Greylock.

> There are many such lime-kilns in that tract of country, for the purpose of burning the white marble which composes a large part of the substance of the hills. Some of them, built years ago, and long deserted, with weeds growing in the vacant round of the interior, which is open to the sky, and grass and wildflowers rooting themselves into the chinks of the stones, look already like relics of antiquity, and may yet be overspread with the lichens of centuries to come. It is a lonesome, and, when the character is inclined to thought, may be an intensely thoughtful occupation; as it proved in the case of Ethan Brand, who had mused to such strange purpose, in days gone by, while the fire in this very kiln was burning.

Two of New England's most famous writers, Hawthorne and Melville, met in the Berkshires. Melville came from New York City to live near Pittsfield in 1850 in a big old home with a gigantic chimney which he wrote of in his short piece "I and My Chimney." Soon after his arrival the two writers were formally introduced at the home of Stockbridge lawyer David Dudley Fields and they became instant friends.

Like Hawthorne's, Melville's work was influenced by his travels about the countryside. His *Piazza Tales* and his novels *Pierre* and *Israel Potter* were written there. In fact, the tales get their name from the rambling piazza Melville had built around his home in order to better view the beautiful scenery. Some contend that he was even influenced by the shape of Mount Greylock, which was always before him, while writing *Moby Dick*, since they believe it resembles a giant sperm whale.

Not far to the east of the Berkshires is Bryant Mountain, named after the poet William Cullen Bryant, who was born within the shadow of the mountain at Cummington. It is easy to see why an artist brought up in this transcendentalist's countryside would write, as Bryant did in "Thanatopsis," "To him who in the love of Nature holds/Communion with her visible forms, she speaks/A various Language." But not many would guess that this poem was written by a lad of seventeen.

Southeast lies Westfield, home of Edward Taylor, generally considered the finest poet of the Colonial period. Taylor arrived in America from his native England in 1668, when he was twenty-six years old. He arrived in Boston, went to Harvard, where he was ordained, and then set up his ministry at Westfield. He lived there for the rest of his life, writing a considerable amount of poetry, but making it available only to family and friends.

It was not until the 20th century that Taylor's poetry became known to the general public. His heirs had heeded his wish that his works not be published and one of them, grandson Ezra Stiles, president of Yale, hid them so securely at the university that they were not discovered there until 1937. They were published two years later to critical acclaim.

Although unknown to them, Taylor clearly presaged later New England writers' view of nature as the material manifestation of a hidden metaphysics that would be revealed to one who studied it:

> I kening through Astronomy Divine
> The Worlds bright Battlement, wherein I spy
> A Golden Path my Pensill cannot line
> From that bright Throne unto my Threshold ly.
> And while my puzzled thoughts about it pore
> I finde the Bread of Life in't at my doore.

> When that this Bird of Paradise put in
> This Wicker Cage (my Corps) to tweedle praise
> Had peckt the Fruite forbid: and so did fling
> Away its Food; and lost its golden dayes,
> It fell into Celestiall Famine sore,
> And never could attain a morsell more.

> Alas! alas! Poore Bird, what wilt thou doe?
> This Creatures field no food for Souls e're gave:
> And if thou knock at Angells dores, they show
> An Empty Barrell: they no soul bread have.
> Alas! Poore Bird, the Worlds White Loafe is done,
> And cannot yield thee here the smallest Crumb.

In this sad state, Gods Tender Bowells run
  Out streams of Grace: And he to end all strife,
The Purest Wheate in Heaven, his deare-dear Son
  Grinds, and kneads up into this Bread of Life:
  Which Bread of Life from Heaven down came and
  stands
Disht in they Table up by Angells Hands.

The quaint little college town of Amherst contains a sprawling red-brick mansion, witness to wealth, culture, and respectability. In it Emily Dickinson spent a good part of her 55 years rejecting the Puritan God of New England but writing about those very New England preoccupations, death and nature. At the age of twenty-three she wrote Thomas W. Higginson, her only important connection with the literary life of her time, "I seldom leave home any more." She spent years without wandering outside her home, save when she made visits to her garden. Hearsay has it that she visited her garden by traversing her long scarlet rug, thus maintaining her connection with her home. She concealed her mind, as well as her person, from all but a few friends. Even Higginson saw her but two times in his life. During her lifetime she permitted only four of her more than 600 poems to be printed.

Four years after her death Higginson was asked to make selections from her numerous poems so that a book of her verse might be published. Although often puzzled by the cryptic nature of her poems, the seemingly monotonous rhythms and the apparently careless grammar and rhyme, he took on the assignment with relish. "After all," he wrote, "when a thought takes one's breath away, a lesson on grammar seems an impertinence." When the book was published in 1891, Emily Dickinson became an overnight literary sensation in New England.

At the time people were reading her poems, the powerful New England vision of human affairs, begun by the Puritans and tempered considerably by Emerson, had begun to shift under pressure from changes in the structure of society. Industrialism and immigration had altered the face of Puritan Anglo-Saxon New England forever. Dickinson, though, worked within the larger literary tradition of New England. She seized on the ingredients of the Protestant vision as symbols for her poetry of terror and ecstasy. She could not accept the Puritan God, whom she describes in one poem as "burglar, banker, father." And her readers had moved far enough from the cloistered world of their past to be able to appreciate irreverences like this:

      Drowning is not so pitiful
        As the attempt to rise.
      Three times, 'tis said, a sinking man

> Comes up to face the skies,
> And then declines forever
> To that abhorred abode
> Where hope and he part company,—
> For he is grasped of God.
> The Maker's cordial visage,
> However good to see,
> Is shunned, we must admit it,
> Like an adversity.

In "Apparently with no surprise" she again takes up the subject of nature, specifically the biting New England cold, which she depicts as an enemy of long standing. Nature is seen as brutal, uncaring, and metaphysically motivated.

> Apparently with no surprise
> To any happy flower,
> The frost beheads it at its play
> In accidental power.
>
> The blond assassin passes on,
> The sun proceeds unmoved
> To measure off another day
> For an approving God.

Emily Dickinson and her tight little world on Main Street in Amherst are certainly one of the enigmas of American literature. Yet, her vision of the world is easily situated in New England letters, once it is understood how the Puritan and transcendentalist views of nature formed so essential a part of her New England character.

Certainly the presence of Harvard University, the oldest college in the country, has contributed to the literary stature of Cambridge. The Puritan migration to Massachusetts was one of the most unusual in the annals of colonization. More than 100 of these early settlers in Cambridge and Boston were college graduates from prestigious Oxford and Cambridge in England. It was in honor of the university city on the banks of the Cam in Britain that New Towne, Massachusetts, became Cambridge in 1638, two years after Harvard was founded.

Subsequently the university became the magnet which drew some of the nation's most illustrious professors and scholars from Edward Taylor, the poet, in 1668 to hundreds of others through the years. Through the Harvard campus have passed such illustrious figures as Charles Eliot Norton, William James, Louis Agassiz, Henry Wadsworth Longfellow, George Pierce Baker (Eugene O'Neill's drama teacher), George Ticknor, James Russell Lowell, George Santayana, Archibald MacLeish, and John Kenneth Galbraith.

Harvard College as it appeared in a wood engraving from 1679.
New York Public Library

Harvard's students have been even more famous in the literary world. The yearbooks list such names as Ralph Waldo Emerson, Richard Henry Dana, Oliver Wendell Holmes, Francis Parkman, T. S. Eliot, Walter Lippmann, J. P. Marquand, Frank Norris, Thomas Wolfe, William H. Prescott, Wallace Stevens, E. E. Cummings, Henry James, Edward Everett Hale, Henry David Thoreau, Henry Adams, Robert Frost, and presidents John Adams, John Quincy Adams, Theodore and Franklin Roosevelt, and John F. Kennedy.

As Van Wyck Brooks asked, where else could one catch sight of literati like James Russell Lowell, author of *The Bigelow Papers*, strolling with William Dean Howells, *The Atlantic* editor, over to Henry James's house on Quincy Street; or bump into Oliver Wendell Holmes and Richard Henry Dana leaving Longfellow's Craigie House (Washington's headquarters in 1775–76) at 105 Brattle Street?

Both Lowell and his neighbor, Henry Wadsworth Longfellow, became identified with a group of writers known as the Fireside Poets, which included Oliver Wendell Holmes, John Greenleaf Whittier, and William Cullen Bryant—all native New Englanders. Their work, as the name implies, was often read aloud by a family audience as it gathered around the nightly fire in the dead of winter. This audience especially loved poems dealing with home, family, nature, spiritual love, and patriotism—probably one of the reasons why later critics often dismissed the Fireside Poets as superficial. Nevertheless, a closer inspection of some of their works reveals an interesting insight into New England thinking and sensitivity. For example, Lowell's political satire, *The Bigelow Papers* illustrates a brilliant mastery of the Yankee dialect, suggesting that no soil but New England's could have produced its rich idiom.

> An' you've got to get up airly,
> Ef you want to take in God
>
> I spose you wonder ware I be; I can't tell, for the soul o' me
> Exactly ware I be myself,—meanin' by thet the holl o' me.
>
> Wen I left hum, I hed two legs, an' they worn't bad ones neither,
>
> (The scaliest trick they ever played wuz bringin' on me hither,)
>
> Now one on' em's I dunno ware;—they thought I wuz adyin',
>
> An' sawed it off because they said it wuz kin' o' mortifyin';
>
> I'm willin' to believe it wuz, an'yit I don't see, nuther,
>
> Wy one shoud take to feelin' cheap a minnit sooner'n t'other,
>
> Sence both wuz equilly to blame; but things is ez they be;
>
> It took on so they took it o-f, an' thet's enough fer me.

With the publication of *The Bigelow Papers,* Lowell found himself in the camp of idealistic, scholarly New Englanders who preached and fought for liberal causes, especially the abolition of slavery, with tenacity, wit, and Yankee shrewdness. Commenting on the result of his satire, Lowell wrote:

> The success of my experiment soon began not only to astonish me, but to make me feel the responsibility of knowing that I held in my hand a weapon instead of the fencing stick I had supposed.

Finally, Lowell's characters show a keen awareness of two different types of New Englanders.

> I needed on occasion to rise above the level of mere patois, and for this purpose conceived the Rev. Mr. Wilbur, who should express the more cautious element of the New England character and its pedantry, as Mr. Bigelow should serve for its homely common-sense vivified and heated by conscience.

Longfellow's work—today too quickly dismissed as superfical and saccharine—typifies the spirit of New England literary conscience in the 19th century. Influenced by and torn between Puritanism and romanticism, Longfellow accepted the Christian belief that man was caught between the currents of good and evil. Many of Longfellow's poems exhibit this balance that he found in the world between good and evil, work and rest, happiness and despair. Or as Longfellow's poem "Haunted Houses" acclaims:

> Our little lives are kept in equipose
> By opposite attractions and desires.
> The struggle of the instinct that enjoys,
> And the more noble instinct that aspires.

Using poetry as a vehicle for teaching, Longfellow, along with many of his fellow New Englanders, believed that without a moral lesson the written word was nearly without value, and certainly without direction:

> Trust no Future, howe'er pleasant!
> Let the dead Past bury its dead!
> Act,—act in the living Present!
> Heart within, and God o'erhead!
> . . .
>
> Tell me not, in mournful numbers,
> "Life is but an empty dream!"
> For the soul is dead that slumbers,
> And things are not what they seem.

Perhaps this is why Longfellow, like Lowell, taught school as well as wrote for a living.

And, among his other, rather prolific accomplishments, he could list a translation of *The Divine Comedy* into English, which he undertook in 1861 after a deep personal tragedy. His wife was burned to death in July of 1861 after her dress caught fire while she was sealing boxes containing curls of her children's hair. Longfellow himself was horribly burned about the face and hands when he tried to smother the flames. Three days later, on the anniversary of their wedding, Fanny Longfellow was buried in Mt. Auburn Cemetary. Longfellow was so upset he could not attend the funeral.

Another well-known resident of Cambridge was Margaret Fuller, a brilliant and creative woman who became a leading transcendentalist. She was a close friend of Emerson, a tireless assistant to Bronson Alcott, a gifted teacher, and a committed feminist. For two years she edited *The Dial*, that highly influential and respected journal of poetry, criticism, and philosophy, begun by members of the famous Transcendental Club in March, 1835. In 1845, she published her greatest work, *Woman in the Nineteenth*

Century, in which she predicted that America would one day become the place where woman would overcome social injustice and male tyranny.

> That now the time has come when a clearer vision and better action are possible—when man and woman may regard one another as brother and sister, the pillars of one porch, the priests of one worship.
> I have believed and intimated that this hope would receive an ample fruition than ever before in our own land.
> And it will do so if this land carry out the principles from which sprang our national life.
> I believe that at present women are the best helpers of one another.
> Let them think, let them act, till they know what they need.

Although not the finest stylist, Margaret Fuller wrote with passion and her book remains a lasting monument to her challenging spirit and sharp, incisive mind. Her unique relationship with Brook Farm community has been the subject of many scholarly articles and books, but Hawthorne's *The Blithedale Romance* remains the most discussed account of her part in that unusual utopian, agrarian, self-supporting community of workers and thinkers. Obviously, Hawthorne did not like Margaret Fuller, and his portrait of her as the dark and fiery Zenobia is far from flattering.

> Zenobia bade Hollingsworth good-night very sweetly, and nodded to me with a smile. But, just as she turned aside with Priscilla into the dimness of the porch, I caught another glance at her countenance. It would have made the fortune of a tragic actress, could she have borrowed it for the moment when she fumbles in her bosom for the concealed dagger, or the exceedingly sharp bodkin, or mingles the ratsbane in her lover's bowl of wine or her rival's cup of tea.

Hawthorne later confessed that the days he spent in the company of Margaret Fuller at Brook Farm were more of a trial than an enjoyment. Nevertheless, this unusual community played an important part in influencing major New England writers and thinkers. Begun in 1841 at West Roxbury, nine miles south of Boston, by George Ripley, a transcendentalist Unitarian minister in Boston gifted with a soul-searching New England intelligence, Brook Farm was home for a time to Hawthorne, Emerson, Theodore Parker, William Ellery Channing, Bronson Alcott and Charles Anderson, Dana and John Sullivan Dwight, to mention only a few. A dismal failure financially, the Brook Farm experiment is regarded as a monument to the New England spirit of idealism, liberty, and intelligence.

Transcendentalism was perhaps best described by Ralph Waldo Emerson in his essays "Nature" and "The Transcendentalist."

> It is a secret which every intellectual man quickly learns, that beyond the energy of his possessed and conscious intellect he is capable of a new energy (as of an intellect doubled on itself), by abandonment to the nature of things; that beside his privacy of power as an individual man, there is a great public power on which he can draw, by unlocking, at all risks, his human doors, and suffering the ethereal tides to roll and circulate through him; then he is caught up in the life of the Universe, his speech is thunder, his thought is Law, and his words are universally intelligible as the plants and animals.

Certainly, transcendentalism spoke about the power of the individual and the need for self-reliance as well as the more traditional New England virtues of spiritual freedom, intuition, moderation, and enduring, persistent thought. Many transcendentalists believed in the immanence of a divinity in both nature and man, and sought for the great "oversoul" that made reality whole and unified. They thought that man could find truth in his feelings and emotions and insisted that to live by the physical senses alone led to certain death, for the soul of nature is metaphysical. Rejecting traditional religions, they denied the need for formal worship and instead insisted that God and the individual needed no emissary.

> Standing on the bare ground,—my head bathed by the blithe air, and uplifted into infinite space,—all mean egotism vanishes. I become a transparent eyeball; I am nothing; I see all; the currents of the Universal Being circulate through me; I am part or parcel of God. The name of the nearest friend sounds foreign and accidental: to be brothers, to be aquaintances, master or servant, is then a trifle and a disturbance. I am the lover of uncontained and immoral beauty. In the wilderness, I find something more dear and connate than in streets and villages. In the tranquil landscape, and especially in the distant line of the horizon, man beholds somewhat as beautiful as his own nature.

Of all the people associated with transcendentalism, Ralph Waldo Emerson was perhaps the closest to being a living embodiment of its tenets. Like his father before him he studied for the ministry at Harvard's Divinity School, which later enabled him to become pastor of Boston's Second Unitarian Church. But Emerson soon grew dissatisfied with his role as a clergyman and began having doubts about the truth of Christian doctrine and the institutionalized church. Inspired by his good friend William Ellery Channing, who began to question even the liberal Unitarian beliefs, he left the ministry in 1832 and took a 10-month tour of Europe, where he broadened his cultural and intellectual scope and began to write seriously. When he returned to America, he started firing off lectures and essays to a public which neither appreciated nor understood him. John Quincy Adams and Andrew Norton said he was a "vile atheist" and dismissed his ideas. Others said he was conceited and insane. But Emerson, undaunted, continued to write and lecture, delivering in 1838 an address to Harvard's graduating divinity students that argued against conventional religious practices and threatened to undermine the entire establishment. This speech caused a whirlwind of controversy around him and his ties with the institutional church.

One of Cambridge's most famous inhabitants was E. E. Cummings, the poet who incorporated unconventional syntax and typography into his art. Cummings was a New England poet in the unbroken line extending from Emerson and Thoreau through Dickinson and Robinson. He savored his past, drew from it, but at the same time confronted the 20th century. His father, the Reverend Edward Cummings, was, like Emerson, a nationally known Unitarian minister of his time who was a firm believer in the Emersonian tenets of self-reliance and self-transcendence. Cummings himself adhered to his father's belief in the strength of the individual, and like Emerson and other New England writers, saw in nature a moral to be drawn for mankind's benefit, if properly understood.

> what if a much of a which of a wind
> gives the truth to summer's lie;
> bloodies with dizzying leaves the sun
> and yanks immortal stars awry.
> Blow king to beggar and queen to seem
> (blow friend to fiend: blow space to time)
> —when skies are hanged and oceans drowned,
> the single secret will still be man
>
> what if a keen of a lean wind flays
> screaming hills with sleet and snow:
> strangles valleys by ropes of thing
> and stifles forests in white ago?
> Blow hope to terror: blow seeing to blind
> (blow pity to envy and soul to mind)
> —whose hearts are mountains, roots are trees,
> it's they shall cry hello to the spring

Cambridge was famous for its Gold Coast, in the days before Harvard built its great houses. James Alan McPherson, the popular contemporary black writer, lived there long after its day of glory when he was a student at Harvard. He wrote his frequently anthologized short story "Gold Coast" there in 1968 in an old building near Harvard Square where Conrad Aiken once had lived. The grandeur was gone when McPherson lived there, but the glorious past of Cambridge remained in the woodwork, or rather in the style of the old apartments, each with a small fireplace, large bathrooms with chain toilets, and a lobby with a high ceiling with thick redwood beams, a marble floor, fancy ironwork, and an old-fashioned house telephone. McPherson's poignant story is about the old, locked into the rusty relics of the past with little hope for the future, as are many of the residents of Cambridge and nearby Boston and large cities throughout the nation.

On an inlet of the Atlantic Ocean lies Salem, the scene of the notorious witch trials of 1692. Unquestionably its most famous dweller was Nathaniel Hawthorne, born in 1804 without a "w" in his name. His great-grandfather, John Hathorne, was one of the three judges who had condemned women to death as witches during Salem's infamous trials. Thus, Hawthorne was deeply affected, even in his blood, by the Puritan history and ideals. In reading his famous novel, *The Scarlet Letter*, his obsession with guilt with the history of Puritan New England, becomes frighteningly apparent:

A 19th century portrayal of one of the trials for witchcraft held in Salem during the famous witchhunt of the 17th century.
New York Public Library

He had all the puritanic traits, both good and evil....His son, too, inherited the persecuting spirit, and made himself so conspicuous in the martyrdom of the witches, that their blood may fairly be said to have left a stain upon him. So deep a stain, indeed, that his old dry bones, in the Charter Street burial-ground, must still retain it, if they have not crumbled utterly to dust. I know not whether these ancestors of mine bethought themselves to repent, and ask pardon of Heaven for their cruelties...at all events, I, the present writer, as their representative, hereby take shame upon myself for their sakes, and pray that any curse incurred by them—as I have heard, and as the dreary and unprosperous condition of the race, for many a long year back, would argue to exist—may be now and henceforth removed.

When Hawthorne was growing up in Salem, the town was beginning to lose much of the splendor it had had in bygone days. This once-famous trading center had been the chief American port used by privateers for attacking British shipping during the American Revolution and the War of 1812. But with the wars over, its wharves and warehouses succumbed to idleness and decay. Yet, as one of the oldest towns in America, Salem was alive with history and the ghosts of the past. Legends and tales of Gothic horrors echoed through the winding streets and across the moss-covered, crumbling houses. Many old women, half insane, walked the streets mumbling to themselves or sat for hours, as Hawthorne once claimed he did, in the cemetery on Charter Street, where crosses and skulls loomed in the shadows.

It was in *The House of the Seven Gables* that Hawthorne put Salem on the literary map:

Halfway down a bystreet of one of our New England towns stands a rusty wooden house, with seven acutely peaked gables, facing towards various points of the compass, and a huge, clustered chimney in the midst. The street is Pyncheon Street; the house is the old Pyncheon House; and an elm tree, of wide circumference, rooted before the door, is familiar to every town-born child by the title of the Pyncheon Elm.

Who would have thought that to the north of Salem lay the one-time world of Rudyard Kipling? Yet it was in Gloucester, a town that for more than 300 years has maintained the most active fishing fleet in New England, that Kipling, a visitor to this community of narrow, winding streets looking to the sea, was inspired to write *Captains Courageous*, one of the world's classics for children. The physician who delivered Kipling's first daughter, Josephine, during a raging blizzard in December of 1892, Dr. James Conland, introduced the author to Gloucester and urged him to write the novel, which was based in part on experiences Kipling had while living there. The conclusion of the novel celebrates a ceremony enacted every August—a commemoration and expiation, a typical New England role—when wreaths are cast on the outgoing tide in memory of the fishermen lost at sea.

> The widows—they were nearly all of that season's making —braced themselves rigidly like people going to be shot in cold blood, for they knew what was coming. The summer boarder girls in pink and blue shirt waists stopped tittering over Captain Edwardes's wonderful poem, and looked back to see why all was silent. The fishermen pressed forward as that town official who had talked to Cheyne bobbed up on the platform and began to read the year's list of losses, dividing them into months. Last September's casualties were mostly single men and strangers, but his voice rang very loud in the stillness of the hall.

Ipswich, to the northeast of Gloucester, became the home of yet another Harvard graduate named John Updike. In Updike's novel *Couples*, a gilded weathervane in the shape of a golden rooster presides over the wasteland that is Tarbox, with metaphysical overtones that echo meaningfully in the tradition of New England literature:

> It turned in the wind and flashed in the sun and served as a landmark to fishermen in Massachusetts Bay. Children in the town grew up with the sense that the bird was God. That is, if God were physically present in Tarbox, it was in the form of this unreachable weathercock visible from everywhere. And if its penny (eye) could see, it saw everything, spread below it like a living map.

Haverhill, the moment a blizzard strikes, is the true home of John Greenleaf Whittier. One of poetry's most famous snowstorms breaks across "a universe of sky and snow" in "Snow-Bound":

> Shut in from all the world without
>   We sat the clean winged hearth about,
>   Content to let the north wind roar
> In baffled rage at pane and door.

Whittier—poet, mystic, dedicated abolitionist, Quaker, humanitarian and influential citizen—was born there on a 148-acre homestead on December 17, 1807 and spent his first 29 years in this New England paradise, storing enough memories of blustery days and storm-stranded nights to last a lifetime. Young Whittier worked the farm like any boy, but in his spare time he wrote. After he had sent one of his poems to William Lloyd Garrison, founder of *The Liberator*, an abolitionist newspaper in Boston, his recognition as a poet was assured.

Concord is where, as Emerson said in his poem, the "embattled farmers ... fired the shot heard 'round the world." It was also the home of some of America's best-known writers—Thoreau, Hawthorne, Bronson and Louisa May Alcott, Emerson and William Ellery Channing. Channing's sister-in-law Margaret Fuller and others, including Whittier, Longfellow, Bret Harte, Henry James and Walt Whitman, spent time in Concord.

Henry David Thoreau was the only major writer actually born in Concord. Perhaps it is fair to say that the town affected him as it did no other creative spirit. He lived most of his life in Concord, attending Concord Academy, then going to Harvard, where he won the friendship of Emerson. After graduation, he returned to his native village, where he taught school for a time.

From 1841 to 1843 he lived in Emerson's home, serving as a general handyman and gardener, but working with his head as well as with his hands. He began to keep a journal of his observations and reactions and to contribute articles to *The Dial* and help Emerson with editorial assignments. There he came in contact with transcendentalists like Margaret Elizabeth Peabody, Orestes Brownson Fuller, Bronson Alcott, and Theodore Parker.

Encouraged to write and think, Thoreau began to develop creatively at a slow but steady pace. It was not until the spring of 1845, however, when he went to Walden Pond, two miles south of Concord village to begin his two-year, two-month, two-day experiment of living "away from civilization" that Thoreau came into his own and wrote the work that would insure his place in American literature.

Although he soaked up all the observations and impressions he would record in *Walden* while living in the woods, the work was written later, mostly in his family home in Concord. Today it remains one of the best nature books in American literature. At the same time, it confronts nature as a philosophical problem—a typical New England approach.

> The wonderful purity of nature at this season is a most pleasing fact. Every decayed stump and moss-grown stone and rail, and the dead leaves of autumn, are concealed by a clean napkin of snow. In the bare fields and tinkling woods, see what virtue survives. In the coldest and bleakest places the warmest charities still maintain a foothold. A cold and searching wind drives away all contagion, and nothing can withstand it but what has a virtue in it, and accordingly, whatever we meet with in cold and bleak

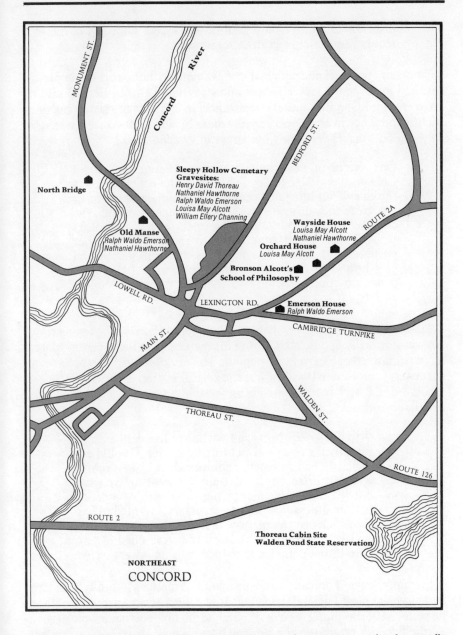

Sleepy Hollow Cemetary Gravesites:
Henry David Thoreau
Nathaniel Hawthorne
Ralph Waldo Emerson
Louisa May Alcott
William Ellery Channing

North Bridge

Old Manse
Ralph Waldo Emerson
Nathaniel Hawthorne

Wayside House
Louisa May Alcott
Nathaniel Hawthorne

Orchard House
Louisa May Alcott

**Bronson Alcott's
School of Philosophy**

Emerson House
Ralph Waldo Emerson

MONUMENT ST.

Concord River

BEDFORD ST.

ROUTE 2A

LOWELL RD.

LEXINGTON RD.

MAIN ST.

CAMBRIDGE TURNPIKE

THOREAU ST.

WALDEN ST.

ROUTE 126

ROUTE 2

**Thoreau Cabin Site
Walden Pond State Reservation**

NORTHEAST
CONCORD

Concord was the scene for a gathering of early American literary giants, and an historically appropriate one at that. As Emerson wrote of it:

> Here once the embattled farmers stood,
> And fired the shot heard round the world.

Here also were found the writers, thinkers, and teachers who first declared their independence from European culture by creating an American literature.

places, as the tops of mountains, we respect for a sort of sturdy innocence, a Puritan toughness.

Thoreau's political and personal involvement with the anti-slavery issue resulted in several essays. His best known is "Civil Disobedience," said to have inspired Gandhi's passive resistance. In it Thoreau related his one-night experience in the Concord jail, where he was imprisoned for refusal to pay a poll tax. He explains his arrest in *Walden*.

> One afternoon, near the end of the first summer, when I went to the village to get a shoe from the cobbler's, I was seized and put into jail, because ... I did not pay a tax to, or recognize the authority of, the State which buys and sells men, women, and children, like cattle, at the door of its senate-house. I had gone down to the woods for other purposes. But, wherever a man goes, men will pursue and paw him with their dirty institutions, and, if they can, constrain him to belong to their desperate odd-fellow society.

Like Robinson's "Miniver Cheevy," Thoreau was born at the wrong time. He was not really appreciated during his own age, but half a century later, his writings became extremely popular. His philosophical perspective on nature, as expressed in *Walden*, was the crystallization of the transcendentalists' ideals; and it came to be increasingly a part of New England's cultural heritage.

> I went to the woods because I wished to live deliberately, to front only the essential facts of life, and see if I could not learn what it had to teach, and not, when I came to die, discover that I had not lived. I did not want to live what was not life, living is so dear; nor did I wish to practice resignation, unless it was quite necessary. I wanted to live deep and suck out the marrow life, to live so sturdily and Spartan-like as to put to rout all that was not life...to drive life into a corner and reduce it to its lowest terms.

In many ways Thoreau was what some Americans think of as the stereotypical New Englander. He was frugal, he was fascinated by nature, he believed in the simple joys of life, and he did not feel that people needed all the luxuries present in the average home. Three chairs were sufficient for Thoreau—one for solitude, two for friendship, and three for company. When there were more than two guests, the rest stood.

Not far from Walden is the Orchard House, the residence of philosopher Bronson Alcott and his daughter Louisa, author of *Little Women*. Although the novel was written in the cottage behind it, the Orchard House is its principal setting. The book was almost totally autobiographical and the major characters were modeled on Louisa Alcott's own family. Meg was her sister Anna, Jo was herself, Beth her sister Elizabeth, and Amy her sister May. Her father was one of the first prominent figures in the transcendentalist movement and the founder of the great Boston Temple School. Bronson Alcott was certainly unique. Once a Connecticut peddler, he later became a brilliant educational reformer and a highly influential social philosopher. Nevertheless, he was always poor and his family was forced to subsist on apples and ideas.

Eight years after Emerson began his first book of essays, *Nature*, in the upstairs study of his grandfather's home, the Old Manse, Nathaniel Hawthorne and his new bride took up residence there. It was to be the happiest time in the writer's life, when the peace and tranquility of his environment coincided with the "almost idyllic" joy of his inner spirit. His stay there, with his memories of the town's solitary river flowing behind his house, his walks along the moonlit streets with his young bride, the morning sunlight coloring his orchard and garden and dancing off the willow branches outside his window are all recalled in *Mosses from an Old Manse*—all, of course, seen from this typical metaphysical and somewhat ironic perspective on nature.

> There was in the rear of the house the most delightful little nook of a study that ever afforded its snug seclusion to a scholar. It was here that Emerson wrote "Nature"; for he was then an inhabitant of the Manse, and used to watch the Assyrian dawn and Paphian sunset and moonrise from the summit of our eastern hill. When I first saw the room, its walls were blackened with the smoke of unnumbered years, and made still blacker by the grim prints of Puritan ministers that hung around.
>
> Perhaps the reader, whom I cannot help considering as my guest in the Old Manse, and entitled to all courtesy in the way of sight showing,—perhaps he will choose to take a nearer view of the memorable spot. We stand now on the river's brink. It may well be called Concord,—the river of peace and quietness; for it is certainly the most unexcitable and sluggish stream that ever loitered imperceptibly towards its eternity,—the sea.

In the heart of Hawthorne's first winter there, he, Emerson, and Thoreau frequently met to go skating on the frozen Concord River. One day Hawthorne's daughter captured in her journal a delightfully allegorical moment of sport as she watched her father, wrapped in his cloak, "move like a self-impelled Greek statue, stately and grave," while Emerson, "evidently too weary to hold himself erect," stooped forward, "half lying on

Emerson's comfortable study in Concord reflects both his broad reading and his style of living. Thoreau found Emerson's house a welcome haven during his Walden adventure.
The Society for the Preservation of New England Antiquities

the air," and a far more agile Thoreau executed "dithyrambic dances and Bacchic leaps," showing off his skill.

> And finally Boston—
> > And this is good old Boston,
> > > The home of the bean and the cod,
> > Where the Lowells talk only to the Cabots
> > And the Cabots talk only to God.
> > > —John Collins Bossich (Patterned on a
> > > toast given at the 25th anniversary of
> > > the Harvard class of 1880)

Boston, the Hub City, the site of the famous tea party, the American Athens, the cradle of American history and, to some, of American snobbery. "The Bostonian who leaves Boston ought to be condemned to perpetual exile," William Dean Howells has Bromfield Corey say chauvinistically in *The Rise of Silas Lapham*, set in Boston of the 19th century. Henry Adams described "Bostonitis" in his famous *Education* as a chronic irritability, "which in its primitive Puritan forms seemed due to knowing too much of his neighbors and thinking too much of himself."

Edgar Allan Poe and Ben Franklin were born there and Eugene O'Neill died there. It was the adopted home of one of Ireland's most colorful patriots, the poet John Boyle O'Reilly (1844–1890), who escaped from a penal colony in the Australian bush to come to America and edit the Boston *Pilot*, then the largest Catholic newspaper in the nation. Mary Baker Eddy founded the Christian Science religion there in 1879.

Literature and education have always been foremost in Boston's culture. In 1635 the Boston Public Latin School was established, the oldest public school in the nation. The following year Harvard became the first institution of higher education in America. Roxbury Latin School is the oldest existing private school in the country. The nation's first high school opened there in 1821. As well as the first book published in America, Boston produced the first newspaper in the 13 colonies, the *Boston News-Letter* in 1704.

Scores of famous novels have been set in Boston, including *The Late George Apley* by J.P. Marquand. Here we find a man limited and molded by Boston and its environs: Beacon Hill, Back Bay, Milton, and Cambridge.

> George William Apley was born in the house of his maternal grandfather, William Leeds Hancock, on the steeper part of Mount Vernon Street, on Beacon Hill, on January 25, 1866. He died in his own house, which overlooks the Charles River Basin and the Esplanade, on the water side of Beacon Street, on December 13, 1933. This was the frame in which his life moved, and the frame which will surround his portrait as a man. He once said of himself: "I am the sort of man I am, because environment prevented my being anything else."

There were also Henry James's *The Bostonians* and Upton Sinclair's *Boston*, inspired by the execution of Sacco and Vanzetti in 1927. Sinclair was quick to point out that it was not the community he was attacking in his quasi-fictional account of the famous trial. In the preface to the two-volume novel he wrote:

> It should be said at the outset that what is great in Boston finds due recognition in this story. Those who have made

the city's glory have never been its rulers, but always a "saving minority."

Boston was also the home of America's counterpart of Samuel Pepys, Samuel Sewall, whose *Diary* is a social history of more than half a century of early Boston. Born in England, Sewall was brought to America at the age of nine in 1663 by his father, who wanted to avoid the consequences of the Restoration. With Nathaniel Hawthorne's ancestor, John Hathorne, and William Straughton he was one of the jurists who sentenced 19 women and men to death at the infamous Salem witch trials. The blood of these innocents rested heavily on his soul and five years later he publicly confessed his "error" in the Old South Church, the only one of the judges to do so.

Sewall's Boston was clustered about three hills: Copp's, Fort and Beacon. The Towne House (now State House), which he visited frequently, was the center of its activities. Years later, under its windows angry British soldiers slaughtered six Americans, including the black man Crispus Attucks, immortalized in a poem by Boyle O'Reilly. From its balcony the Declaration of Independence was read. Sewall thus is interesting not just for himself but for the way his *Diary* illuminates the years of transition from Puritan theocracy to royal province, as well as the accompanying resentment that was to lead to the Revolution. He was, for example, probably the first in America to speak out against slavery, recording in his diary on June 22, 1716: "I essay'd to prevent Indians and Negroes being rated with horses and hogs; but I could not prevail."

Many of the sites that have been part of Boston's literary history are still there. Hawthorne often walked through the King's Chapel Burying Ground while planning *The Scarlet Letter*. He was struck by the tombstone of Elizabeth Pain, accused of the murder of her child in 1683. A large "A" emerged from the upper left corner of the gravestone.

Just southwest of King's Chapel is the Parker House, where members of the Saturday Club—Emerson, Holmes, Lowell, Dana, and Howells—frequently met and entertained guests like Sarah Orne Jewett and Willa Cather. Two blocks to the east, at School and Washington Streets, stands the Older Corner Bookstore, where the first works of many of the members of the Saturday Club were sold.

North of the famous Boston Common, where residents are still legally permitted to graze their cows, lies elegant Beacon Hill. On the corner of Beacon and Bowdoin, next to the State House, stood the home of Major Molineux of Hawthorne's "My Kinsman, Major Molineux." Note the usual careful attention to detail that Hawthorne hangs from a moral judgment about the power of imagining.

And first he threw his eyes along the street. It was of more respectable appearance than most of those into which he had wandered, and the moon creating, like the imaginative power, a beautiful strangeness in familiar objects, gave something of romance to a scene that might not have possessed it in the light of day. The irregular and often quaint architecture of the houses, some of whose roofs were broken into numerous little peaks, while others ascended, steep and narrow, into a single point, and others again were square; the spire snow-white of some of their complexions, the aged darkness of others, and the thousand sparklings, reflected from bright substances in the walls of many; these matters engaged Robin's attention for a while....

Although Thayer Academy in South Braintree holds a respected place among New England's finest preparatory schools, it has the dubious distinction of having expelled from its student body one of America's greatest living writers. Seventeen-year-old John Cheever, born May 27, 1912 in Quincy, a few miles south of Boston, was dismissed from Thayer after he fell behind in his studies and was caught smoking on the school's premises. It was the end of Cheever's formal schooling and his beginning as a writer. Drawing on his failures and frustrations at Thayer, Cheever wrote "Expelled," his first published short story, which anticipated both the style and the themes of his later fiction. His subtle but deeply moralistic strain indicates his affinity with other New England writers from Melville and Hawthorne to John Updike and John Gardner, and his characters often reflect the eccentricities considered native to the region.

Across from Plymouth Rock to the east is Provincetown, at the northern tip of the Cape, where today artists and tourists come from all over the world to enjoy the beauty of the shoreline and the festivities of this cultural center. It was here in 1915 around a driftwood fire after a picnic supper on the beach that a group of writers, disgusted with the bourgeois Broadway theater—and even with the new Washington Square Theater in New York's Greenwich Village—decided to put on their own plays "just for the hell of it" and converted an old wharf, containing a gray fishhouse and a small shack, into a theater. Each of the writers, who included Susan Glaspell and Wilbur Daniel Steele—his wife, Margaret, had been using the fishhouse as an art gallery—chipped in five dollars for repairs to convert the dock into a playhouse. And thus the Wharf Theater, the launching pad for many of the early plays of Eugene O'Neill, was born. It is still there, with few changes, presenting the plays of O'Neill and other Provincetown pioneers each summer.

Provincetown during its artistic heyday in the 1920's.
The Society for the Preservation of New England Antiquities

Nantucket has long been a favorite setting for many writers; but who has not read *Moby Dick* without being struck by Melville's rather biting description of it?

> Nantucket! Take out your map and look at it. See what a real corner of the world it occupies; how it stands there, away off shore, more lonely than the Eddystone lighthouse. Look at it—a mere hillock, and elbow of sand; all beach, without a background. There is more sand there than you would use in twenty years as a substitute for blotting paper.

VEVAY, SWITZERLAND, is a long way from Newport, Rhode Island, but Henry James, in *Daisy Miller*, found similarities in the two resorts. Alluding to it as "an American watering place," he wrote that the sights and sounds of Newport are echoed in the little Swiss town on the shores of Lake Geneva. James was not the only writer attracted to Newport. George Berkeley, the Irish philosopher, lived on a farm near the seaport from 1729 to 1731. Legend has it that the great thinker wrote most of his philosophical masterpiece *Alciphron* while resting on the nearby hanging rocks that overlook the sea.

While riding on the seashore at Newport, Longfellow was inspired to write his famous ballad, "The Skeleton in Armor." In the preface to the poem he noted:

> A year or two previous a skeleton had been dug up at Fall River, clad in broken and corroded armor; and the idea occurred to me of connecting it with the Round Tower at Newport, generally known as the Old Wind-Mill.

Longfellow's final version of "The Skeleton in Armor" is full of romantic allusions to the Vikings and "wild Baltic strands," but it is the ancient tower of Newport dating back to the 12th century with which he ends his sad tale of the Viking and the blue-eyed maid.

> Three weeks we westward bore,
> And when the storm was o'er,
> Cloud-like we saw the shore
>   Stretching to lee ward;
> There for my lady's bower
> Built I the lofty tower,
> Which, to this very hour,
>   Stands looking seaward.
>
> There lived we many years;
> Time dried the maiden's tears;
> She had forgot her fears,
>   She was a mother
> Death closed her mild blue eyes,
> Under that tower she lies;
> Ne'er shall the sun arise
>   On such another!

CONNECTICUT, WITH VILLAGE GREENS and white church steeples, has not been without its share of literary giants over the past two centuries. Such notables as Eugene O'Neill, Mark Twain, Harriet Beecher Stowe, the Connecticut Wits, Noah Webster, Charles Dudley Warner, Samuel Griswold Goodrich, and Wallace Stevens all made their homes there, as do the contemporary writers John Hawkes and Arthur Miller.

New London was the boyhood home of Eugene O'Neill and served as the setting for two of his plays, the autobiographical *Long Day's Journey into Night* and his only full-length comedy, *Ah, Wilderness.* O'Neill did not like New London or most of its residents. When he returned from Europe in

This Dutch print provides an early view of Hartford looking north-northwest from the Connecticut River.
The Connecticut Historical Society

1931 he revisited Monte Cristo Cottage and was so depressed just looking at it from the street that he left without going inside. He particularly disliked the social leaders of the town—Chatfield in *Long Day's Journey* is a takeoff on a New London family name—and once told a friend that he looked forward to going back there some day with a "flock of painted whores, hiring a tally-ho of six horses, and having the girls ride up State Street and throw dimes to the crowd." He wanted to be there to laugh, he said, as the social elite of the town and their ladies scrambled in the street for the coins.

Hartford, the state capital and the home of many of Connecticut's men and women of letters, played host to the famous Connecticut or Hartford Wits, who originally called themselves the Friendly Club of Hartford and held weekly meetings in a tavern on Dorr (now Market) Street to discuss literary topics and trade gossip. They flourished during the last quarter of the 18th century and the first quarter of the 19th. Among them were Joel Barlow—best known for his *Hasty Pudding*—Timothy Dwight, John Trumbull, Lemuel Hopkins, Richard Alsop, and David Humphreys.

Although the language may appear a bit arch for today's audiences, *Hasty Pudding*, with its talk of "gaudy prigs," "noisy swine," "pamper'd pigs" and "cooling milk" is delightful to the palate because of its rich and fattening New England nourishment.

E'en in they native regions, how I blush
To hear the Pennsylvanians call thee Mush!
On Hudson's banks, while men of Belgic spawn
Insult and eat thee by the name Suppawn,
All spurious appellations, void of truth;
I've better known thee from my earliest youth:
Thy name is Hasty-Pudding! thus my sire
Was wont to greet thee fuming from the fire;
And while he argued in thy just defence
With the logic clear, he thus explained the sense:—
"In haste the boiling cauldron, o'er the blaze,
Receives and cooks the ready powdered maize:
In haste 'tis served, and then in equal haste,
With cooling milk, we make the sweet repast.
No carving to be done, no knife to grate
The tender ear, and wound the stony plate;
But the smooth spoon, just fitted to the lip,
And taught with art the yielding mass to dip,
By frequent journeys to the bowl well stored,
Performs the hasty honors of the board."
Such is they name, significant and clear,
A name, a sound to every Yankee dear,
But most to me, whose heart and palate chaste
Preserve my pure hereditary taste.

There are who strive to stamp with disrepute
The luscious food, because it feeds the brute;
In tropes of high-strain'd wit, while gaudy prigs
Compare thy nursling man, to pamper'd pigs;
With sovereign scorn I treat the vulgar jest,
Nor fear to share thy bounties with the beast.
What though the generous cow gives me to quaff
The milk nutritious; am I then a calf?
Or can the genius of the noisy swine,
Though nursed on pudding, claim a kin to mine?
Sure the sweet song, I fashion to thy praise,
Runs more melodious than the notes they raise.

In the early years of the 20th century, a young Harvard graduate worked diligently in Hartford as an insurance man. He gradually made his way toward the top of his company, becoming a vice president of the Hartford Accident and Indemnity Company after 18 years of service. He stole time at night to write poetry, but had small success in getting it published at first. Even in the year of Wallace Stevens's death, 1955, just two months shy of his seventy-sixth birthday, his poetry was not universally recognized, as it is today. He was never listed in *Who's Who*, as many lesser writers are. His own colleagues in the insurance business found it difficult to believe that there was a real live poet among them. "What, Wally a poet?" one protested quite forcefully. "We don't talk about poetry here."

His double life did not diminish the quality of his verse. His finest poems, included in his collections *Harmonium*, *The Man with the Blue Guitar* and *Transport to Summer*, were not meat, however, for casual browsing by the unprepared reader. Stevens himself insisted he wrote only for those willing and able to take some pains to understand his own poetic labors, and so, when his early books failed to win wide sales, he was not surprised. In fact, he rather enjoyed relating anecdotes about the obscurity of his verse, such as the one about the letter he received after the publication of his "The Emperor of Ice-Cream." The secretary of the ice cream manufacturers' association wrote to Stevens asking him to explain it and state frankly whether he was for or against ice cream.

Although certainly not a local colorist, he was occasionally inspired by his town and state. Poems like "An Ordinary Evening in New Haven," "Conversation with Three Women of New England," "Connecticut," and "Of Hartford in a Purple Light" are a few examples of poems inspired by his environment. In the latter, observe how the town takes on a feminine quality when fused with purple light.

> The stage-light of the Opera?
> It is like a region full of intonings
> It is Hartford seen in a purple light.
>
> A moment ago, light masculine,
> Working, with big hands, on the town,
> Arranged its heroic attitudes.
>
> But now as in an armour of women
> Purple sets purple round. Look, master,
> See the river, the railroad, the cathedral...

Stevens's vision of a particular physical place is thus passed through moral or metaphysical lenses. Almost all New England writers would recognize this process as their own.

THE
MIDWEST

Jon Spayde

For thousands of Americans who do not know the land, and for thousands who do, the expatriate novelist Glenway Wescott summed up his native Midwest more or less accurately when he called it "nowhere, an abstract nowhere. However earnestly writers proud of being natives of it may endeavor to give it form and character, it remains out of focus, amorphous, and a mystery." Its affectionate nicknames (the Heartland; the Midland; America's Breadbasket) evoke a wholesomeness that is ballasted with complacency, a heartiness that comes from "being close to the land," a downright reasonableness that is genuine but narrow. We mean all of this when we say, again and again, that the Midwest is flat.

The flat Midwest is every bit as successful a literary creation as the Paris of the bohemians and Pushkin's scary Petersburg. Like those creations, it is the result of a series of abstractions, a selection of qualities that, at a certain moment, affected writers more powerfully than other qualities, obsessed them, even, and so passed memorably into fiction.

The image, though by now available everywhere, comes originally from a few very good books written over the span of a single generation: Hamlin Garland's *Main-Travelled Roads*; *Spoon River Anthology*, by Edgar Lee Masters; Sherwood Anderson's *Winesburg, Ohio*, which is deeply and richly in Masters's debt; the Minnesota satires of Sinclair Lewis: *Main Street* and *Babbitt* and the rest. It is an image very beautifully articulated by these writers, and there is a great deal of truth in it, even now.

But a very little attention to Midwestern history will convince anyone of the limitations of the image. The provincial heartland sustained cities like Cincinnati and St. Louis, where Hegel was read and discussed in German before he was available to Harvard boys. The rock-ribbed Protestant heartland is Catholic in Dubuque and Omaha and in the tiny Czech, Polish, and

The Serpent Mound of the Adena, nearly 3,000 years old, in Adams County, Ohio.
Ohio Historical Society

French farm towns of Iowa, as well as in Chicago and St. Louis. There are Sicilian social clubs in south Des Moines and Jewish congregations on the middle Mississippi that date back to the revolutionary days of 1848. The Midwest gave birth and support to Mother Bloor of the American Communist Party, to Big Bill Haywood of the Industrial Workers of the World, and to the only State Bank in America, that of North Dakota. It would be easy to document, from New Harmony to the Iowa Amanas, to the Grange, the Non-Partisan League, and the Federal Theater Project, that Midwestern energy has been as often expanded in re-thinking social reality as it has been in exploring the way things are.

THE BEGINNINGS OF THE RECORD, and even a kind of narrative, can be found on Pleasant Ridge in the Effigy Mounds National Monument in Iowa. Or at Great Serpent Mound in Adams County, Ohio. There stands the monumental "concrete poetry" of an Indian civilization nearly three thousand years gone.

The Serpent Mound of the Adena people (ca. 1000 B.C.) is a snake effigy sculpted in earth, delicately sinuous, 1,254 feet long and five feet high. Writing in the heyday of speculation about the origin and function of these great monuments, William Pidgeon (*Traditions of DE-COO-DAH,* 1858) called them "the hieroglyphical sign(s) through which the traditions were taught, and the knowledge of past events preserved." They seem a laborious kind of writing, even if sacred and hieroglyphical. Yet from an aerial view of the Pleasant Ridge grouping, it's hard not to think that a story of some kind is being told, for instruction or delight: a long line of beasts—bears—is crossed at a dramatic angle by a flight of three graceful birds, two flying far ahead of the bear column, one involved in a circular melee at the column's rear.

No one knows why the bird and beast mounds are there, and what they were intended to tell their people. It's tempting, if a little fanciful, to think of them as a hieroglyphic prophecy of the story Midwestern writing will have to tell again and again: a story emerging solidly and a little self-consciously from the earth, like a sod house out of the short-grass prairie; the story of a progression of strong, courageous animals formed into a social group that coheres even as it moves forward. Now and again a brilliant bird flies up from among them, circles over them, happy to be free and flying away. But some of the best of the bird-spirits can never get wholly away: they circle back again and again, endlessly—and rather unhappily—fascinated by the stolid, stupid, sacred assembly of the bears.

These latter spirits, writers like Hamlin Garland, Sherwood Anderson, Willa Cather, and Curtis Harnack, made the myth by which the Midwest is best known in our literature: the myth of the yearning spirit imprisoned in the prairie village, drawing both strength and discontent out of the beautiful earth.

But before that myth was made came the first myths that white men believed about the interior. This fragment comes from Father Vimont's account of the journey of Jean Nicollet from French Canada to the western shore of Lake Michigan at Green Bay:

> He embarked in the Huron country, with seven savages, and they passed by many small nations, both going and returning. When they arrived at their destinations, they fastened two sticks in the earth, and hung gifts thereon, so as to relieve these tribes from the notion of mistaking them for enemies to be massacred. When he was two days journey from that nation, he sent one of those savages to bear tidings of the peace, which word was especially well received when they heard it was a European who carried the message; they despatched several young men to meet the Manitouirinou—that is to say, "the wonderful man." They meet him, they escort him, and carry his baggage.

The Indians, like their luckless cousins of Mexico, exalted their invaders. But Nicollet was no less ambitious in his conception of the natives of Green Bay:

> He wore a grand robe of China damask, all strewn with flowers and birds of many colors....

A French map of the Midwest drawn in 1757, showing geographical features, various Indian tribes, and French settlements in what was known as La Louisiane.
New York Public Library

Nicollet had prepared himself to meet the wise Mandarins of a China that had captured the imagination of philosophical and mercantile Europe, thanks in great part to the writings of the indefatigable, globe-circling Fathers of the Society of Jesus, who had installed themselves in Peking as well as Montreal. They wrote the earliest accounts of the exploration of the Mississippi Valley as well, which, while it failed to be China, succeeded admirably for one hundred sixty years as the jewel of the French Empire.

The *Jesuit Relations,* as these 73 volumes of narrative are known, record the slow and stunningly courageous penetration of a wilderness many times the size of France by handfuls of men in fragile boats, powered by the rhythmic pull of arms and shoulders. Once the French had reached Green Bay, the way was open via the Fox River, a single short portage, and then the Wisconsin, into the fabled "Father of Waters," the "Mesipi," the vast Western river about which there had been nothing but tantalizingly detailed and persistent rumors. Even Nicollet's Green Bay hosts had talked of it. The Jesuit Jacques Marquette and the son of a Quebec wagon-maker, Louis Joliet, paddled, portaged, and found it. On the new river lived creatures both familiar and frightening:

> We saw only deer and cattle, bustards and swans without wings, because they drop their plumage in this country.

From time to time, we came upon monstrous fish, one of which struck our canoe with such violence that I thought it was a great tree, about to break the canoe to pieces. On another occasion, we saw on the water a monster with the head of a tiger, a sharp nose like that of a wildcat, with whiskers and straight, erect ears; the head was gray and the neck quite black; but we saw no more creatures of this sort.

On the 25th of June the explorers discovered human footprints on what is now the Illinois side of the river, and, Crusoe-like, followed them inland to a cluster of three villages of the Illinois people. What followed was a ritual of welcome and a feast. Marquette's record establishes a tradition in Midwestern literature: the loving account of the big, sit-down dinner:

When we reached the village of the great captain, we saw him at the entrance of his cabin, between two old men, all three erect and naked, and holding their calumet turned toward the sun. He harangued us in a few words, congratulating us upon our arrival. He afterward offered us his calumet, and made us smoke while we entered his cabin, where we received all their usual kind attentions....

The council was followed by a great feast, consisting of four dishes, which had to be partaken of in accordance with all their fashions. The first course was a great wooden platter full of sagamite, that is to say, meal of Indian corn boiled in water, and seasoned with fat. The master of ceremonies filled a spoon with sagamite three or four times, and put it to my mouth as if I were a little child. He did the same to Monsieur Jollyet. As a second course, he caused a second platter to be brought, on which were three fish. He took some pieces of them, removed the bones therefrom, and, after blowing upon them to cool them, he put them in our mouths as one would give food to a bird. For the third course, they brought a large dog, that had just been killed; but when they learned that we did not eat this meat, they removed it from before us. Finally, the fourth course was a piece of wild ox, the fattest morsels of which were placed in our mouths.

It's quite remarkable how long-lived the discovery-narrative is in the literature of the Mississippi Valley. From these *Jesuit Relations* through the travel journals of European visitors, the emigrant guides, the local colonists and beyond—the great land is constantly described, the habits of natives ceaselessly scrutinized. Slowly the outsider—Jesuit, European novelist, Eastern visitor—becomes an insider: a narrator born in the midland. But this narrator is too often an outsider in another sense: a village girl riding into Chicago, an artist returning to the Wisconsin town of his boyhood, or a local lad who is somehow "different." Through all the shifts of perspective in the literary record of the Midwest, there remains, in nearly every account, something of the cautious wonder of the explorer—and more often than not, a little bit of his self-righteousness, too.

There was much to wonder about. The great river. The prairie:

> Prairie travel resembles that of the sea. The Compass is the guide, the direct course is not always the best, and the probabilities of finding wood, water, grass, and a road compare with those of obtaining favourable and moderate winds and a smooth sea. At night when the wind is down, you can hear a scream for miles, and conversation is audible from a wagon coming over the horizon, so tiny you can blot it out by one finger. The silence is enormous; women whisper to each other afraid of breaking it.... You can see a storm far off raging in thunder and sulpherous light, while where you are standing a struck match will burn steadily in the open air.

The land is generous—think of Marquette's meal!—but it is also paradoxical, mercurial. No one has captured this quality better than the Minnesota poet Meridel LeSueur, from whose 1945 book *North Star Country* this quote comes. LeSueur. elsewhere finds an emblem for the perplexity of prairie life:

> The Indians had a curious little god, Ha-yo'-ka, expressive of the perversity of prairie weather. He wore a green cocked hat, went naked in winter, and in summer wrapped a buffalo robe around him. The little prairie hills were his home. In joy he sighed and in sorrow laughed. He felt confident when beset by dangers and quaked with fear in safety. You can see him now in those little whirlwinds that tear across the prairie with nobody in them.

Overhead, and unforgettable to anyone who has seen it once, the tragic and comic drama of clouds and wind.

> The great thunderheads, birds of wind in the sky, were thought by the Indians to be giants who dug the ditches of the rivers, and when they died became thunderbirds, the lightning the flash of their eyes, the thunder the sound of their terrible song. Those that did not live in the sky became the lonely boulders found standing without reason upon the plains.

In the long French decades, before the westward land rush at the beginning of the 19th century, the human environment was no less stormy and strong, as the poet Kenneth Rexroth reminds us in his history of modern American poetry:

> New France was a very peculiar kind of France, and bore more resemblance to Kievan Russia with its Varangian, Kazar, and Bulgar river-borne fur traders than anything to be found in the homeland. Its forts and trading posts were communities of armed merchant adventurers. Most of the women were Indians, and later also Negroes and mixed bloods. A masculine, anarchistic, sensual culture grew up of the same character as the Cossacks', or before them the Vikings'. No other people assimilated and were assimilated so completely, by not just Indians, Negroes and Spanish, but by the American land.

"Anarchic" and "sensual" are not words one usually uses about the Midwest in our own day, but there can be no doubt about its assimilative power. It is well to remember that the land opened to American settlement after the French and Indian War (when the English took it), the Revolution (when the Americans took it from the English) and the treaties of 1795 (when General "Mad Anthony" Wayne took Ohio and Indiana from the Indians) and the Louisiana Purchase of 1803, was ready for a human and cultural mixture of unprecedented magnitude and speed. An already polyglot and multicultural river basin, a Kievan wilderness, accepted in a century millions of men and women representing every American subculture and every nation in Europe.

THE HUMAN STREAM OUT OF THE FIRST AMERICAN FRONTIER—the hilly western regions of the Seaboard Colonies and Kentucky—into the second, the Ohio and Indiana country, moved an English-born pioneer named Morris Birkbeck to remark in 1817: "The Old America seems to be breaking up and moving West."

Between 1814 and 1819, the post War-of-1812 rush, perhaps the most frantic of all, saw tens of thousands of moving men and women on Forbes' Road to Pittsburgh and the headwaters of the Ohio. On this great river they floated, in keelboats and barges, into the southern reaches of Ohio, Indiana, and Illinois; these forested "downstate" regions were populated with hardy Pennsylvania Scotch-Irish and Germans many years before anyone ventured into the frightening tall-grass prairie to the north. The Ohio became a river of legend as well as migration and commerce, and out of Ohio traffic grew the city of Cincinnati, the first cultural, and—after a fashion—literary capital of the Midwest.

The Ohio has been described as "beyond all competition, the most beautiful river in the universe, whether we consider it for its meandering course through an immense region of forests, for its clean and elegant banks, which offer innumerable delightful situations for cities, villages, and improved farms: or for those many other advantages, which truly entitle it to the name originally given it by the French, of 'La Belle Riviere,' that is, 'The Beautiful River.'" This description was penned several years since, and it has not generally been thought an exaggerated one. Now the immense forests recede, cultivation smiles along its banks, towns every here and there decorate its shores, and it is not extravagant to suppose, that the day is not very far distant when its whole margin will form one continued village.

Thus wrote pilot and publisher Zadok Cramer in the 1811 edition of *The Navigator,* a practical guide to flatboat and keelboat navigation, republished yearly to keep current of the ever-changing course of the river. The little god Ha-yo'-ka presided over the world of the boatmen, too.

The river traffic not only brought settlers to the frontier and wealth to Cincinnati (situated at the confluence of the Ohio and the Miami, a prime northward highway into the Ohio country), it also brought visitors from far and wide. Many of them were literary men and women, for this was the heyday of the descriptive sketch of Western travel. And there were the English, French, Swedish, or German accounts of the curious new nation,

Cincinnati began as a river town handling trade along the Mississippi, and it remained so in the 19th century.
New York Public Library

which was so paradoxically divided between a robust Jeffersonian cult of liberty and chattel slavery. Nearly everyone visited Cincinnati, the western Metropolis, after a fascinating steamboat ride. Dickens, for one:

> Cincinnati is a beautiful city; cheerful, thriving, and animated. I have not often seen a place that commends itself so favourably and pleasantly to a stranger at the first glance as this does: with its clean houses of red and white, its well-paved roads, and foot-ways of bright tile.

In 1834, a generation after the first great age of Ohio traffic, but still just before the opening of the northern prairies to widespread cultivation, the English writer and abolitionist Harriet Martineau was moved to praise Cincinnati society in warm terms:

> The tea-table was set out in the garden at Dr. Drake's. We were waited upon, for the first time in months, by a free servant. The long grass grew thick under our feet; fire flies were flitting about us, and I doubted whether I had ever heard more sense and eloquence at any Old World tea-table than we were entertained with as twilight drew on. As we walked home through the busy streets, where there was neither the apathy of the South nor the disorder consequent upon the presence of a pauper class, I felt strongly tempted to jump to some hasty conclusions about the happiness of citizenship in Cincinnati. I made a virtuous determination to suspend every kind of judgement: but I found each day as exhilarating as the first, and when I left the city, my impressions were much like what they were after an observation of twenty-four hours.

A slightly more jaundiced and more down-to-earth view of the city comes from the pen of Frances Trollope, who was no tourist but a serious emigrant from England who published a best seller called *Domestic Manners of the Americans* in 1832. It is worth quoting at length because of its raciness and balance—in Trollope's account Cincinnati is a real American city, praiseworthy, appalling, full of surprises, and going about its daily tasks without apology:

> Though I do not quite sympathise with those who consider Cincinnati as one of the wonders of the earth, I certainly think it a city of extraordinary size and importance, when it is remembered that thirty years ago the aboriginal forest occupied the ground where it stands; and every month appears to extend its limits and its wealth.... From June to December tomatoes (the great luxury of the

American table in the opinion of most Europeans) may be found in the highest perfection in the market for about sixpence the peck....

In Cincinnati Marquette's Mississippi monsters have been transformed into mechanical waxwork figures in an urban "museum":

> [Mr. Dorfeuille] has constructed a pandemonium in an upper story of his museum, in which he has congregated all the images of horror that his fertile fancy could devise: dwarfs that by machinery grow into giants before the eyes of the spectator; imps of ebony with eyes of flame; monstrous reptiles, devouring youth and beauty; lakes of fire, and mountains of ice; in short, wax, paint and springs have done wonders....

In her delicate, British, eminently even-handed manner, Trollope anticipates later descriptions of the city that will dominate the post-Civil War Midwest: Chicago, the world's hog butcher.

> It seems hardly fair to quarrel with a place because its staple commodity is not pretty, but I am sure I should have liked Cincinnati much better if the people had not dealt so largely in hogs...mounting a certain noble-looking sugar-loaf hill, that promised pure air and a fine view, we found the brook we had to cross, at its foot, red with the stream from a pig slaughter-house, while our noses, instead of meeting the thyme that loves the green hill's breast, were greeted by odors that I will not describe, and which I heartily hope my readers cannot imagine; our feet, that on leaving the city, had expected to press the flowery sod, literally got entangled in pigs' tails and jawbones: and thus the prettiest walk in the neighborhood was interdicted forever.

Taken together, these and other visitors' accounts of Cincinnati amount to a vision of the ambivalence of the Midwestern city and of the Midwestern culture itself. The blood of newly slaughtered hogs runs past elegantly appointed tea-tables. New England civility and German intellectuality mingle in the streets with crude hucksterism and the stink of the barnyard.

Cincinnati literature (to use the phrase at all may overstate the case for it) tried to come to terms with the rough new realities of the river culture. One John P. Foote established the Cincinnati *Literary Gazette* in 1824; Timothy Flint followed in 1827 with the *Western Monthly Review*, which John T. Flanagan calls "a dignified and respectable imitation of the eastern periodicals." Morgan Neville's description of the legendary keelboatman

Two of the steps in the work of a Cincinnati slaughterhouse.
New York Historical Society

Mike Fink, however, is the product of literary Cincinnati that has stayed in American folklore for the longest time. It comes from James Hall's *The Western Souvenir*, a literary annual for the Christmas season of 1829. In one sense it is just one of a thousand steamboat-journey narratives; but it is also a brave attempt to come to terms with a new language and a new man:

> As the boat drew near the shore, the escape steam rever-
> berated through the forest and hills, like the chafed
> bellowing of the caged tiger. The root of a tree, concealed
> beneath the water, prevented the boat from getting suffi-
> ciently near the bank, and it became necessary to use the
> paddles to take a different position.
> "Back out! Manee! and try it again!" exclaimed a voice
> from the shore. "Throw your pole wide—and brace off!—or
> you'll run against a shag!"
> This was a kind of language long familiar to us on the
> Ohio. It was a sample of the slang of the keel-boatmen.
> The speaker...was leaning carelessly against a large
> beech; and, at his left are negligently pressed a rifle to his
> side, presented a figure, that Salvator would have chosen
> from a million, as a model for his wild and gloomy pencil.
> His stature was upwards of six feet, his proportions
> perfectly symmetrical, and exhibiting the evidence of
> Herculean powers. To a stranger, he would have seemed a

complete mulatto. Long exposure to the sun and weather on the lower Ohio and Mississippi had changed his skin; and, but for the fine European cast of his countenance, he might have passed for the principal warrior of some powerful tribe....

"SOME DAY A WISE MAN, one who has not read too many books but who has gone about among men, will discover and set forth a very interesting thing about America," says Sherwood Anderson in his 1920 novel *Poor White*. "The land is vast and there is a national hunger for vastness in individuals. One wants an Illinois-sized man for Illinois, an Ohio-sized man for Ohio ...."Anderson is wrong on one score: this hunger appears in book after book, poet after poet. It is one of the most durable traditions in Midwestern writing, reaching all the way from Neville to Twain's satirical "Child of Calamity" to the Lincoln cult, to Dreiser's monster financier Cowperwood and Vachel Lindsay's William Jennings Bryan. There is a very modern, very ironical version in James Wright's contemporary poem-cycle on Warren Harding.

Before this giant could come to birth and into his American birthright, something had to happen to the language. This incomparable character had to escape the bondage of comparison with the drawings of Salvator and with Hercules; this meant that the literary explorer had to give up his search for "the thyme that loves the green hill's breast" and struggle for ways to realize the hog bones and the boatmen; to cease merely to describe or report them; to make prose and poetry of both.

It was that unhappy spirit Samuel Clemens who tried hardest. One critic called him "the Lincoln of our literature."

Twain had a contemporary from downstate Indiana, a middling scholar who was his literary inferior in every way, named Edward Eggleston. Six years after the conclusion of the Civil War, in 1871, he published a book called *The Hoosier Schoolmaster*. This novel, which is considered to be the first Midwestern narrative of "local color," is all about the misadventures and eventual triumph of a young log-schoolhouse master in the Indiana hinterland along about the middle 1830s. Rarely has a story of robbery, revenge, and true love been told with so little dramatic or character-building skill. But, then, novel-writing was not really in Eggleston's line, as Twain might have said. What he was was a dedicated folk-philologist, and he rendered the Hoosier dialect with a fearful authenticity. This little exchange, early in the book—

"Nough said,"[1] was Bill's reply.
"You durn't[2] do it," said Bud.
"I don't take no sech a dare,"[3] returned Bill...

—explodes at the bottom of the page into a flower garden of footnotes:

> [1]*"Nough said"* is more than enough said for the French translator, who takes it apparently for a sort of barbarous negative....I need hardly explain to any American reader that *enough* said implies the ending of all discussion by the acceptance of the proposition or challenge.

> [2]*Durn't, daren't, dasent, dursent,* and *don't dast* are forms of this variable negative heard in the folk-speech of various parts of the country. The tenses of this verb seem to have got hopelessly mixed, long ago, even in literary use, and the speech of the people reflects this historic confusion.

> [3]*To take a dare* is an expression used in senses diametrically. Its common sense is that of the text. The man who refuses to accept a challenge is said to take a dare, and there is some implication of cowardice in the imputation. On the other hand, one who accepts a challenge is said also to take the dare.

With Eggleston the life of the Ohio River country, Hoosier-land, no less than its dialect, enters the sphere of dignified fiction. While the best things—the only readable things—in *The Hoosier Schoolmaster* are all verbal things: puns, etymologies, malapropisms—Eggleston does establish the central theme of most of the rest of Midwest fiction, too: an earnest and aspiring young spirit coping as best he can with village torpidity, hypocrisy, venality, and banality, and now and then winning little victories:

> Out of all the books he had ever read he told story after story...they all listened with great eyes while he told of Sinbad's adventures, of the Old Man of the Sea, of Robinson Crusoe, of Captain Gulliver's experiences in Liliput, and of Baron Munchausen's exploits.
> Ralph had caught his fish. The hungry minds of these backwoods people were refreshed with the new life that came to their imaginations in these stories.

From here on, Midwestern writers will begin a long critique of Midwestern culture. For some reason—a reason not too difficult to imagine—an important part of that critique will have to do with failure to appreciate the values represented by writers, and books, and the brilliant and lyrical ideas that writers have.

Even by Eggleston's day the life of the Midwest had changed radically. While his novel looked back at the old broad leaf forest Hoosier world of spelling bees and "squires" in ancient powdered wigs, American settlement and agriculture had moved north then west, first into regions at the top edge of the prairie—notably Michigan, which was soon to grow rich from orchards and iron—then onto the forbidding grasslands themselves:

> The tough vinelike roots of the bluestems and prairie clovers twanged with a thousand ringing sounds as each step of the horses pulled the sharp blade forward through the sod of ten thousand years. As the soil was turned, a black ribbon reinforced with the living foundation of the prairie thudded into the trench made by the preceding round of the plow. Bee nests were upturned, mice scurried from their ruined homes, and raucous gulls swarmed behind, picking up worms, insects and other small creatures evicted from the sanctuary of their grassland homes.

Bees, mice, and bugs were not the only things disturbed by this unprecedented movement onto the "true prairie" of upper Ohio, Indiana, and Illinois, of Minnesota and Iowa, and then beyond into the short-grass lands of Nebraska, Kansas, and the Dakotas. As the pioneers went West into land that was more and more difficult and costly to break to the plow, new relationships developed between the farmer and the wider economy. The tragic historian of these new relationships is the novelist, story writer, and Populist Hamlin Garland. In this scene from his most famous story he makes his bedeviled dirt-farmer pronounce "Indiana" just as Eggleston had transcribed the word. But the experience he communicates is literally and figuratively hundreds of miles away from Eggleston's river-and-forest world:

> "I didn't like the looks of the country, anyhow," Haskins said, partly rising and glancing at his wife. "I was ust t' northern Ingyannie, where we have lots a timber 'u' lots o' rain, 'u' I didn't like the looks o' that dry prairie. What galled me the worst was goin' s'far away acrosst so much fine land layin' all through here vacant."

The story, "Under the Lion's Paw," can stand for what was happening in the latter 1880s. It is the story of the relationship between a man, the land, and a mortgage. If the rush into the valley of the Ohio had been made in the spirit of Jeffersonianism, with every flatboat or steamboat-borne family picturing to itself a tidy and self-sufficient farmstead in a shady river bottom, this northwest rush would be presided over by other spirits: Ha-yo'-Ka, the thunderheads, the grasshoppers, the dust storms, Herbert Spencer, the "social" Darwin, Henry George, Karl Marx, Thorstein Veblen, and the financial, technical, and commercial forces that were creating an "industrial" agriculture. Even Iowa, that most generous of prairie states, with fully one-quarter of the earth's finest growing soil, could let the farmer down.

The sod dugout was a practical kind of prairie housing. It was relatively warm and protected inhabitants from tornadoes and severe storms.
Nebraska State Historical Society

Herbert Quick, a memoirist from the 1920s, recalls a conversation in which he was told, "Anyone who was fool enough to move into such a hell of a country as Iowa deserved to starve."

The late 1880s and the 1890s, hard times on the farm, put their stamp on our image of the Midwest. Garland's writing, by far the most distinguished fiction that had yet been created about the region, came out of his political convictions (asked to address a Populist Party convention in Omaha, he simply read "Under the Lion's Paw" to the assembled delegates). He recounted, memorably, the journey to South Dakota that led to his first and most famous collection of stories, *Main-Travelled Roads*:

> On my way westward, that summer day in 1887, rural life presented itself from an entirely new angle. The ugliness, the endless drudgery, and the loneliness of the Farmer's lot smote me with stern insistence. I was the militant re-former.
>
> The farther I got from Chicago, the more depressing the landscape became. It was bad enough in our former home in Mitchell County, but my pity grew more intense as I passed from northwest Iowa into southern Dakota. The houses, bare as boxes, dropped on the treeless plains, the

barbed-wire fences running at right angles, and the towns were assemblages of flimsy wooden sheds with painted pine battlement, produced on me the effect of an almost helpless and sterile poverty.

Garland, a strong new voice, was also something of a dead end, as the tone of the excerpt above suggests. There was to be only one other first-rate fictional chronicler of the bleak western prairie—Willa Cather—but a host of depressing farm novels full of crop failure, foreclosure, grasshopper horror, self-mutilation, insanity, and suicide. If any one of Garland's words rang out in the subsequent 30 years of farm fiction, it was the word "sterile." The finest writers turned away from the farm, although a hardy band of regionalists in Iowa did their level best to call them back to it between 1915 and the end of the New Deal.

HARD TIMES AND NEW TIMES were drawing Midwesterners into the cities; and one great city in particular. Garland caught as well as anyone the peculiar relationship between prairie land and the metropolis on the western shore of Lake Michigan:

> Chicago has three winds that blow upon it. One comes from the East, and the wind goes out to the cold gray-blue lake. One from the North, and men think of illimitable spaces of pinelands and maple-clad ridges which lead to the unknown deeps of the arctic woods.
> But the third is the West of the Southwest wind, dry, full of smell of unmeasured miles of growing grain in summer, or ripening corn and wheat in autumn. When it comes in winter the air glitters with incredible brilliancy. The snow of the country dazzles and flames in the eyes; deep blue shadows everywhere stream like stains of ink. Sleigh bells wrangle from early morning till late at night, and every step is quick and alert. In the city, smoke dims its clarity, but it is welcome.

"The approach to Chicago"—by train always, and from the north or the west—became a stock scene, beginning with Garland's *Rose of Dutcher's Coolly.* Rose, a Wisconsin girl, first sees the city emblematically:

> It was this wonderful thing again, a fresh, young and powerful soul rushing to a great city, a shining star of steel obeying the magnet, a clear rivulet from the hills hurrying to the sea. On every train at the same hour, from every direction, others, like her, were entering on the same search to the same end.

"See that cloud?" some one said; "that's Chicago."

Rose looked—far to the south-east a gigantic smoke-cloud soared above the low horizon line, in shape like an eagle, whose hovering wings extended from south to east, trailing mysterious shadows upon the earth. The sun lighted its mighty crest with crimson light, and its gloom and glow became more sharply contrasted. Towards this portentous presence the train rushed, uttering an occasional shrill neigh, like a stallion's defiance.

Passing, swiftly, to a very similar scene in Theodore Dreiser's *The Titan* we can see that observation and calculation have arrived to replace vision; the Midwestern image is coming to be intricate, the Midwestern eye sharp; now what is wanted is data for the eye, and no more metaphors:

The tracks, side by side, were becoming more and more numerous. Freight cars were assembled here by thousands from all parts of the country—yellow, red, blue, green, white. (Chicago, he recalled, already had thirty railroads

Downtown Chicago near Dearborn Street in 1909.
Chicago Historical Society

terminating here, as though it were the end of the world.]
The little, low one and two story houses, quite new as to
wood, were frequently unpainted and already smoky—in
places grimy. At grade crossings, where ambling streetcars
and wagons and muddy-wheeled buggies waited, he noted
how flat the streets were, how unpaved, how sidewalks
went up and down rhythmically—here a flight of steps, a
veritable platform before a house, there a long stretch of
boards laid flat on the mud of the prairie itself. What a city!
Presently a branch of the filthy, arrogant, self-sufficient
little Chicago river came into view, with its mass of
sputtering tugs, its black, oily water, its tall red, brown and
green grain elevators, its immense black coal pockets and
yellowish-brown lumberyards.

No more metaphors, perhaps; but it's necessary to be honest about Dreiser,
the first and greatest biographer of Chicago. He was a writer with a canny
eye, and no small detail of the newly rich city escaped him: the fall of a
shadow on a building; the sweet smell of twilight air; the jingle of a gold-
plated harness. Yet he could stand up and "gas" about the city, like an orator
out of the 1850s:

> The city of Chicago … To whom may the laurels as laure-
> ate of this Florence of the West yet fall? This singing flame
> of a city, this all-America, this poet in chaps and buckskin,
> this rude, raw Titan, this Burns of a city!

It sounds like a good joke: "Florence" is a comparison nearly too silly to
laugh at, and one hopes that "singing flame" and "Burns" are satirical
allusions to the Great Fire of 1893. But probably not. Probably Dreiser was
serious, and singing like this seemed right to him. To brag and to boast are
almost "natural" prairie urges, and for the Midwestern farmer, passed
through the hell of 1895 and the loss of so many of his old, outsized dreams,
Chicago was where a lively mind could turn to find the old prairie sense of
unlimited possibility, the wide free field for human scope and energy.
Dreiser's Cowperwood went there with his strawberry-blonde mistress, and
made a killing out of the street railways. The city that symbolized the
embroilment of the prairie yeoman in finance, agricultural technology,
railway and elevator rates, and the manipulable "laws" of supply and
demand was now, paradoxically, the center of Midwestern energy and
optimism. Mike Fink, the "Ringtailed Roarer," and the "Child of Calamity"
were now city men.

And yet, the Dreiserian eye and ear could come close to perfection in
recording the dirty, delimited, daily reality of the city. John Berryman has
rightly said that the two ward heelers Kerrigan and Tiernan, in *The Titan*

are "the most effective ward leaders in American literature, handled with...complete understanding."

> In the first and second wards of Chicago at this time... were two men, Michael (alias Smiling Mike) Tiernan and Patrick (alias Emerald Pat) Kerrigan, who, for picturesqueness of character and sordidness of atmosphere, could not be equaled elsewhere in the city, if in the nation at large. Smiling Mike Tiernan, proud possessor of four of the largest and filthiest saloons of this area, was a man of large and genial mold...his chief present joy consisted in sitting behind a solid mahogany railing at a rosewood desk in the back portion of his largest Clark Street hostelry—the Silver Moon. Here he counted up the returns from his various properties—saloons, gambling resorts, and houses of prostitution....
>
> The character of Mr. Kerrigan, Mr. Tiernan's only rival in this rather difficult and sordid region, was somewhat different. He was a small man, quite dapper, with a lean, hollow, and somewhat haggard face, but by no means sickly body, a large, strident moustache, a wealth of coal-black hair parted slickly on one side, and a shrewd, genial brown-black eye—constituting altogether a rather pleasing and ornate figure whom it was not at all unsatisfactory to meet...his saloons harbored the largest floating element that was to be found in the city—longshoremen, railroad hands, stevedores, tramps, thugs, thieves, pimps, rounders, detectives and the like....

Chicago could offer the young Midwestern mind two valuable freedoms— freedom from the social bonds of the small town, and (at other times) freedom from a certain abstract high-mindedness inherited from New England or Leipzig.

And yet, the ties that bind continued to bind, and the winds remained high, and Chicago merely served to test and prove these prairie-born continuities. Of all the good writers of Chicago's "Robin's-Egg Renaissance" (1911-1916) there isn't one that the big city turned into a decadent.

MASTERS, SANDBURG, LINDSAY, LEWIS, ANDERSON, FLOYD DELL—all met in Chicago. They shared an upbringing and an epoch, and among them they managed to give voice to almost all of the sides of the many-sided Midwestern mind. Among them Dell and Sandburg were the most willing to take on the reality of the big city. Yet all of them were haunted equally by a place and state of mind called the Village—and it is the Village that is the major Midwestern work of architecture, sculpture, philosophy, and fiction.

If anyone was the promoter and critical patron of what we have come to call "The Chicago Renaissance," it was Floyd Dell, from Davenport, Iowa. Prodigy, village aesthete, Socialist, newspaperman, Dell epitomizes the energy and youthful hopefulness of the early Chicago period. As editor's assistant and later editor of the Friday Literary Review of the Chicago *Evening Post*, while still in his early twenties, he was in a position to see and comment upon everything:

> Under Francis Hackett [Dell's predecessor], the Friday Literary Review was giving expression to a growing youthful body of American literary taste, which had nourished itself upon the very best European literature and had civilized modern standards. That growing body of taste had hitherto been almost voiceless, and was supposed not to exist. Literary criticism was almost entirely either academic or mere puffery; to be alive and to have any knowledge of literature was a combination almost unknown; to bring social ideas to bear upon aesthetic products was something very new indeed.
>
> At some time in those ... days, I met Carl Sandburg, and he read some of his poems from manuscript. They were all impressionistic, misty, soft-outlined, delicate.... Carl Sandburg had not struck yet the note he was soon to strike in 'Chicago—hog-butcher of the world'.... Dreiser told me of a Chicago lawyer named Edgar Lee Masters, who was a poet; America would hear from him soon, said Dreiser.... A hitherto unknown novelist swam into my ken, Sherwood Anderson, with the manuscript of a novel, 'Windy MacPherson's Son,' which I immediately admired; it had things in it about the Middle West which never got into fiction, and a soul-questioning quasi-Dostoievskian note in it too which I admired devoutly....

This group, including Vachel Lindsay, who in 1912 was still writing delicate lyrics about butterflies, prairie flowers and eternal beauty, and Sinclair Lewis, who was getting ready to turn his own Dreiserian eye to the service of satire, was writers of Youth—not only were they young men, but so were their protagonists; and the problems their protagonists had were the problems of late adolescence. Willa Cather, who belonged to the Chicago group only by occasional association and by virtue of parallel goals, caught this youthful spirit in a poem called "Prairie Spring":

> Evening and the Flat land,
> Rich and sombre and always silent;
> The miles of fresh-plowed soil,
> Heavy and black, full of strength and harshness;
> The growing wheat, the growing weeds,

> The toiling horses, the tired men;
> The long empty roads,
> Sullen fires of sunset, fading,
> The eternal, unresponsive sky.
> Against all this, Youth,
> Flaming like the wild roses,
> Singing like the larks over the plowed fields,
> Flashing like a star out of the twilight....

If Cather catches something of the spirit of the Chicagoans, the background is nonetheless wrong. The young men of the Renaissance were not farm boys. They came from towns, and in most cases the towns they came from were of some size and importance in their regions. Dell, from Davenport, had by far the richest urban experience before coming to Chicago. Davenport was, and is, an industrial city with a large German-Jewish population descended from the revolutionary "Forty-Eighters." Socialist thought was a part of the hometown scene; as Dell explains in his autobiographical novel *Moon-Calf*:

> There had always been Socialists in Port Royal [Davenport]—not few enough to make them oddities, and not so many as to have any effect upon the practical politics of the town.... Central branch of Local Port Royal lay in the trough of the wave of events; putting up candidates for elections, holding street meetings in earnest competition with the Salvation Army and the sellers of patent medicines....

As he went about writing exquisite little poems, attending local meetings in the Davenport *Truner-Halle*, working in a candy factory, and reporting about Judaism, labor, and German theater for the Davenport paper, Dell developed a love for the city and a gratitude to it that he never abandoned, even as he and his associates became involved in something called "The Village Revolt." Dell's friend the scholarly Rabbi Nathan of Port Royal (based upon Rabbi Fineshriber) sums up the city:

> Port Royal has a quality of its own. I suppose this is partly due to the pioneers from New England, who brought with them ideals and a respect for learning; but it is more due, I think, to the Germans, who left home because they loved liberty, and brought with them a taste for music, discussion, and good beer. There are so many of the Germans, and they have so much enthusiasm, that they dominate the town.... It is true, they have never been able to convert the descendants of New England to gymnastics and choral singing; but they have laid out these magnificent parks, and built our library—which, you will have noticed, is well stocked with free-thought literature....

Davenport, so similar in many respects to Cincinnati, represents the earliest sort of Midwestern settlement: the river town. But the railroads made and destroyed communities too, a generation later in the 1850s. When huge numbers of Scandinavians came into the midland after the Civil War, they arrived on the trains. And they built up and filled up railroad towns like Carl Sandburg's Galesburg, Illinois. If Dell found what he needed in Davenport—a lively high-mindedness, a diversity of intellectual purposes and cultural strains—Sandburg got what he wanted out of Galesburg too: a mixture of human beings and of human languages. A mixture that got richer, it seemed, with every new trainload of "young strangers."

> This small town of Galesburg, as I look back at it, was a piece of the American Republic. Breeds and blood strains that figure in history were there for me, as a boy, to see and hear in their faces and their ways of talking and acting. People from New England and their children owned much of the town and set the main tone in politics, churches, schools and colleges. I heard Yankee old-timers and how they talked "through the nose." Up from Kentucky and Tennessee had come English and Scotch-Irish breeds who were mostly Democrats in favor of the saloons and farther back in favor of Stephen A. Douglas as against Lincoln. Many Swedes had become voters and a power in politics and business. Their Republican leader for years was a banker, Moses O. Williamson, known as "Mose." He was on the Illinois State Committee of the Republican Party, and if you wanted a State or Federal office the word was "See Mose." And the Irish? I had Irish schoolteachers and playmates. I would stand still in the Q (Chicago, Burlington and Quincy Railroad) yards to watch the switchman, Tom Carmody, walk. He was a prize-winning dancer and his way of walking had a music to it....At parties, sociables, picnics, political rallies, among the shopmen, or in a cigar store, Mark [Connelly], the young Irishman, would give his Swedish dialect stories. He was as good as any Swede at imitating a green Swede....

The roster of races that Sandburg had nothing to do with in his boyhood testifies further to the richness of Galesburg mix:

> Frenchy Juneau and his father were the only French I knew. I didn't get to know any Poles, Bohemians, Slovaks, Russians, Hungarians, Spanish, Portuguese, Mexicans, South Americans, or Filipinos....Often in the 1890's I would get to thinking about what a young prairie town Galesburg was—nearly twenty thousand people, and they

had all come in fifty years. Before that it was empty rolling prairie. And I would ask: Why did they come? Why couldn't they get along where they had started from? Was Galesburg any different from the many other towns, some bigger and some smaller? Did I know America, the United States, because of what I knew about Galesburg?

Sandburg's question—Did I know America, can one know America out of one's youthful knowledge of an American village?—haunted the Chicago writers. The Village was the test-case; it was made to stand for many things about America, and the writers who created it explored its terrain with a fierce and unrelenting geographic fervor.

There is a curious characteristic of Midwestern literary history: A highly successful image, like that desperate "sterility" portrayed in Hamlin Garland's stories, preempts not only most previous images, but even blinds the reader and commentator to parts of the work in question—Garland's, here—that don't fit the image. And then, the image goes on to affect every similar work that follows.

The success of Sinclair Lewis's *Main Street* in 1920 has so colored our understanding of Edgar Lee Masters and Sherwood Anderson, older and younger contemporaries, that it is sometimes maintained that these three writers are the main line in a literary revolt against the village that included many lesser lights—Glenway Wescott and Carl Van Vechten, among others, as well. Sandburg and Lindsay stand outside the revolt (though Lindsay's life has been made by biographers into a parable of the defeat of genius by Babbitry), and hence a faint pall of sentimentality is made to hang over their work. The hard edge of the Midwestern vision, it is held, is an articulate anger at Midwestern narrowness of spirit.

Lewis owes a great deal to Hamlin Garland. To Garland's description of a sleepy Wisconsin village in "Up the Coulee," he adds a socially sharpened eye for detail. Garland:

> The town caught and held his eyes first. How poor and dull and sleepy and squalid it seemed! The one main street ended at the hillside at his left and stretched away to the north, between two rows of the usual village stores, un-relieved by a tree or a touch of beauty. An unpaved street, drab-colored, miserable, rotting wooden buildings, with the inevitable battlements—the same, only worse, was the town.
>
> The same, only more beautiful still, was the majestic amphitheater of green wooded hills that circled the horizon, and toward which he lifted his eyes....

Lewis, on the main street of Gopher Prairie, Minnesota:

Axel Egge's General Store, frequented by Scandinavian farmers. In the shallow dark window space heaps of sleazy sateens, badly woven galateas, canvas shoes designed for women with bulging ankles, steel and red glass buttons upon cards with broken edges, a cottony blanket, a graniteware frying-pan reposing on a sun-faded crepe blouse.

Billy's Lunch. Thick handless cups on the wet oilcloth-covered counter. An odor of onions and the smoke of hot lard. In the doorway a young man audibly sucking a toothpick.

Ye Art Shoppe, Prop. Mrs. Mary Ellen Wilks, Christian Science Library open daily free. A touching fumble at beauty. A one room shanty of boards recently covered with rough stucco. A show-window delicately rich in error: vases starting out to imitate tree-trunks but running off into blobs of gilt—an aluminum ash-tray labeled "Greetings From Gopher Prairie."

And like Garland, Lewis found poignancy in the contrast between the squalid settlement and the lovely land on which it squatted like an impertinence. Carol Kennicott takes a buggy ride with her doctor husband, beyond the confines of the little town, out onto the cultivated prairie:

As the sun warmed the world of stubble into a welter of yellow they turned from the highroad, through the bars of a farmer's gate, into a field, slowly bumping over the uneven earth. In a hollow of the rolling prairie they lost sight even of the country road. It was warm and placid. Locusts trilled among the dry wheat-stalks, and brilliant little flies hustled across the buggy. A buzz of content filled the air. Crows loitered and gossiped in the sky.

Garland's people are struggling victims of social squalor; Lewis's are darned proud of Gopher Prairie; so the continuing critique of the Village necessarily shifts from social to psychological circumstances. For Lewis the Village is not just an objective environment, but one that produces a particular state of mind in its inhabitants. What remains the same, however, is the sense that the Midwestern village by its very nature cannot open upon the world; that it represents a kind of spiritual dead end that can only be avoided or escaped. It is no accident that both writers are obsessed with physical reality—the stuff of daily geography—and the limits it imposes upon life—Garland in a bold and generalizing way, Lewis in the nitty gritty of detail.

Lewis shares much more with Garland than with any of the other Chicago writers, who were up to something else. The contrast with Edgar Lee Masters is especially striking.

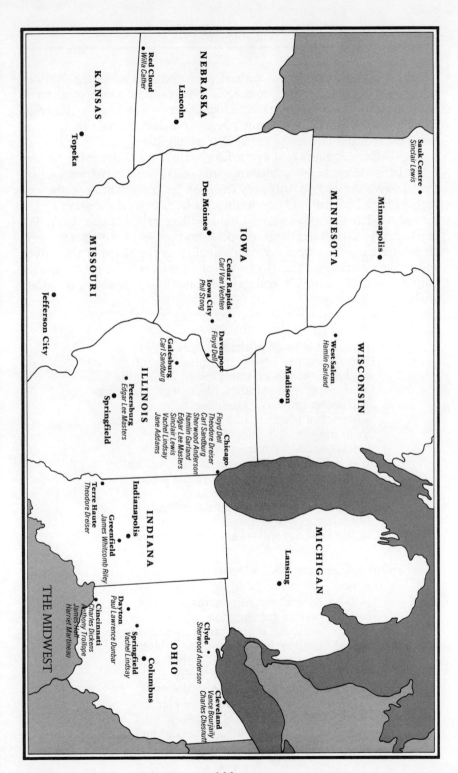

THE MIDWEST

KANSAS

Topeka •

NEBRASKA

Red Cloud
Willa Cather •

Lincoln •

Sauk Centre •
Sinclair Lewis

MINNESOTA

Minneapolis •

Des Moines •

IOWA

Cedar Rapids •
Carl Van Vechten

Iowa City •
Phil Stong

Davenport •
Floyd Dell

WISCONSIN

West Salem •
Hamlin Garland

Madison •

MISSOURI

Jefferson City •

Galesburg •
Carl Sandburg

ILLINOIS

Petersburg •
Edgar Lee Masters

Springfield •

Chicago •
Floyd Dell
Theodore Dreiser
Carl Sandburg
Sherwood Anderson
Hamlin Garland
Edgar Lee Masters
Sinclair Lewis
Vachel Lindsay
Jane Addams

Terre Haute •
Theodore Dreiser

Indianapolis •

INDIANA

Greenfield •
James Whitcomb Riley

MICHIGAN

Lansing •

Clyde •
Sherwood Anderson

Cincinnati •
Charles Dickens
Anthony Trollope
James Hall
Harriet Martineau

Dayton •
Paul Lawrence Dunbar

Springfield •
Vachel Lindsay

Columbus •

OHIO

Cleveland •
Vance Bourjaily
Charles Chesnutt

-111-

For some reason, there was no real poetry written about the Midwest until 1914, except for the numerous 19th century verses written in Miltonic diction and praising towns like Davenport as "Queen City of the Western World!" or Will Carleton's Hoosier dialect poems that spawned the likes of Edgar Guest and James Whitcomb Riley.

In 1914 Carl Sandburg won a prize for certain of his "Chicago Poems," and Edgar Lee Masters began publishing parts of a durable masterwork called *Spoon River Anthology*, in *Reedy's Mirror*, St. Louis. These poems, collected into a book in 1915, are soliloquies from beyond the grave by 244 former residents of a downstate Illinois village called Spoon River. The dead are given one last chance to speak, and consequently they strive in their utterances to give a necessary finality to the shape of their lives, testifying sometimes to the narrowness of those lives in the village, and the courage it took to revolt against the constricting demands of village society:

> *Dorcas Gustine*
> I was not beloved of the villagers,
> But all because I spoke my mind,
> And met those who transgressed against me
> With plain remonstrance, hiding nor nurturing
> Nor secret griefs nor grudges.
> That act of the Spartan boy is greatly praised,
> Who hid the wolf under his cloak,
> Letting it devour him, uncomplainingly.
> It is braver, I think, to snatch the wolf forth
> And fight him openly, even in the street,
> Amid dust and howls of pain.
> The tongue may be an unruly member—
> But silence poisons the soul.
> Berate me who will—I am content.

Some spirits rejoice, like Fiddler Jones:

> How could I till my forty acres
> Not to speak of getting more,
> With a medley of horns, bassoons and piccolos
> Stirred in my brain by crows and robins
> And the creak of a wind-mill-only these?
> And I never started to plow in my life
> That some one did not stop in the road
> And take me away to a dance or picnic.
> I ended up with a broken fiddle—
> And a broken laugh, and a thousand memories,
> And not a single regret.

And the freedom of death makes possible communion with remote but sympathetic spirits:

> *Lucius Atherton*
> When my moustache curled,
> And my hair was black,
> And I wore tight trousers
> And a diamond stud,
> I was an excellent knave of hearts and took many a
>   trick.
> But when the gray hairs began to appear—
> Lo! a new generation of girls
> Laughed at me, not fearing me,
> And I had no more exciting adventures
> Wherein I was all but shot for a heartless devil,
> But only drabby affairs, warmed-over affairs
> Of other days and other men.
> And time went on until I lived at Mayer's restaurant,
> Partaking of short orders, a gray, untidy,
> Toothless, discarded rural Don Juan...
> There is a mighty shade here who sings
> Of one named Beatrice;
> And I see now that the force that made him great
> Drove me to the dregs of life.

A contemporary Iowa City poet named Chuck Miller says:

> ...lately been thinking of what it means to be a Midwest-
> ern writer with exemplars such as Meridel LeSueur and
> Sherwood Anderson and his Mid-America Chants and too
> that sense you get from Edgar Masters of the bitterness of
> life here, the straight forward beauty of it, and the crush-
> ing narrowness of it at the same time.

What Masters is up to is a struggle against the "crushing narrowness" and an expansion of the "straight forward beauty" into something universal—at least as universal as the great literary Europe represented by Dante's Beatrice and the eternal myth of Don Juan—and both "at the same time." He seeks thus to transmute even the negativity of his vision into the timeless, the mythic, the literary—that is, to make it positive and enduring.

In the miraculous year 1912, Floyd Dell had a chance to meet Arnold Bennett, a novelist that his Chicago generation admires, in a Loop hotel:

> He asked me whether I had been born in Chicago or in a
> small town. In a small town I said; and then he assured
> me—though I hadn't asked him—that I could write novels

...that it was growing up in a small town that gave me the knowledge of people necessary for novel writing.

Bennett's remark suggests in an appropriately prosaic way certain advantages that poets and novelists of the Chicago scene had: they came into a great literary city from communities that were small enough to remember clearly. From communities that had received the impress of a number of cultures. Communities that were, thanks to Boston and Heidelberg, highminded enough to sustain both hypocrisy and good free libraries. The bright Midwestern lad could see Jeffersonian idealism extolled and betrayed in a single day; and at night he could open up Shaw or Mencken or Friedrich Nietzsche and try to make sense of what he had seen. He personalized ideas, because in his town there were ten atheists, twelve socialists, one unforgettable librarian, and, perhaps, an editor like the one Sandburg remembers:

> Gersh Martin died in 1894 at sixty-six years of age, his life given to liberty, free speech, printer's ink, and hard liquor. In the six years that he owned, edited, and wrote his weekly, the *Press and People,* I saw him many a time on Main Street or Boone's Avenue walking around to get news items, gossip, and advertising, or "another little drink"....He had been a canal mule-driver, a tramp printer, and when he came to Galesburg he made a newspaper pay by dipping his pen in an ink bottle and writing "hot stuff." He would breeze straight into scandals that other papers wouldn't touch. The churches and colleges, politicians and "city fathers," the Women's Christian Temperance Union, they heard from him, some reading him on the sly while saying, "I wouldn't read that dirty sheet." A Baptist Sunday-school superintendent found short in his accounts the *Republican-Register* took as "another good man gone wrong," but the *Press and People* had it, "No, another bad man found out."

One poet had the not-wholly-unreasonable dream that a community of this sort, an idealized and idealistic Midwestern village, could best embody and promote what he considered to be both the aesthetic principles of the Declaration of Independence and a vision of a new America. Thus it was that Vachel Lindsay set about very deliberately to become the prophet of Springfield, Illinois. In 1912 he left on the first of a series of westward "tramps" on foot, exchanging his diaphanous verses for food and lodging. Upon his return to Springfield (he lived in his childhood home until he was middle-aged) Lindsay issued a proclamation "Of the New Village, and the New Country Community, as Distinct from the Village":

This is a year of bumper crops, of harvesting festivals. Through the mists of the happy waning year, a new village arises, and the new country community, in visions revealed to the rejoicing heart of faith.

And yet it needs no vision to see them. Walking across this land I have found them, little ganglions of life, promise of thousands more. The next generation will be that of the eminent village. The son of the farmer will be no longer dazzled and destroyed by the fires of the metropolis. He will travel, but only for what he can bring back. Just as his father sends half-way across the continent for good corn, or melon-seed, so he will make his village famous by transplanting and growing this idea or that. He will make it known for its pottery or its processions, its philosophy or its peacocks, its music or its swans, its golden roofs or its great union cathedral of all faiths.

It was clear to Lindsay that his own city would one day contain all of these glories. He drew visionary pictures of huge heavenly censers scattering frankincense over the Sangamon County Court House and the Illinois State Capitol. He admonished his townsmen in "On the Building of Springfield":

> Let not our town be large...remembering
> That little Athens was the muses' home,
> That Oxford rules the heart of London still,
> That Florence gave the Renaissance to Rome.
>
> Some city on the breast of Illinois
> No wiser and no better at the start
> By faith shall rise redeemed, by faith shall rise
> Bearing the western glory in her heart:—

In 1929 Frank Luther Mott, a University of Iowa professor closely associated with the regionalist literary magazine *The Midland,* praised Vachel Lindsay succinctly:

> Mr. Lindsay, if one may be allowed the word, is openly and proudly and purposefully a "bunker." He believes, in other words, in building up and elaborating all the fine legendary materials we have.

As well he had to; for Lindsay also appointed himself the poetic custodian of all American myths. In another love song to Springfield called "Springfield Magical" he wrote:

In this, the City of my Discontent,
Down from the sky, up from the smoking deep
Wild legends new and old burn round my bed
While trees and grass and men are wrapped in sleep.

Poem titles show him ranging widely over the myths he seeks to collate and extend—American myths that should form both the American poet and the American village: "General Williams Booth Enters Into Heaven"; "John L. Sullivan, The Strong Boy of Boston"; "In Praise Of Johnny Appleseed"; "Our Mother Pocahontas"; "In Which Roosevelt Is Compared To Saul"; and not the myths of the past only; Lindsay wrote what is probably the first and last book to interpret the cinema in terms of the teachings of Emanuel Swedenborg and the Egyptian hieroglyph (*The Art Of The Motion Picture* .

Lindsay's particular kind of myth-making depended upon the wealth of southern and central Illinois thought and history that he studied most of his life. The Swedenborgianism that colored his vision—and brought him spiritually close to one of the first Midwestern mythmakers, Johnny Appleseed—was common in southern Illinois after the Civil War, according to Edgar Lee Masters's eloquent biography of Lindsay. The Lincoln-cult turned politics into moral pageantry, and a pervasive optimism about human institutions made the magical Springfield a plausible, if not possible, dream.

In a book called *Poor White*, published in the same year as Lewis's *Main Street*, Sherwood Anderson wrote what was both an appreciation and a sort of epitaph of the Midwestern spirit as it had been shaped in the days of Masters's and Lindsay's youth, the 1870s and 1880s:

> In even the smallest of the towns, inhabited only by farm laborers, a quaint interesting civilization was being developed. Men worked hard but were much in the open air and had time to think. Their minds reached out toward the solution of the mystery of existence. The schoolmaster and the country lawyer read Tom Paine's *Age of Reason* and Bellamy's *Looking Backward.* They discussed these books with their fellows. There was a feeling, ill-expressed, that America had something real and spiritual to offer the rest of the world. Workmen talked to each other of the new tricks of their trades, and after hours of discussion of some new way to cultivate corn, shape a horseshoe or build a barn, spoke of God and his intent concerning man. Long-drawn-out discussions of religious beliefs and the political destiny of America were carried on.

Masters, Lindsay, and Anderson were all three of them *modern* writers in the sense that they had to create for themselves out of disparate fragments

*Sherwood Anderson in his later years retired to a small Virginia town to edit two
newspapers, one Republican and the other Democratic.*
Culver Pictures, Inc.

a community of limited size and a specific history, and trust that that
community could somehow represent the macrocosm. Only then could
they seek out the great myths and rework them, as writers always have.
Masters's talkative shades are, in their high-minded and slightly prim
Midwestern way, trying to become James Joyce's mythic Dubliners.
Lindsay's incomplete "universal" book *The Golden Book of Springfield*
reminds us not only of Thoreau's plan for a great book about Concord, but
also of William Carlos Williams's cosmic expansion of the Springfield-size
town of Paterson, New Jersey. The difference is that Lindsay, being a
Midwesterner, actually thought that his dream city could be built. He was
a cloudy-headed kind of Frank Lloyd Wright.

Lewis, on the other hand, set his own task to be the debunking of this
dream, which he accomplished easily by simply pointing to the world the
Midwesterners had made of their characteristic kind of community. The
image he made has the finality of good satire: it is unanswerable and
definitive because it captures enough of the essential nature of the place
that even its unwilling targets must recognize themselves in its portrayal.

Sherwood Anderson, who cared about time and history in a way that Lewis did not, told the story of the origin of Gopher Prairie, being careful to show that dreams do not die even if institutions change, tracing the transformation of Midwestern optimism:

> The air of Bidwell began to stir with talk of new times. The evil things said of the new life coming were soon forgotten. The youth and optimistic spirit of the country led it to take hold of the hand of the giant, industrialism, and lead him laughing into the land. The cry, "get on in the world," that ran all over America at that period...rang in the streets of Bidwell.

The giant, who towered over the figure of Lincoln, changed everything:

> At the town of Gibonsville, near Bidwell, Ohio, and at Lima and Finley, Ohio, oil and gas fields were discovered. At Cleveland, Ohio, a precise, definite-minded man named Rockefeller bought and sold oil. From the first he served the new thing well and he soon found others to serve with him....From all sides the voice of the new age that was to

Findlay, Ohio, the site of one of the first big oil strikes in the United States in the 1880s. The town literally found oil in its own backyard.
Ohio Historical Society

do definite things shouted at them. Eagerly they took up the cry and ran with it. Millions of voices rose. The clamor became terrible, and confused the minds of all men. In making way for the viewer, broader brotherhood into which men are someday to emerge, in extending the invisible roofs of the towns and cities to cover the world, men cut and crushed their way through the bodies of men.

The mind of the Midwest is haunted by history in a curious way. The past is always a verb, something that is always shaping the present and, more importantly, men's perceptions of the present. Three generations take you back to virgin prairie. Memory is the memory of transformation, of hard work to remake something. It is also the memory of what the weather did, or how the Minneapolis Grain Exchange ruined the wheat price in 10 hours. It is the memory of a railroad town that filled up in 25 years, or of a coal village in southeastern Iowa that folded up two years after the season ran out.

Midwestern conservatism may be tight enough to hold down communities on a windy prairie; Midwestern community spirit may be cohesive enough to pull a town through a drought or tornado. But when a new wind blows, the Main Street businessman can become a savage competitor, the wheat farmer can start to talk like a Red. The little red god Ha-yo'-Ka will dance in the dust storm that blows over the ruined land. It is a fascinating accident of history that the prairie land, which is so splendidly rich and so dreadfully changeable, should have been settled by people with the paradoxical set of needs to tear them in different directions: the need to put down roots and, at the same time, the desire to transform themselves every generation.

SHERWOOD ANDERSON'S WORK in the 1920s completed the now familiar literary image of the Midwestern village, in an uneasy compromise between satire and nostalgia; the Ohio town of *Poor White* is both the calm cradle of an admirable democratic culture and, later, a new home for industrialism and the machine-mind.

In the bitter age of the Depression that followed, America would survey, explore, and examine itself as never before in its history. There were, for example, no reliable statistics about the number and nature of the unemployed. So researchers went out into America to find them, talk to them, and decide whether they were typical. Documentarists sought out American strengths that the Crash had not weakened. A bewildering number of documentary works, examining American economic, geographical, and cultural reality from the standpoint of the eyewitness, issued from every ideological camp, and for a variety of purposes: radical critique, New Deal propaganda, wartime consensus-building. In the process, the nation pro-

vided itself with materials for forming an unprecedentedly detailed awareness of itself, class by class, region by region, town by town, mile by mile.
The project that typifies the age and the effort is the great series of State
Guides produced under the W.P.A. by the Federal Writers' Project. In the
pages of the Guides, towns and cities that had stood in Midwestern
literature before 1929 as the grim citadels of Main-Streetery had decom-
posed into bright, swarming clusters of life. From the *Ohio Guide:*

> [In Cleveland] the white stock of native parentage com-
> prises only a quarter of the population; 8 per cent are
> Negroes and the remaining 67 per cent are either foreign-
> born or the offspring of foreign or mixed parentage. Once
> almost entirely Nordic and Celtic in make-up, Cleveland
> was transformed by the expanding steel industry into one
> of the racially most diversified communities in the United
> States. Forty-eight nationalities have representation here,
> more than 40 languages are spoken in the city. First in
> number are the Czechoslovaks, followed by the Poles,
> Italians, Germans, Yugoslavs, Irish, and Hungarians.
> Where they concentrate in nationality groups, their na-
> tive languages are spoken almost as commonly as English.
> A large section on the South Side is peopled primarily by
> Poles and Czechoslovaks; the Yugoslavs and Lithuanians
> have concentrated in an area of three square miles near
> the lake on the East Side. Between the Flats and West 65th
> Street on the west side is a densely populated section
> containing chiefly Germans, Irish and Rumanians. "Little
> Italy" lies south of Euclid Avenue just east of University
> Circle. The Russians and Greeks congregate principally in
> the vicinity of Prospect Avenue and East 14th Street, the
> Jews around East 105th Street north of Euclid Avenue, and
> around Kinsman Road west of Shaker Heights.

The Guides sought America in the detail, as much in somnolent rural Iowa
as in Ohio's biggest city. In this, they followed the earlier examples of Dell
and Sandburg and Dreiser. Legend and "folk-say" mixed happily with
demonstrable fact to grant every little wide place in the road its vividness
and dignity. From the *Iowa Guide:*

> At 101 m. is the junction with State 138, gravelled. Right
> on this road is MYSTIC, 3 m. (896 alt., 1,953 pop.), estab-
> lished in the 1880's as a mining center, following the
> discovery of a rich vein of coal. According to one story,
> Dennis Vandyke named the town for his birthplace, Mys-
> tic, Conn., but according to another version, Vandyke
> thought an "aura of mystery hovered over the locality"

when he first came and he wished to perpetuate this
impression in the name. Some of the miners here think
there will be a fatality if a woman enters a coal mine...
some will not allow members of their families to work in
the mine on the day before Christmas (Swedish); a bird or a
bat flying into the house is a warning of death to come....

Surely this toned-down myth-making is a relief from the grandiose visions
of a Vachel Lindsay; perhaps it is paradoxical that the documentary labor of
these years revealed and released the imaginative energy of the region
better than so-called imaginative literature did. Meridel LeSueur's *North
Star Country*, an informal history and assemblage of "documents" from the
life of Minnesota and the upper Midwest, is full of similar folk-life, like
these hallucinatory beasts from the lonesome brains of lumbermen:

There are animals seen only by a few. It was easy to see
strange animals in the solitude of the woods. Many went
crazy. It was said that only the Finns could stand to work
alone. These animals were variously seen but were never
caught for museums, or their bones found for study:
The *ax-handle hound* prowled around lumber camps
looking for ax or peavey handles to eat. The *argopelter*
lived in hollow trunks and threw things at the jacks. A
hangdown was found hanging like lichen from a limb and
could be caught only by placing a tub over it. The stone-
eating *gyascutus* was like a deer, with rabbit ears, teeth
like a lion, and telescopic legs for hill grazing. It was never
seen except after snake bite.

The confluence of documentarism and art in the Midwest during this
period produced a term that struggled, with varying degrees of success, to
become a movement: regionalism. Writing in 1935 from Iowa City, Iowa,
the Midwestern (and perhaps national) capital of the movement, the
painter Grant Wood attempted a definition:

Each section has a personality of its own, in physiography,
industry, psychology. Thinking painters and writers who
have passed their formative years in these regions, will, by
care-taking analysis, work out and interpret in their productions these varying personalities. When the different
regions develop characteristics of their own, they will
come into competition with each other; and out of this
competition a rich new American culture will grow. It was
in some such manner that Gothic architecture grew out of
the competition between different French towns as to
which could build the largest and finest cathedrals.

The roots of this tendency, which might be called local color made programmatic, are deep and tangled. In Iowa, which was to provide regionalism with its institutional headquarters (the University of Iowa) and its artist-hero (Wood), the local-literature impulse first emerged between the covers of Johnson Brigham's *Midland Monthly*, published in Des Moines between 1894 and 1899. The *Monthly* was a modest showcase for the two main tendencies in late 19th-century Midwestern literature: orthodox "local color" with a Hamlin Garland bite, and local humor, as purveyed by the likes of Emerson Hough and Ellis Parker Butler (author of "Pigs is Pigs").

In a conscious effort to continue the work of Brigham and to participate in the excitement that was being spread abroad by the Chicago Renaissance, John T. Frederick of the English Department at the University of Iowa established *The Midland* at Iowa City in 1915. This, the first of many literary little reviews out of Iowa City, was to run until 1933.

While Chicago acted as a magnet for visionary enthusiasts of the future (Lindsay, Sandburg) and satirists of the present (Lewis) and lyricists of the past or passing (Masters, Anderson), Iowa City made itself into a center for earth-worship. *The Midland* refused satire and went for depth; refused the city and plumbed the contemporary rural reality for resonant material. This plumbing could get dark and thick, as the Iowa humorist Phil Stong recalls in his *Hawkeyes*:

> During my college years, 1915–19, all of us little farm-hands were trying to make the *Midland.* The method was to summon up memories of the most miserable and feckless family we had ever heard of around the home town, adorn them with some tragic graces and see that one or all of the outfit (1) went crazy, (2) murdered the others, (3) committed suicide, incest or arson before the end of the story. It was Eugene O'Neill gone mad in the pigpens; yet Frederick was such an excellent editor that he made the business seem plausible.

The calmer *Midland* stories tended to follow a Hamlin Garland recipe made nostalgic: a prodigal returns to the rural homeland. Only home was a farm, not a village, and the young wanderer usually gives up city life at the end and decides to end his days among the corn-rows. Such stories made liberal use of a great Midwestern set-piece, land-praise:

> Low rolling hills, fold after fold, smooth brown and autumnal, some plowed to soft earth-color, some set with corn stalks of pale tarnished gold. Along the farther ones, the woods lay like a colored cloud, brown, russet, red and purple-tinged.
>
> This was glorious. This was getting back at things! This

was happiness! What farmer could ever escape his longing for the land, for the vision and smell of it, for the sounds of it, for the vision of it all laid out in soft ridges and planted ready to yield!

During its relatively long life, *The Midland* welcomed to its pages a number of first-rate writers, among them Stanley Burnshaw, Babette Deutsch, Howard Mumford Jones, Mark Van Doren, and the young Loren Eiseley. Yet most of what *The Midland* intended was being done better by Willa Cather. Whatever its deficiencies, its demise in 1933 coincided almost exactly with the rise of *Midland* values and theories onto the national stage, the institutionalization of what Grant Wood rather awkwardly called "farmer material."

Hard times in cities turned American eyes fondly back to the farm: bean-rows looked more promising than bread-lines. Farm holidays and foreclosure sales happened everywhere, yet it was the hard, dry,western Midwest —the Dakotas, Kansas, Nebraska—that produced the worst images of rural decay in the mind of America. Eastern Iowa, Grant Wood country, blessed with God's best topsoil, became the center and symbol of optimistic agrarianism in the Depression years. As the 1930s drew past the mid-mark, Iowa became an honest, modest cultural oasis, too.

Part of the reason is that the art-and-welfare bureaucracy in Washington was loaded with eminent Iowans: Henry Wallace, Secretary of Agriculture and hence the ultimate boss of the Farm Service Administration and its famous Photographic Unit; Harry Hopkins, Administrator of the W.P.A.; and Hallie Flanagan, the fiery head of the Federal Theatre.

Hopkins and Flanagan travelled to Iowa City to formally inaugurate the Federal Theatre on the University campus. It was to be, in its director's words, "national in scope, regional in emphasis, and democratic in allowing each local unit freedom." At Iowa, the writers who had been working under Wilbur Schramm in the School of Letters (the famous Writers' Workshop under Paul Engle would get underway in 1937), and the young directors, actors, and technicians at the University Theatre under E. C. Mabie, were called upon to collaborate in the making of regional and American plays.

With Flanagan looking on, Grant Wood teaching in the art department, the humanist critic Norman Foerster teaching English, the curtain constantly going up on new productions in Mabie's beautiful University Theatre, and Schramm and Engle busy building the most famous writing school in the world, Iowa City was a good place to make art in the latter 1930s. Regionalism was a catchword, often heard and often repeated; it had become, after all, national cultural policy. Firmly Midwestern works like E. P. Conkle's *Prologue to Glory*, a play in the continuing Midwest tradition of the Lincoln-cult, emerged. But regionalism falls into perspective if it is recalled that among the most distinguished projects at Iowa in the 1930s were Tennessee Williams's *Glass Menagerie*, and productions of the *Medea* and Ibsen's *Peer Gynt*. The Iowa artists were no more constrained by W.P.A. policy than James Agee was by the ideological premises of *Fortune* magazine, for whom he began to write *Let Us Now Praise Famous Men*.

WHEN AMERICA WENT TO WAR, regionalism was put to new uses. Particularism, the competition of regions, was put aside as Americans began to meld their different voices into a unified chorus of "national policy." LeSueur's *North Star Country* mentioned earlier was part of a series called *American Folkways*, under the general editorship of Erskine Caldwell. The roster of authors was distinguished: the sociologist Oscar Lewis covered the *High Sierra*, and Carey McWilliams, who was later to edit *The Nation* with distinction, contributed *Southern California Country*. Progressives all, these authors tended to see the war effort as a kind of populist triumph. LeSueur, in particular, rings Whitman-like changes on the theme of the upper Midwest as the crucible of a strong new people:

> The men of the north country who have come through this turbulent gap into the vent of the future, in so swift a time, are grandsons of Norwegians who married the daughter of a German forty-eighter, whose father's mother married a Polander, whose daughter very likely married an Irishman whose father was a Finn. These tall sons, and they grow tall here, fold up in the cockpit of a plane and get a bead's eye, not only on the enemy but on the future.
>
> The village has new life.... Merchants, bankers, housewives, high-school kids put their shoulders to the wheel in new forms of cooperation, developing from the machine and from necessity, expressing itself further in pooling of parts, collective use of machinery, and county planning.

Whatever "new life" the village-collective might have had, inside or outside of LeSueur's prose, it did not survive the postwar world any better than those patriotic leftists who spoke for it did. America shrank into separated clusters of ego-satisfactions; the West Coast boomed, and both Interstate freeways and improved air schedules made it possible, even desirable, to zip from coast to vivid coast without passing through the local color of Midwestern villages at all.

For poets and prose-writers, however, there remained one vital village, a good place to study for a year or two: Iowa City, where the Writers' Workshop boomed along, nurturing Roth and Vonnegut and Flannery O'Connor and W.D. Snodgrass and, eventually, a host of writers from Asia, Africa, and Central Europe. Iowa was the harbinger of the by now well-established intimate relationship between writers and colleges. It did not produce a lot of writing about the Midwest, but it did inspire a lot of poems called "Iowa" or "Iowa City." Most of the people who wrote and lived there liked it; there was, and is, a nice balance there between the things of the mind and the life of the soil. The Workshop teacher and novelist Vance Bourjaily kidded that balance gently in his recent novel *Now Playing At Canterbury:*

> In those crop fields, beside this pasture, the corn is ankle-
> high and finger-fat, the fist-sized soybean plants are Kelly
> green against black dirt. We had better wish them well.
> There's a tithe growing out there to keep the big State
> University moving on its earnest, complicated mission—
> for a cup of soybeans, your kid can triangulate a star, for an
> ear of corn, memorize two lines of Lermontov.

ANOTHER CONTEMPORARY LITERARY CENTER in the Midwest is Minneap-olis, the metropolis of the North Star Country. From Garland to Lewis, this region has sustained a hard vision that tends toward the somberly satirical. James Wright continues this tradition in "The Minneapolis Poem":

> I wonder how many old men last winter
> Hungry and frightened by namelessness prowled
> The Mississippi shore
> Lashed blind by the wind, dreaming
> Of suicide in the river.
> The police remove their cadavers by daybreak
> And turn them in somewhere.
> Where?
> How does the city keep lists of its fathers
> Who have no names?
> By Nicollet Island I gaze down at the dark water
> So beautifully slow.
> And I wish my brothers good luck
> And a warm grave.

Richard Grossman's book *Tycoon Boy* is notable because it makes grim poetry of the world of American business: board rooms, Xerox machines, after-work poker parties, promotional brochures. This passage is from "The Work Force":

> Awe comes into Mpls in the form of a cup
> prepared for snow. It is a wake
> where everyone is afraid to sleep:
> the body is grim and covered with white wool.

In my office the light is the same
but outside where you can see the windows
the work force staggers a Corpse
lounges over the bins and files of Gelco.

These examples, about ten years apart, typify a strong direction in contemporary poetry with a Midwestern setting: the tendency to mourn. While the central traditions of Midwestern regional writing always concerned themselves, directly or indirectly, with the threat of death or the reality of sterility, poets since the war have been looking at the landscape more and more from the cypress groves, as it were, of Edgar Masters's Spoon River cemetery. Edward Dorn wrote a beautiful poem, very much in Masters's debt, "The Air of June Sings":

> Across the road in a strawberry field two children are
> stealing their supper fruit, abreast in the rows, in the fields
> of the overlord, Miller his authentic name, and I see that
> name represented here, there is that social side of burial,
> too, long residence, and the weight of the established local
> dead. My eyes avoid the largest stone, larger than the
> common large, Goodpole Matthews, Pioneer, and that
> pioneer sticks in me like a wormed black cherry in my
> throat, No Date, nothing but that zeal, that trekking and
> Business, that presumption in a sacred place, where chil-
> dren are buried, and where peace, as it is in the fields and
> the country should reign....

Sinclair Lewis at his harshest sounds almost like Sandburg when his Babbitt is compared with these incredibly grim visions of Business in the arms of Death.

The Iowa-Nebraska poet Ted Kooser puts himself securely in another tradition when he uses the objects of common life to tell a story that might have come out of *Main-Travelled Roads*. But here again the story is told from the standpoint of a graveyard wanderer, reading in "Abandoned Farmhouse" the various items that serve as tombstones of a vanished life:

> He was a big man, says the size of his shoes
> on a pile of broken dishes by the house;
> a tall man too, says the length of the bed
> in an upstairs room; and a good, God-fearing man,
> says the Bible with a broken back
> on the floor below the window, dusty with sun;
> but not a man for farming, say the fields
> cluttered with boulders and the leaky barn.
>
> Something went wrong, says the empty house
> in the weed-choked yard. Stones in the fields

say he was not a farmer; the still-sealed jars
in the cellar say she left in nervous haste.
And the child? Its toys are strewn in the yard
like branches after a storm—a rubber cow,
a rusty tractor with a broken plow,
a doll in overalls. Something went wrong, they say.

When Midwestern poets do not write epitaphs, they often write of
loneliness; and if not loneliness, then meditative solitude. The Minneso-
tan Robert Bly, important for both his publishing work and his translations
from Spanish, Scandinavian, and other modern poetries, is a finder of the
"deep" image, the revelation that rises up apparently unbidden, at the very
moment the mind stops searching for it. That is the theme of a poem
elaborately entitled "After Drinking All Night with a Friend, We Go Out In
A Boat At Dawn To See Who Can Write The Best Poem."

Beneath the waters, since I was a boy,
I have dreamt of strange and dark treasures,
Not of gold, or strange stones, but the true
gift, beneath the pale lakes of Minnesota.

This morning also, drifting in the dawn wind,
I sense my hands, and my shoes, and this ink—
Drifting, as all of this body drifts,
Above the clouds of the flesh and the stone.

One Midwestern elegist who handles loneliness and abandonment better than most and who still can reach back into a populous human world is
the novelist Toni Morrison, whose *Sula* opens with this unforgettable
paragraph that moves through memory back into the life of a community
and its people, and culminates in a stroke of characterization that brings all
the dead alive at once.

In that place, where they tore the nightshade and black-
berry patches from their roots to make room for the
Medallion City Golf Course, there was once a neighborhood. It stood in the hills above the valley town of Medallion and spread all the way to the river. It is called the
suburbs now, but when black people lived there it was
called the Bottom. One road, shaded by beeches, oaks,
maples and chestnuts, connected it to the valley. The
beeches are gone now, and so are the pear trees where
children sat and yelled down through the blossoms to
passersby. Generous funds have been allotted to level the
stripped and faded buildings that clutter the road from
Medallion up to the golf course. They are going to raze the
Time and a Half Pool Hall, where feet in long tan shoes

once pointed down from chair rungs. A steel ball will knock to dust Irene's Palace of Cosmetology, where women used to lean their heads back on sink trays and doze while Irene lathered NuNile into their hair. Men in khaki work clothes will pry loose the slats of Reba's Grill, where the owner cooked in her hat because she couldn't remember the ingredients without it.

Morrison's village of black saints and sinners is a new, rich departure in the tradition of Village literature; some of the richness probably comes from the subtle influence of that sometime Iowan, Tennessee Williams, upon the settings and the characterizations. The people of the Bottom are by turns desperate, murderous, exuberant, tender, and suicidal; sometimes their hard lives make them mean, and sometimes they feel what Thomas McGrath, a North Dakota poet, calls "unreasonable content." Here is part of his own satirical tribute to the Village Revolt, "Ah—To The Villages", which sums up rather well the Midwestern writer's ambivalence about the emptiness that is at once his most famous traditional theme, a myth made by outsiders, a powerful daily reality, and a windmill to tilt with, like Don Quixote or Vachel Lindsay:

> Leaving the splendid plaza and the esplanade—
> The majestic facades of metropolitan unease—
> Let us to the vast savannahs of despair
> Repair; and let us seek
> The panoramas of malaise, the continental anguish,
> The hysteria and the nausea of the villages.

> Somewhere—perhaps where Omaha, like a disease,
> And the magnificent, brumal names of Fargo, of
>   Kalamazoo,
> Infect the spirit with magnificent ennui—
> A baroque splendor attends our small distress:
> We dress in the grand extravaganzas of cafard.

> Still, there will come evenings without true
>   discontent—
> The sparrows loud in the dust and the crows gone
>   cawing home
> To the little wood; the lights ending at the prairie,
>   and—
> As the divine and healing night comes down—
> The town reeling with unreasonable content.

THE SOUTH
&
BORDER STATES

BUTLER BREWTON

BETWEEN THE YEARS 1763 AND 1767, Charles Mason and Jeremiah Dixon, two English astronomers, settled a boundary-line dispute between Pennsylvania and Maryland by surveying the land. The line that Mason and Dixon established settled the quarrel by separating Pennsylvania both from Maryland and from what later became West Virginia, and by establishing the north-south division between Maryland and Delaware. Ever since, this boundary has been known as the Mason-Dixon Line, and during the Civil War it separated the slave and nonslave states. The South then adopted "Dixie" (perhaps from Dixon) as its provincial term, and the song by the same name as its anthem:

> Oh, I wish I was in the land of cotton.
> Old times there are not forgotten,
> Look away, look away, look away, Dixie land.

Old times are indeed at the essence of the South: the memory of them, the pressure of them, informs the entire way of life that is called Southern. The land speaks volumes.

Themes typical of Southern literature grew out of a number of special moments in American history. These moments generated sudden and radical changes in the life and attitudes of the South. The peculiar treatment of the thematic concerns by an assortment of authors led to the development of a body of American literature sufficiently unique to be described as Southern. There is a mood, a tone, a color in the writings eternal as that which can be observed in the personalities of the people themselves, and this special flavoring forms the distinctive character of the literature.

The four periods most essential to this character were the years leading up to the Civil War, the Civil War itself from 1861 to 1865; the Reconstruction period; and the years after 1895 to the death of Dr. Martin Luther King, Jr. in 1965. Obviously these historic periods brought changes to regions besides the South, but Southern literature has been obsessed with the issues these periods stirred: slavery; the decline of agriculture and the myth of the independent yeoman farmer; the Ku Klux Klan, Jim Crow, and Civil Rights; and the overwhelming sense that some vague Golden Age of the past has been irrevocably lost. From these concerns is woven the texture of the Southern soul, and consequently they form the basic pattern at the core of the literature.

The antebellum South is a haze of contradictory memories. Endless rows of white cotton where the slaves worked under the whip from sunup to sundown sustained the Southern economy, though the rich cane and tobacco fields flourished, too. The rich planters behaved like feudal lords and led leisurely lives of luxury. They and their families bought the latest in refinement and culture while their agricultural methods stripped the soil of its natural minerals in order to capture European markets. Even to this day the land bears the mark of abuse and overuse, and the slaves— forced into servitude for life terms, brutalized, emasculated, and stripped of every human right—became the ugliest mar on the Southern as well as the nation's conscience.

Harriet Beecher Stowe, "the little woman who wrote the book that made this great war," as Abraham Lincoln called her, shocked the South. *Uncle Tom's Cabin*, Stowe's classic, is probably the most influential book ever written in America. The book appeared in March 1852 and immediately sold millions. Lavishly praised in her home state of Massachusetts, Stowe was brutally insulted, too. She once received an envelope containing a Negro's ear with a scrawl to the effect that this was one of the effects of any so-called defense of the "damned niggers." Stowe had written in the author's preface to *Uncle Tom's Cabin*:

> The object of these sketches is to awaken sympathy and feeling for the African race, as they exist among us; to show their wrongs and sorrows, under a system so necessarily cruel and unjust as to defeat and do away the good effects of all that can be attempted for them, by their best friends, under it.

Stowe's treatment of the antebellum South shows the total dominance that whites had over the life and death of their slaves, and a further reading in *Uncle Tom's Cabin* would show that even the poverty-stricken whites who worked as slave drivers, even the poor white trash who sharecropped for subsistence-level wages, thought themselves superior to the slaves. That complete power of the slaveholder led to the development of all manner of subterfuge. For example, the slaves sent their escape plans to each other in codes that made the masters think they were simply fanatical Christians:

> Git on board little chillun.
> Git on board little chillun.
> Git on board little chillun.
> There's room for many-a-more.

These songs or spirituals grew into a complex Southern tradition. Other examples include "Swing Low Sweet Chariot," "Steal Away to Jesus," and "I Got A Home in Dat Rock."

When General Robert E. Lee finally surrendered the Southern forces to General Ulysses S. Grant in 1865 at Appomatox, it marked the end of an era. The plantations lay in burnt ruins. Confederate soldiers wandered wearily back home to find that all they had known and fought for had been whirled away like a black smoke by a terrible wind. The often painful transition period following the Civil War became the subject matter of much of Southern literature. One Georgian woman, Margaret Mitchell, chronicles the emotions of this change in her book *Gone with the Wind*.

Reflecting the South's historical development from antebellum through Reconstruction and including the development of the Ku Klux Klan, *Gone with the Wind* was heralded by readers everywhere as the Great American Novel. It is the story of Scarlett O'Hara, the spoiled, ruthless daughter of a wealthy plantation owner. She becomes a woman just in time to witness the Civil War sweeping away the life for which her upbringing has prepared her. After the fall of Atlanta, Scarlett returns to Tara (her plantation), and by stubborn shrewdness saves it from both Sherman's raid and the carpet-baggers. This demanding process, however, takes its toll: it hardens her. She has come near to starvation of body and spirit, and she vows never to let it happen again.

Virtually all of the characters in *Gone with the Wind* symbolize some aspect of the nature of the South. Ashley Wilkes, the lover with whom Scarlett is obsessed throughout her life, suggests the dream of the antebellum Southern aristocracy. He is dignified, chivalrous, sensitive, proud. He dies psychically but remains alive as a symbol of what the South has lost but will forever seek: the golden era of the Southern manner and the Southern way. The cry of the South to this day remains "The South shall rise again!" Even the name Ashley suggests both that which has been burned, and that which, like the mythological phoenix, will rise to new glory out of its own ashes.

Rhett Butler, the sophisticated profiteer, is attracted to Scarlett, and she finally marries him to insure her own survival. Clearly this event comments on the kinds of accommodations that the South was forced to make for economic need. Scarlett survives, but the marriage proves to be a failure. It ends when Scarlett, after a series of indiscretions, convinces Rhett that she can never truly be his love because of her eternal devotion to the memory and image of Ashley. But, at the same time, Scarlett pleads to Rhett to remain with her, since his existence, his being near her, guarantees her security.

Yet, in the true spirit of the eternal will of the South, Scarlett, after musing over her loss of Rhett and her near loss of life, steels herself by deflecting her hopes into the future—a future where anything is possible.

The South, destroyed just as Scarlett was, nevertheless was no nearer to being completely defeated than she; and it is this attitude that defines the distinctive quality of Southern literature. Countless works explore this nostalgia, this unrelenting desire of the South to recapture the world lost by the Civil War.

The last of the special moments in the South's history came at the turn of the century, Booker T. Washington, a former slave, founded the famous Tuskegee Institute in Alabama. He became accepted as the spokesman for and leader of blacks, largely because of his position on separation of the races. The South had been worried about the aspirations of its black population, and so Washington's promise to the nation, that blacks would not attempt either to interact socially or politically with whites or to merge into the mainstream of American life, helped guarantee the policy of separatism that existed officially until the Supreme Court's decision in *Brown v. Board of Education* in 1954. Not until the 1960s and the efforts of such civil rights advocates as Martin Luther King, Jr. and Malcolm X did segregation and racial discrimination begin to ease. But the Washington era outlined many of the themes in Southern literature.

Though he was born in Ohio in 1872, Paul Lawrence Dunbar portrayed in his poetry a tone recurrent in Southern life and literature. So typical of rural Southern life was the slow humdrum religious and pastoral image that his readers readily accepted Dunbar's dialect as authentically Southern. No doubt, Dunbar wished to protest certain aspects of post-Reconstruction—a period that he saw as one marked by utter contempt for poor people and blacks—but most readers seem to have missed this subtle point and continued to trust as accurate the simplicity and ignorance voiced by the poems. Dunbar's black preacher in the poem, "An Antebellum Sermon," for instance, speaks to his racially mixed congregation:

> So you see de Lawd's intention
> Evah since de worl' began
> Was dat His almighty freedom
> Should belong to evah man,
> But I think it would be bettah,
> Ef I'd pause agin to say,

Dat I'm talking 'bout ouah freedom
In a Bibleistic way.

ACROSS THE POTOMAC RIVER, south of Washington, lies Virginia. In 1607, the English sea captain, John Smith, traveling with three ships and 105 men, docked in Virginia and within that year authored the first book written in North America, *A True Relation.* This work documented Smith's explorations down the Potomac and Rappahannock Rivers and Chesapeake Bay. Smith, a flamboyant figure who met all the criteria of a folk hero, often reported accounts of his adventures that seem to have been exaggerations or even outright lies. Few believed him when, for instance, he declared 20 years after his journey to the New World that, upon first arriving in Virginia, other leaders of the English expedition had two gallows made for his execution for attempted mutiny. "But Captaine Smith could not be perswaded to use them," he boasted. The incident is unaccountable in history, yet in the 1612 edition of Smith's *Map of Virginia* he does tell of his imprisonment for subversive behavior at sea.

John Smith assisted in founding the first permanent English colony at Jamestown, a peninsula in the James River a few miles southeast of what is now the sprawling tobacco capital, Richmond. Smith, up on criminal charges and never able to work in concert with other leaders, exhibited his real strengths in expeditions among Indians to procure corn and other food for the half-starved settlers and in inventing colorful episodes now well-etched into America's literary heritage. His *A Generall Historie of Virginia, New England and the Summer Isles* includes his own account of the romantic Captain John Smith being rescued from death by Pocahantas, the beautiful daughter of Chief Pawhattan. The tale, true or not, has since become an American legend; but the existence of Pocahantas herself is not in doubt. Her marriage to John Rolfe in 1614 aided in establishing good relations with the Indians. In 1617 she died in England, from the exhaustion and illness brought on by her touring.

Virginia has been called both the mother of presidents and the mother of states: George Washington, Patrick Henry, James Madison, and numerous others who were essential to the American Revolution were all Virginians. Among them, of course, is Thomas Jefferson, whose multifaceted genius found expression in almost every area of human endeavor from architecture to botany to writing. He designed both his own home, Monticello, and the campus of the University of Virginia; he studied with care the possibilities of improving various agricultural products; and he authored the Declaration of Independence, in which he drew on Locke and Enlightenment philosophy to create one of the most elegant and enduring statements of human aspiration ever written.

Virginia boasts its scenic geographic regions as well as its fascinating history. The Appalachian Plateau, the Appalachian Ridge and Valley Region, the Blue Ridge, the Piedmont and Atlantic Coastal plain are distinctive areas that attract thousands of tourists each year. The Dismal Swamp is one lesser known region that has always held great interest for naturalists, tourists, and writers. It teems with wildlife, stumps, pines, and mythology. Some writers have told of the ghost of an Indian maiden who paddles a white canoe through the misty water as her lover follows. But there are also less attractive memories connected with the swamp. Henry Wadsworth Longfellow and Harriet Beecher Stowe wrote of antebellum days when slaves, attempting to hide from their masters, were hunted down by dogs as they stumbled though the mud there. The first several lines of Longfellow's poem, "The Slave in the Dismal Swamp," give a vivid description of this agonizing ordeal:

> In dark fens of the Dismal Swamp
> The hunted Negro lay;
> He saw the fire of the midnight camp,
> And heard at times a horse's tramp
> And a bloodhound's distant bay,
>
> Where will-o-the-wisps and glow worms shine,
> In bulrush and in brake;
> Where waning masses shroud the pine
> And the cedar grows, and the poisonous vine
> Is spotted like the snake;
>
> Where hardly a human foot could pass,
> Or a human heart would dare,
> On the quaking turf of the green morass,
> He crouched in the rank and tangled grass,
> Like a wild beast in his lair.

Harriet Beecher Stowe's novel *Dred: A Tale of the Great Dismal Swamp* tells of the rebellious slave Dred who provided refuge for other runaway slaves in the swamp. One model for Stowe's character was Nat Turner, the leader of a slave insurrection.

It should not have been surprising that the natural response of slaves to their condition of servitude would be uprisings and attempts to gain freedom. David Walker's *Appeal* in the 1820s, a document that blasted the institution of slavery, has often been cited as a major motivation for the Southhampton, Virginia, slave insurrection in 1831 led by Nat Turner, a renegade mystic. It is reported in Styron's *Confessions of Nat Turner* that this slave felt himself to be a kind of Moses selected by some divine power to deliver his people from bondage, and upon the occasion of a solar eclipse in February, 1831, and in the atmosphere of Walker's *Appeal*, Turner became convinced that this was the moment ordained for his God-appointed

The Dismal Swamp, frequently used as an escape route by both convicts and slaves.
New York Public Library

task. On August 21, he and his followers began their revolt by killing his owner and the entire household, and in rapid succession murdered other slave-holding families in the area. Sixty whites were killed before state and federal troops overpowered the main body of the rebels. But 100 slaves were slaughtered and 13 slaves and three free blacks were hanged immediately. On October 30, two slaves revealed where Turner had taken refuge and in less than two weeks he was executed. Following this uprising in Virginia, the entire South strengthened its Black Codes (laws to limit the movement and activities of blacks), and white citizens literally stayed awake nights in fear of possible repeat rebellions.

NORTH CAROLINA, to the south of Virginia and at the northern edge of South Carolina, finds its literary trademark in the claim that the state is "a vale of humility between two mountains of conceit." Despite this tongue-in-cheek attitude, North Carolinians have not been amused by William Byrd's insulting account of the state in his *History of the Dividing Line:*

> Surely there is no place in the world where the inhabitants live with less labor than in North Carolina. It approaches nearer to the description of Lubberland than any other, by the great felicity of the climate, the easiness of raising provisions, and the slothfulness of the people.

Surely if William Byrd could have envisioned North Carolina's future literary activity, he might have found less basis for such an assessment. Among North Carolina's literary offspring are Charles Chesnutt, Thomas Wolfe, and Paul Green, whose outdoor drama still celebrates one of America's most mysterious subjects—"The Lost Colony" that disappeared from history. North Carolina can even claim Carl Sandburg, who chose to spend the last years of his life there.

Charles Chesnutt, born in 1858, was actually a native of Ohio, but was forced to move with his relatives when they had to return to North Carolina to earn a livelihood. Chesnutt prided himself on being a mulatto and explored in his writing the special tensions experienced by Americans whom he felt were too white to be accepted as black and too black to be accepted as white. The Tragic Mulatto theme underlies practically all Chesnutt's major novels and short fiction, including *The House Behind the Cedars, The Marrow of Tradition,* and *The Wife of His Youth and Other Stories of the Color Line.* His most significant contribution to American literature may be the tales of his *The Conjure Woman,* which are based on North Carolina folklore. These tales are narrated by Uncle Julius, a shrewd ex-slave who uses them to instruct and manipulate his northern employer. *The House Behind the Cedars* examines a problem that became a haunting theme in Southern literature—the child of racially mixed blood. Tryon, white and a leading chracter in the novel, reads from a medical journal:

> Turning the leaves idly, he, Tyron, came upon an article by a Southern writer, upon the perennial race problem that has vexed the country for a century. The writer maintained that owing to a special tendency of the Negro blood, however diluted, to revert to the African type, any future amalgamation of the white and black races, which foolish and wicked Northern negrophiles predicted as the ultimate result of the new conditions confronting the South, would therefore be an ethnological impossibility; for the smallest trace of Negro blood would inevitably drag down the superior race to the level of the inferior, and reduce the fair Southland, already devastated by the land invader, to the frightful level of Hayti, the awful example of Negro incapacity.

The Thomas Wolfe Memorial, 48 Spruce Street in Asheville, is an ordinary white frame house and is known in Asheville as the "Old Kentucky Home." Most visitors, however, see it as "Dixieland," the boardinghouse run by Mrs. Eliza Gant in Wolfe's *Look Homeward, Angel.* The residents of Asheville resented Wolfe's raw and honest portrayal of certain people in his hometown. Because it was such a blunt expose, the book was banned from the public library in Asheville.

Criticism simply made *Look Homeward, Angel* even more popular, however, and Wolfe eventually was warmly welcomed back to Asheville. The nostalgia for a lost past, and the mixed emotions brought out by his return, surface in *Of Time and the River:*

> When they got down off the mountain into South Carolina they were very drunk. On a dusty sand-clay road between some cotton fields they stopped the car, and walked out into the fields to piss. The cotton stood stiff and dry and fleecy in its pods, the coarse brown stalks rose up in limitless planted rows, and underneath, he could see the old and homely visage of the red-clay earth.
>
> At one edge of the field, and seeming very far away and lonely-looking, there was a negro shanty, and behind this a desolate wooded stretch of pine. Over all the earth at once, now that the roar of the engine had stopped, there was an immense and brooding quietness, a drowsed autumnal fume and warmth, immensely desolate and mournful, holding somehow a tragic prophecy of winter that must come, and death, and yet touched with the lonely, mournful and exultant mystery of the earth.
>
> Eugene reeled back toward the car again...ending up in a passionate oration about the hills, the fields, the cotton and the earth—trying to tell them all about "the South" and making of the stalks of cotton and "the South" a kind of symbol....
>
> But at that moment, all Eugene was trying to say about his years away from home, and his return, and how he had discovered his own land again and was, "by God," one of them—waving the stalks of cotton as he talked, and finding the whole core and kernel of all he wished to say in these stalks of cotton....

CHARLESTON, FOUNDED IN 1670, still boasting its gracious homes, gardens, and historical sites, was at once the commercial and political center of the Old South. It sired the almost European-style culture that identifies the South Carolinian to this day. It is the city where the first cannons of the Civil War launched the argument against Fort Sumter, and it was in Charleston that Denmark Vesey, a slave, plotted his almost successful seizure of the armory to free his fellow slaves in the state. Likewise, it was in this famous old city that a group of gentlemen writers known as the Charleston School flourished in the years before Sherman's infamous march to the sea.

*An early 19th century engraving showing Charleston as a
thriving seaport and expansive city.*
New York Historical Society

Recent years have seen literary emphasis again focused on Charleston, where a group of authors, known as the Poetry Society of South Carolina, worked. One of the group, DuBose Heyward, a lifetime Charlestonian, born of an aristocratic family, lived at 76 Church Street at the time he wrote *Porgy*. Heyward, like many other Southern writers, chose for his subject Southern blacks. In fact, it seems that Heyward was more a recorder of the actual than a creator of the fictional when he wrote *Porgy*, which later became the Broadway hit *Porgy and Bess*. Some Charlestonians maintain that Porgy was a real person whose name was Sam Richardson and who lived in a tenement at 89-91 Church Street. Heyward knew Richardson, the heavy-set black man who was neither virtuous nor villainous, when he had a little goat wagon and sat around begging.

Heyward was drawn to blacks as literary subjects at least in part because of an experience he had:

> There had been some small robberies from freight yards on the waterfront tracks. I was making my way to work when I heard someone shout, "Look out!" I saw a large Negro racing directly toward me. A second later a policeman rounded the corner, aimed coolly and carefully and fired. The man lurched forward and died, almost at my feet.

After that, Heyward knew what he was meant to do in life: he would give himself to writing and his first work would be about the slum Negro of the South. Heyward goes on:

> As for myself, from earliest memory Negro life fascinated me. As a boy, swimming from the wharves and watching the seething life on the great cotton piers, I was caught by the color, the mystery and movement of Negro life. Negroes in long lines trucking cotton on the wharves; dim figures in a deserted warehouse squatting over a crap game; spirituals bringing me up short to listen against the wall of a dilapidated church that I had to pass each night on the way from work.

This subject matter made Heyward's career and insured his immortality in American literature. When Porgy lost his love, Bess, to the lure of New York's glitter, he lamented as the traditional lover on his knees would. Yet the dialect Heyward knew and rendered well revealed Porgy as the noble primitive reaching beyond his limits toward what he considered the best of all things:

PORGY: *(wildly)*. You—Bess?—Yo' ain't means Bess dead?

SERENA: She worse dan dead.

LILY: Sportin' Life carry she away on de Noo Yo'k boat.

They are all silent, gazing at Porgy. He, too, is silent for a moment.

PORGY: Where dat dey take she?

MINGO: Noo Yo'k.

MARIA: Dat's way up Nort'.

PORGY: *(pointing.)* It dat way?

MARIA: It take two days by de boat. Yo' can't find um.

PORGY: I ain't say I can find um. I say, where it is?

MARIA: Yo' can't go after she. Ain't yo' hear we say yo' can't find um.

ANNIE: Ain't yo' know Noo Yo'k mos' a t'ousand mile' from here?

PORGY: Which way dat?

LILY: *(pointing)*. Up Nort'—past de Custom House.

Porgy turns his goat and drives slowly with bowed head toward the gate.

One current literary figure who has arisen from the South to take the literary world by storm is a passionately opinionated and sensitive man of contradictions, James Dickey. *Deliverance*, of course, is Dickey's most famous book, and is set on the white water of an unnamed river north of Atlanta at the Georgia-South Carolina border. Other works include fiction as well as poetry. *Introduction to Stone, Drowning with Others, Helmets, Buckdancer's Choice*, for which he won the National Book Award, and *Poems 1957-1967* have all made Dickey a sought-after lecturer on American literature and a valued member of the University of South Carolina faculty.

With his embroidered shirts and wide-brimmed cowboy hat, Dickey symbolizes the striking contrasts between the new Southern writers and the members of the Charleston School of gentlemen poets. He is as much a part of the growth and changes as the new factories and industries. Like many in the South, Dickey was attracted as a young man to the nostalgic views of the agrarians who wished to keep man in close relation with nature. He is frequently considered a Gothic poet, like other Southern writers who domesticate the grotesque. His poem "The Sheep Child," demonstrates Dickey's power to link past horror with an archetypal world of pastoral myth that cannot be eradicated or forgotten:

> Farm boys wild to couple
> With anything with soft-wooded trees
> With mounds of earth   mounds
> Of pinestraw   will keep themselves off
> Animals by legends of their own:
> In the hay-tunnel dark
> And dung of barns, they will
> Say I have heard tell

> That in a museum in Atlanta
> Way back in the corner of somewhere
> There's this thing that's only half
> Sheep   like a woolly baby
> Pickled in alcohol   because
> Those things can't live   his eyes
> Are open   but you can't stand to look
> I heard from somebody who...

> But this is now almost all
> Gone. The boys have taken
> Their own true wives in the city,
> The sheep are safe in the west hill
> Pasture   but we who were born there
> Still are not sure. Are we,
> Because we remember, remembered
> In the terrible dust of museums?

Merely with his eyes, the sheep-child may
Be saying   saying
I am here, in my father's house ...

WRITERS WHO HAVE CALLED GEORGIA HOME have lived among the remnants of the old South's cultural tradition and its horrible results. Georgia is, after all, the site of General Sherman's famed march, and the devastation of his attack has left its mark as well on the state's literature.

Sidney Lanier was born in Macon in 1809. He was a doctor, but preferred writing poetry. His friend Edgar Allen Poe called him "one of the best and one of the worst poets in America." In ill health most of his life, Lanier, in addition to being a poet, was a talented musician, and played the flute in Baltimore's Peabody Symphony Orchestra for years. This devotion to music is reflected in his ability to capture the sensuous sound patterns and rhythms of music in his verse, and to evoke from the reader the deepest instinctive responses. At the same time, his poetry is far from ethereal, and treats real-life subjects such as the plight of the poor and the growing commercialism of post-Civil War America.

The Marshes of Glynn made famous by Lanier are found in Brunswick. These spacious saltwater marshes are now traversed by causeways and bisected by channels of the Intercoastal Waterways, but the natural scenic beauty that caused Lanier to write "Marshes of Glynn" has survived, making it possible to relive the poet's vivid description of these marshes and the mood they called forth in him, as when he compares the union of the marsh waters and the sea to his own yearnings for union with God. Lanier writes in the first stanza:

> Glooms of the live-oaks, beautiful-braided and woven
> With intricate shades of the vines that myriad-cloven
> Clamber the forks of the multiform boughs,—
> Emerald twilights,—
> Virginal shy lights,
> Wrought of the leaves to allure to the whisper of vows,
> When lovers pace timidly down through the green
> colonnades
> Of the dim sweet woods, of the dear dark woods,
> Of the heavenly woods and glades,
> That run to the radiant marginal sand-beach within
> The wide sea-marshes of Glynn:—

Carson McCullers, considered one of the most important Southern writers, was born in Columbus. *The Heart is a Lonely Hunter* illustrates the Southern reluctance to deal with the strange, the crippled, the unusual, and the tendency to see the people in those categories as inferior or less

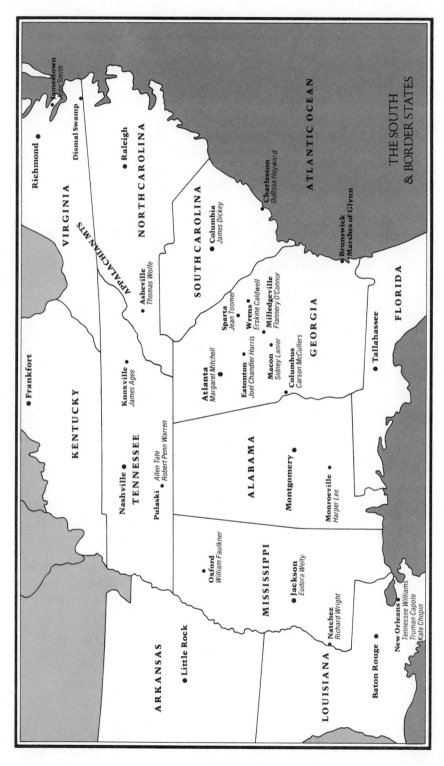

THE SOUTH
& BORDER STATES

ATLANTIC OCEAN

VIRGINIA

Richmond •

Jamestown
John Smith

Dismal Swamp •

NORTH CAROLINA

• Raleigh

Asheville •
Thomas Wolfe

SOUTH CAROLINA

Columbia •
James Dickey

Charleston •
DuBose Heyward

Brunswick •
Marshes of Glynn

KENTUCKY

• Frankfort

Knoxville •
James Agee

TENNESSEE

Nashville •
Pulaski •   Allen Tate
Robert Penn Warren

Atlanta •
Margaret Mitchell

Sparta •
Jean Toomer

Wrens •
Erskine Caldwell

Milledgeville •
Flannery O'Connor

Eatonton •
Joel Chandler Harris

Macon •
Sidney Lanier

Columbus •
Carson McCullers

GEORGIA

• Tallahassee

FLORIDA

ALABAMA

Montgomery •

Monroeville •
Harper Lee

Oxford •
William Faulkner

MISSISSIPPI

Jackson •
Eudora Welty

ARKANSAS

• Little Rock

Natchez •
Richard Wright

New Orleans •
Tennessee Williams
Truman Capote
Kate Chopin

LOUISIANA

Baton Rouge •

APPALACHIAN MTS.

valuable. The story tells of a deaf mute in a small Southern town who loses his only friend—who also happens to be a mute. He then appeals to other "outsiders"—a lonely girl who loves music; a doctor who is black; a young radical—and succeeds in winning their friendship. The book explores the themes of loneliness and isolation, her fundamental concerns in other works like *The Ballad of the Sad Cafe, Clock Without Hands, A Member of the Wedding*, and *Reflections in a Golden Eye*, all written during the 1940s and 1950s. A typical section from *The Heart is a Lonely Hunter* sketches these notions:

> The town was in the middle of the deep South. The sum-
> mers were long and the months of winter cold were very
> few. Nearly always the sky was a glassy, brilliant azure and
> the sun burned down riotously bright. Then the light, chill
> rains of November would come, and perhaps later there
> would be frost and some short months of cold. The winters
> were changeable, but the summers always were burning
> hot. The town was a fairly large one. On the main street
> there were several blocks of two- and three-story shops
> and business offices. But the largest buildings in the town
> were the factories, which employed a large percentage of
> the population. These cotton mills were big and flourish-
> ing and most of the workers in the town were very poor.
> Often in the faces along the streets there was the desper-
> ate look of hunger and of loneliness.

Born in 1925, Flannery O'Connor spent most of her short life in Mill-edgeville. The author of the novels *Wise Blood, The Violent Bear It Away*, and collections of short stories, *A Good Man Is Hard To Find* and *Everything That Rises Must Converge*, she is among the most accomplished American writers. Ill for most of her life, she lived on a country estate called Andalusia, and heaped up honors for her literary activity. Typical of O'Connor's wit and humility is her short story, "A Good Man is Hard to Find," in which the author captures the spirit and attitudes of the Southerners she knew so well:

> "Let's go through Georgia fast so we won't have to look at it
> much," John Wesley said.
> "If I were a little boy," said the grandmother, "I wouldn't
> talk about my native state that way. Tennessee has the
> mountains and Georgia has the hills."
> "Tennessee is just a hillbilly dumping ground," John
> Wesley said, "and Georgia is a lousy state too."
> "You said it," June Star said.
> "In my time," said the grandmother, folding her thin
> veined fingers, "children were more respectful of their

native state and their parents and everything else. People did right then. Oh look at that cute little pickaninny!" she said and pointed to a Negro child standing in the door of a shack, "Wouldn't that make a picture, now?" she asked and they all turned and looked at the little Negro out of the back window. He waved.

"He didn't have any britches on," June Star said.

"He probably didn't have any," the grandmother explained. "Little niggers in the country don't have things like we do. If I could paint, I'd paint that picture," she said.

Many modern writers have lived in Georgia and have used the state as the setting for their works. Much of Jean Toomer's novel *Cane* was set in the backwoods of Georgia. Attempting to explore his own roots, Toomer, a mulatto, found some solace in the sensuousness of black life before disassociating himself from a race he considered too polluted to merit his devotion. "Reapers" demonstrates his poetic talent as he captures a flavor distinctive to the South.

Black reapers with the sound of steel on stones
Are sharpening scythes. I see them place the hones
In their hip-pockets as a thing that's done,
And start their silent swinging, one by one.
Black horses drive a mower through the weeds,
And there, a field rat, startled, squealing bleeds,
His belly close to ground. I see the blade,
Blood-stained, continue cutting weeds and shade.

Erskine Caldwell, notorious in some quarters for his pictures of Southern poor whites, portrayed shiftless, downtrodden, but sometimes comical sharecroppers in *Tobacco Road* and *God's Little Acre*, both published in the early 1930s. Jeeter Lester of *Tobacco Road* embodies many of the most prominent Southern tendencies—tendencies that led to literary caricatures and dead ends:

Jeeter made a false start somewhere nearly every day. He was going to Fuller, or he was going to McCoy, or he was going to Augusta; but he never went when he said he would. If he told Ada at night that he was going to McCoy early the next morning, he would decide at the last minute to go to Fuller or Augusta instead. Usually he would have to stop or walk out over the old cotton fields and look at the tall brown broomsedge, and that made him think about something else. When he did walk out into the sedge, the chances were that he would lie down and take a nap. It was a wonder how he ever got the wood cut that he hauled to Augusta. Sometimes it took him a whole week to cut enough blackjack for a load.

Just then it was the beginning of the new season that was causing him to change his mind so frequently.... The smell of newly turned earth, that others were never conscious of, reached Jeeter's nostrils with a more pungent odor than any one else could ever detect in the air. That made him want to go out right away and burn over the old cotton fields and plant a crop.... Even if he succeeded in borrowing a mule, Jeeter did not know where to begin begging for credit to buy seed-cotton and guano. The merchants in Fuller had heard his plea so many times that they knew what he was going to ask for as soon as he walked in the door, and before he could say the first word they were shaking their heads and going back to where he could not follow them. He did not know what to do about it.

Jeeter postponed nearly everything a man could think of, but when it came to plowing the land and planting cotton, he was as persistent as any man could be about such things. He started out each day with his enthusiasm at fever pitch, and by night he was still as determined as ever to find a mule he could borrow and a merchant who would give him credit for seed-cotton and guano.

Perhaps the most famous literary creations to come out of Georgia are *Tales of Uncle Remus* and *Gone with the Wind.* Joel Chandler Harris was born in 1848 in Eatonton to a mother who had just been deserted by her husband, and his early life was plagued by financial hardship and a poor education. He loved to read, however, and eventually landed a job as an assistant in the printing office where *The Countryman* was published. The office was located on a plantation populated by blacks who made up tales about the plantation animals, and gave them, as Aesop had in ancient Greece, human characteristics. Harris seized upon the richness of this black folklore and used it to capture a reading audience throughout the world. Harris's tales featured an old slave named Uncle Remus telling stories to a little boy about Br'er Rabbit and Br'er Fox and Br'er Bear. "The Briar Patch" and "The Tar Baby," the best known stories of the collection, first appeared in a newspaper, *The Constitution*, on which Harris worked. Today the stories are out of fashion, partly because Harris's picture of the happy, gentle slave entertaining his master's child is too sentimental. Yet Harris made an important contribution to American literature by preserving in writing many of the Southern black folk tales.

Another writer whose subject was the Civil War South is Frank Yerby, a black man, born in 1916 in Augusta. One of the best-selling contemporary novelists, he won an O. Henry Award in 1944 for his short story "Health Card." Despite his artistic skill, Americans did not take well to black writers, especially protest writers, at that time. Yerby hid his identity as an Afro-American and turned to writing romantic historical novels that featured white characters, and his works sold so well that some of them were made into motion pictures. He is best known for his works *The Foxes of Harrow, Pride's Castle,* and *The Vixen.*

In one of his works, *Benton's Row,* Yerby juxtaposed what the South has eternally struggled to believe with what it actually is. At one point, Benton, the protagonist, reflects:

> So it was that after his death, perhaps even before, he was to slide back again into myth and legend, his stature augmented in the minds of his progeny to that of a folk-hero, more, even into demigod, princely in his valor, sage-like in wisdom, strong beyond the possibility of mere humanity, fair with that commanding male beauty attributed always to the offspring of the dim ancestral gods.
>
> He, the man himself, was none of these things. It was merely that he gave the legend shape, force, direction, by believing implicitly of himself all the things that were afterwards said of him....

WITH A LITERARY HISTORY THAT GOES BACK as far as the 17th century, Florida has long been a major haunt for writers from all over the country. Jonathan Dickinson, when his group of Quakers was cast up on the coast near what is now Palm Beach after they were wrecked en route from Jamaica to Pennsylvania, recorded the tragedy in *God's Protecting Providence* in 1699. Not only was this book one of America's first best sellers, but it was also the first account of the Indians of the southeastern coast. Other early writers who followed him celebrated the rich and various plant and animal life, striking sympathetic chords in the imaginations of Ralph Waldo Emerson and the English Romantics William Wordsworth and Samuel Taylor Coleridge.

Florida has been visited by many writers who sometimes were so taken by what they saw that they adopted it as their home. Harriet Beecher Stowe spent several winters on an orange farm she bought with her husband in 1867. The Stowes's original intent in buying the home, which is at Mandarin on the St. John River, was to create a model for the efficient employment of free black labor. The intent had to give way to the necessity of discouraging the spectators who flocked to see Mrs. Stowe by charging twenty-five cents per person for admission.

On his way to report on the Cuban revolution in 1896, Stephen Crane spent some time in Jacksonville. It was there that Crane met his wife, who at that time ran a popular sporting house in the town. On his way to Cuba, Crane's boat sank off the coast of Florida, an incident that provided Crane with the material on which his masterpiece "The Open Boat" is based.

> Gray-faced and bowed forward, they mechanically, turn by turn, plied the leaden oars. The form of the lighthouse had vanished from the southern horizon, but finally a pale star appeared, just lifting from the sea. The streaked saffron in the west passed before the all-merging darkness, and the sea to the east was black. The land had vanished, and was expressed only by the low and drear thunder of the surf.
> "If I am going to be drowned—if I am going to be drowned—if I am going to be drowned, why, in the name of the seven mad gods who rule the sea, was I allowed to come thus far and contemplate sand and trees? Was I brought here merely to have my nose dragged away as I was about to nibble the sacred cheese of life?

James Weldon Johnson and Zora Neale Hurston, two prominent black authors, were natives of Florida. Johnson was born in Jacksonville in 1871. A songwriter, poet, novelist, teacher, and the first black man to be admitted to the Florida bar since Reconstruction, Johnson could not work as a lawyer in Florida because no one at the time would risk having a black man plead his case before the customarily all-white jury in the South. He did, however, fight successfully to upgrade the quality of black education in Florida and went on to hold high office in the National Association for the Advancement of Colored People (NAACP). Johnson also wrote the lyrics for a tune by his brother Rosamund, a song titled "Lift Every Voice and Sing" that became a sort of black national anthem. Johnson strongly disliked the black dialect poetry in the manner of *Lyrics of Lowly Life* of Paul L. Dunbar so fashionable during his era. He considered the use of dialect demeaning, but at the same time he wished to capture the power of the black slave preacher with his "words of fire." This desire led Johnson to write the frequently anthologized sermon, "The Creation," which is collected in *God's Trombones*.

Johnson gave the reading public a scare with his *Autobiography of an Ex-Colored Man*. He published the work anonymously, pretending that the author was a mulatto who had been able to conceal his identity and marry into a white family. The character fathered children and lived in a white community with a white wife, but feared that his true identity would eventually be discovered.

HARPER LEE WAS BORN IN ALABAMA IN 1926, and studied at the state university. Her first novel, *To Kill a Mockingbird*, told the story of a black falsely accused of raping a white woman, was a tremendous success, and was made into a film starring Gregory Peck. Lee knew her dialects and she knew her people, poor whites and blacks both, as the following excerpt shows:

> Atticus said professional people were poor because the farmers were poor. As Maycomb County was farm country, nickels and dimes were hard to come by for doctors and dentists and lawyers. Entailment was only a part of Mr. Cunningham's vexations. The acres not entailed were mortgaged to the hilt, and the little cash he made went to interest. If he held his mouth right, Mr. Cunningham could get a WPA job, but his land would go to ruin if he left it, and he was willing to go hungry to keep his land and vote as he pleased. Mr. Cunningham, said Atticus, came from a set breed of men.

However poor those people may have been, they had effective and established ways of doing things—Southern ways that were frequently, if unknowingly, violated by outsiders:

> If I could have explained these things to Miss Caroline, I would have saved myself some inconvenience and Miss Caroline subsequent mortification, but it was beyond my ability to explain things as well as Atticus, so I said, "You're shamin' him, Miss Caroline. Walter hasn't got a quarter at home to bring you, and you can't use any stovewood."
>
> Miss Caroline stood stock still, then grabbed me by the collar and hauled me back to her desk. "Jean Louise, I've had about enough of you this morning," she said. "You're starting off on the wrong foot in every way, my dear. Hold out your hand."
>
> I thought she was going to spit in it, which was the only reason anybody in Maycomb held out his hand: it was a time-honored method of sealing oral contracts. Wondering what bargain we had made, I turned to the class for an answer, but the class looked back at me in puzzlement. Miss Caroline picked up her ruler, gave me half a dozen quick little pats, then told me to stand in the corner. A storm of laughter broke loose when it finally occurred to the class that Miss Caroline had whipped me.

Schooling in the more remote rural areas of the South was erratic and makeshift.
Library of Congress/Farm Security Administration

TENNESSEE WILLIAMS WAS BORN IN COLUMBUS, MISSISSIPPI, a state which has been the home of many of America's most popular writers. Williams's plays *Twenty-Seven Wagons Full of Cotton*, later filmed as *Baby Doll*, and *Cat on a Hot Tin Roof* were both set in the Delta region. *The Glass Menagerie* explores in particular detail one of the themes recurring in the works of Southern writers: the weight of the Southern past and its quaint values which fall so heavily upon the shoulders of the young. Amanda, the mother in the play, is invested with great but confused vitality as she clings to another time. Laura, the daughter, is crippled and fragile, like the glass articles she collects. She is a projection of Amanda's dreams, yet Laura's own dreams are even more deluded since they cause her severe weaknesses.

Eudora Welty was born in 1909 in Jackson and lived there most of her life, observing the people and customs of the area. Fascinated by her setting as most Southern writers were and are, Welty captured to perfection the speech patterns and mannerisms of Mississippians in *A Curtain of Green*, *The Robber Bridegroom*, *The Wide Net*, and *Delta Wedding*. Since then she has portrayed Mississippi life in *The Golden Apples, The Optimist's Daughter, Losing Battles,* and *The Ponder Heart.* In addition, she has written essays and reviews later collected as *The Eye of the Story.* Winner of three O. Henry Prizes, the William Dean Howells Medal of the American Academy of Arts and Letters, and the 1973 Pulitzer Prize, Welty, in her writing, seems mesmerized by the poor and primitive, so that what emerges in her work is a picture of the inexhaustible energy and nobility in the black people around her. Her short story "Powerhouse" appears to be a comment on the truism that blacks somehow set free the creative rhythms of life and art for whites. Like many other Southern writers, Welty has been concerned with the potential of black life:

> POWERHOUSE is playing! He's here on tour from the city—"Powerhouse and His Keyboard"—"Powerhouse and his Tasmanians"—think of the things he calls himself! There's no one in the world like him. You can't tell what he is. "Nigger man?"—he looks more Asiatic, monkey, Jewish, Babylonian, Peruvian, fanatic, devil. He has pale gray eyes, heavy lids, maybe horny like a lizard's, but big glowing eyes when they're open. He has African feet of the greatest size, stomping, both together, on each side of the pedals. He's not coal black—beverage colored—looks like a preacher when his mouth is shut, but then it opens—vast and obscene. And his mouth is going every minute: like a monkey's when it looks for something. Improvising, coming on a light and childish melody—*smooch*—he loves it with his mouth.
>
> Is it possible that he could be this! When you have him there performing for you, that's what you feel. You know people on a stage—and people of a darker race—so likely to be marvelous, frightening.

Perhaps the writer who most explored the emasculation of blacks by prejudice was Richard Wright, the most famous black American writer of the modern era. He was born in the historic town of Natchez in 1908—a place considered by many as the most racist section of the country. Wright's partially autobiographical work *Black Boy* is a bitter and horrifying portrait of the spiritual and physical devastation that racism and ignorance wreak on a black child struggling to grow up. When the book first appeared, it was banned from the Natchez Public Library—ironically, the young Wright had never been allowed to read there, since blacks were barred from public facilities in his native state. One Mississippi congressman said of *Black Boy* in 1945:

> It is a damnable lie from beginning to end. It is practically all fiction. There is just enough truth to enable him to

build his fabulous lies about his experiences in the South.
…It is the dirtiest, filthiest, lousiest, most obscene piece
of writing that I have ever seen in print.…But it comes
from a Negro and you cannot expect any better from a
person of this type.

But Southern white racists were not the only faction to criticize Wright
for his hard-hitting indictment of Mississippi life. Leading black intellectuals accused him of formulating a negative view of black life because he
had not taken into account the general progress that the race had made. But
a passage of *Black Boy* states, without apologies, Wright's observations on
the fundamental psychological and social problems confronting blacks:

> I used to mull over the strange absence of real kindness in
> Negroes, how unstable was our tenderness, how lacking in
> general passions we were, how void of hope, how timid our
> joy, how bare our traditions, how hollow our memories,
> how lacking we were in those intangible sentiments that
> bind man to man and how shallow was even our despair.
> After I had learned other ways of life, I used to brood upon
> the unconscious irony of those who felt that Negroes led
> so passionate an existence! I saw that what had been taken
> for our emotional strength was our negative confusions,
> our flights, our fears, our frenzy under pressure.

The most formidable black responses to Wright came from Dr. Alain
Locke and from W.E.B. Dubois. Wright dismissed their criticism by simply
saying, "I am convinced that they [blacks] cannot yet fathom the motives
that made me write this book; they are not emotionally independent
enough to want to face the naked experience of their lives."

There is little doubt that when Americans think of Mississippi writers
they think of William Faulkner. Born in 1897 in Albany, Faulkner made
Lafayette County, surrounding Oxford, immortal as his fictional Yoknapatawpha, while he renamed Oxford itself Jefferson. Some Mississippians
remember Faulkner simply as Bill—the strange, quiet man who sometimes
sat on a bottle crate in the hot morning sun in front of the general store,
acting "right strange." But the sagas of the Sartorises, the Snopses, the
Compsons, and the other denizens of Yoknapatawpha County lives on with
vigor in such novels as *Sartoris, The Sound and the Fury, Sanctuary, Light
in August, Absalom, Absalom, The Unvanquished, Go Down Moses,* and
Intruder in the Dust.

Faulkner got his literary start when he drifted to New Orleans, where he
worked on a newspaper and met Sherwood Anderson. The older, established writer was impressed with Faulkner's first novel *Soldier's Pay,* which
depicts the homecoming of a dying soldier in the manner and tradition of

"lost generation" writers like F. Scott Fitzgerald. Soon, however, the younger writer was doing his own mythmaking with Yoknapatawpha, and in the end Faulkner himself fathered a whole school of writers—most famous among them Robert Penn Warren, Flannery O'Connor, and the numerous Southern Gothic writers. Their concerns typically revolved around the problems of Southern history, its role in forming Southern identity, and the relation of these to the vast changes in American society that changed as well the nature of the South. Nostalgia colors all Southern reminiscences, Faulkner knew; and his writing usually seeks to define and explore the mode of confrontation between the South's idealized past and its declining present. One succinct example of this approach can be found in "A Rose for Emily":

> When Miss Emily Grierson died, our whole town went to her funeral: the men through a sort of respectful affection for a fallen monument, the women mostly out of curiosity to see the inside of her house, which no one save an old manservant—a combined gardener and cook—had seen in at least ten years.
>
> It was a big, squarish frame house that had once been white, decorated with cupolas and spires and scrolled balconies in the heavily lightsome style of the seventies, set on what had once been our most select street. But garages and cotton gins had encroached and obliterated even the august names of that neighborhood; only Miss Emily's house was left, lifting its stubborn and coquettish decay above the cotton wagons and the gasoline pumps—an eyesore among eyesores. And now Miss Emily had gone to join the representatives of those august names where they lay in the cedar-bemused cemetery among the ranked and anonymous graves of Union and Confederate soldiers who fell at the battle of Jefferson.
>
> Alive, Miss Emily had been a tradition, a duty, and a care; a sort of hereditary obligation upon the town, dating from that day in 1894 when Colonel Sartoris, the mayor— he who fathered the edict that no Negro woman should appear on the streets without an apron—remitted her taxes, the dispensation dating from the death of her father on into perpetuity.... When the next generation, with its more modern ideas, became mayors and aldermen, this arrangement created some little satisfaction.

JAZZ, ONE OF AMERICA'S MOST DISTINCTIVE CULTURAL ACHIEVEMENTS, was born in New Orleans, where such great Dixieland groups as the Eagles and Superior Bands and such musicians as Joe "King" Oliver and Louis Armstrong performed and polished their music until it won a vast audience all over the world.

The varied cultural mix—symphony, opera, concerts, and live theater—makes New Orleans a stimulating environment for writers. The city and surrounding territory of preserved plantations such as the Houmas Plantation and the Tchoupitoulas Plantation (now a restaurant); huge azaleas and magnolias, still blooming 30 feet into the air around the mansions; majestic moss-laden live oaks, one over 200 years old, measuring 25 feet in circumference, and hanging over the Houmas house; all these elements carry a visitor back to an earlier time that seems almost physically present.

Louisiana's earliest literature was French and centered largely around the themes of the noble savage and the unspoiled nature found in such abundance throughout it when it was the primitive colony. During the 19th century, what was written in English dealt mostly with the Creoles, descendents of the early French settlers. In the 1750s and early 1760s, the French living in Acadia in Nova Scotia, called Acadians or Cajuns, were driven out of Canada by the English. Many of these Acadians wandered to the then French territory of Louisiana and finally settled in St. Martinville in the Teche country. The Reverend Horace Conolly, a Salem preacher, often related the hardships of two lovers among the wandering Acadians and wanted Nathaniel Hawthorne to write a tale based on the lovers' ordeal. Hawthorne, realizing the material was not to his taste, advised Conolly to tell the story to Henry Wadsworth Longfellow, who liked the story immensely. In 1847, he published *Evangeline: A Tale of Acadia*, in which he featured two lovers, Evangeline and Gabriel, based on real-life characters from the outcast Acadians. Evangeline Oak, a huge old tree, is believed to be where Louis, prototype of Gabriel, met Emmeline (Evangeline) only to tell her when she arrived that he had married someone else. Longfellow's poem, of course, ends more romantically.

Longfellow was an outsider treating the culture, but Kate Chopin, born in St. Louis in 1851, moved to New Orleans after she married a Creole man. Her mother was also Creole, and so Chopin was steeped in Creole culture, Cajun life, and the French Catholic tradition. Her most famous collection of stories, *Bayou Folk* drew on her own experiences in the village of Cloutierville, and was one of the earliest examples of a school that later became prominent in Southern writing—the local colorists or regionalists, who attempted to recapture the peculiar nuances and facets of the unique blend of cultures found in Southern locales like New Orleans.

DAVY CROCKETT OF TENNESSEE has become an American folk hero. Born in 1785, he was a hunter, scout, frontiersman, and eventually a congressman. He wrote many tall tales about himself, and today it is hard to distinguish between the true Crockett and the mythical one. One tale

*Davy Crockett in his full
frontier regalia.*
Tennessee State Library

relates how once when he aimed his rifle at a raccoon in a tree, the animal, recognizing Crockett, said, "Don't shoot, Colonel. I'll come down. I know when I'm a gone coon."

Crockett won a seat in the Tennessee legislature in 1823, and was later nominated as a joke, to run for the U.S. Congress. During his campaign, a flock of noisy guinea hens wandered into a meeting, disrupting Crockett's speech with their clucking, but Crockett turned the disruption in his favor by claiming that the hens were really saying "Crockett." The story endeared him to the public and won him the election. After leaving Congress, he joined 180 other Americans at the Alamo in San Antonio, where they were slaughtered by 5,000 Mexicans on March 6, 1836. Among Crockett's writings are *A Narrative of the Life of David Crockett, An Account of Colonel Crockett's Tour to the North and Down East,* and *Colonel Crockett's Exploits and Adventures in Texas.*

The poet and critic John Crowe Ransom was born in Pulaski. Along with Allen Tate, Robert Penn Warren, and several other poets and critics, Ransom advocated a return to agriculture as the economic base of the South; a rejection of industrialism; and a rejuvenation of Christian moral values in daily life. The Fugitives, as they called themselves, published in 1930 *I'll Take My Stand: The South and the Agrarian Tradition*. The poetry and criticism—called New Criticism—started by the Agrarians have been very influential in modern American literature, especially as a teaching method, since it attempts to focus on "the poem itself" rather than its social or historical context. Robert Penn Warren and Cleanth Brooks wrote two widely used college texts—*Understanding Poetry* and *Understanding Fiction*—that disseminated this viewpoint widely throughout American academia.

Of course, Robert Penn Warren is quite well known for his other writings as well. Poet, essayist, novelist, Warren has had a distinguished literary career spanning some 50 years. His most famous work is *All the King's Men*, which won the Pulitzer Prize in 1946. In it Warren paints a portrait of a Southern politician, a demogogue, based largely on Huey Long's life. He saw sharply in a Faulknerian way the secret rhythms that power life in the South:

> I got to Mason City early in the afternoon and went to the Mason City Cafe, Home-Cooked Meals for Ladies and Gents, facing the square, and sampled the mashed potatoes and fried ham and greens with pot-likker with one hand while with the other I competed with seven or eight flies for the possession of a piece of custard pie.
>
> I went out into the street, where the dogs lay on the shady side under the corrugated iron awnings, and walked down the block till I came to the harness shop. There was one vacant seat out front, so I said howdy-do, and joined the club. I was the junior member by forty years, but I thought I was going to have liver spots on my swollen old hands crooked on the head of the hickory stick like the rest of them before anybody was going to say anything. In a town like Mason City the bench in front of the harness shop is—or was twenty years ago before the concrete slab got laid down—the place where Time gets tangled in its own feet and lies down like an old hound and gives up the struggle. It is a place where you sit down and wait for night to come and arteriosclerosis. It is the place the local undertaker looks at with confidence and thinks he is not going to starve as long as that much work is cut out for him. But if you are sitting on the bench in the middle of the afternoon in late August with the old ones, it does not seem that anything will ever come, not even your own

funeral, and the sun beats down and the shadows don't
move across the bright dust, which, if you stare at it long
enough, seems to be full of glittering specks like quartz.
The old ones sit there with their liver-spotted hands
crooked on the hickory sticks, and they emit a kind of
metaphysical effluvium by virtue of which your categories are altered. Time and motion cease to be. It is like
sniffing ether, and everything is sweet and sad and far
away. You sit there among the elder gods, disturbed by no
sound except the light *rale* of the one who has asthma, and
wait for them to lean from the Olympian and sunlit de-
tachment and comment, with their unenvious and fore-
knowing irony, on the goings-on of the folks who are still
snared in the toils of mortal compulsions. I seen Sim
Saunders done built him a new barn. Then, Yeah, some
folks thinks they is made of money. And. Yeah.

Knoxville was the birthplace of James Agee, novelist, essayist, and film
reviewer, who wrote *Let Us Now Praise Famous Men*, a searing study of
three families of Alabama sharecroppers during the Depression. Agee and
photographer Walker Evans were assigned in 1936 by *Fortune* magazine—
an apparently unlikely sponsor—to produce a series of documentary articles about the life of the sharecroppers in the South. Their material was, not
surprisingly, rejected. Houghton Mifflin published it in expanded form, but
it was hardly an overnight success: sales dwindled to fewer than 50 copies
per year during the 1950s. A new edition published in 1960 brought it into
prominence, and both text and photographs have become classics. Agee's
writing was bitter but pointed, and paid tribute to the power of Evans's
photographs:

> I realize that, with even so much involvement in explana-
> tions as this, I am liable seriously, and perhaps irretriev-
> ably, to obscure what would at best be hard enough to give
> its appropriate clarity and intensity; and what seems to me
> most important of all: namely, that these I will write of are
> human beings, living in this world, innocent of such twist-
> ings as these which are taking place over their heads; and
> that they were dwelt among, investigated, spied on, re-
> vered, and loved, by other quite monstrously alien human
> beings, in the employment of still others still more alien;
> and that they are now being looked into by still others,
> who have picked up their living as casually as if it were a
> book, and who were actuated toward this reading by vari-
> ous possible reflexes of sympathy, curiosity, idleness, et
> cetera, and almost certainly in a lack of consciousness,
> and conscience, remotely appropriate to the enormity of
> what they are doing.

> If I could do it, I'd do no writing at all here. It would be photographs; the rest would be fragments of cloth, bits of cotton, lumps of earth, records of speech, pieces of wood and iron, phials of odors, plates of food and of excitement. Booksellers would consider it quite a novelty; critics would murmur, yes, but is it art; and I could trust a majority of you to use it as you would a parlor game.

Evans's camera and Agee's prose cut through the nostalgia that so often filtered other depictions of the South. It was as if the camera lens focused his prose clearly and irrefutably on a phenomenon that the greatest Southern writers, like Faulkner and Wright, were only too painfully aware of: the alienation of the South, not only from other sections of the country, but even from its own harsh contemporary reality. Agee and Evans unmasked the Southern nostalgia for an idealized rural past as the self-deception that it was. In his later novel *A Death in the Family*, Agee explores many of the same preoccupations—and reveals the same poetic skill—that informed his earlier work. The loving attention to detail is typically Southern, typically Agee:

Depression life in the South was at least as hard as in the rest of the country's farming areas. The sharecroppers, poor to begin with, suffered terribly.
Library of Congress/Farm Security Administration

We are talking now of summer evenings in Knoxville, Tennessee, in the time that I lived there so successfully disguised to myself as a child. It was a little bit mixed sort of block, fairly solidly lower middle class, with one or two juts apiece on either side of that. The houses corresponded: middle-sized gracefully fretted wood houses built in the late nineties and early nineteen hundreds, with small front and side and more spacious back yards, and trees in the yards, and porches. These were soft-wooded trees, poplars, tulip trees, cottonwoods. There were fences around one or two of the houses, but mainly the yards ran into each other with only now and then a low hedge that wasn't doing very well. There were few good friends among the grown people, and they were not poor enough for the other sort of intimate acquaintance, but everyone nodded and spoke, and even might talk short times, trivially, and at the two extremes of the general or the particular, and ordinarily nextdoor neighbors talked quite a bit when they happened to run into each other, and never paid calls. The men were mostly small business-men, one or two very modestly executives, one or two worked with their hands, most of them clerical, and most of them between thirty and forty-five.

But it is of these evenings, I speak.

Supper was at six and was over by half past. There was still daylight, shining softly and with a tarnish, like the lining of a shell; and the carbon lamps lifted at the corners were on in the light, and the locusts were started, and the fire flies were out, and a few frogs were flopping in the dewy grass, by the time the fathers and the children came out. The children ran out first hell bent and yelling those names by which they were known; then the fathers sank out leisurely in crossed suspenders, their collars removed and their necks looking tall and shy. The mothers stayed back in the kitchen washing and drying, putting things away, recrossing their traceless footsteps like the lifetime journeys of bees, measuring out the dry cocoa for break-fast. Whey they came out they had taken off their aprons and their skirts were dampened and they sat in rockers on their porches quietly.

No doubt most of the writers discussed in this section would recognize both the scene Agee describes and the affection that shapes that description. Most of them would also be able to claim it—and Agee's divided sense of loyalty—as their own.

THE MOUNTAIN STATES & SOUTHWEST

CURTIS CASEWIT

THE LITERARY WEST IS NOT ONE of addresses and neighborhoods, nor of salons and soirées. Rather, it is one of boomtowns, canyons, deserts, and wide plains. One characteristic of the region has consistently dominated the attitudes of those who have written about it: it's big, and it does things in a big way.

The area is dotted with reminders of some of the world's most fabulous mineral strikes; the Guggenheim family fortune began in a silver mine in Leadville, Colorado, where Oscar Wilde once lectured to prospectors on aesthetics. The West was also headquarters for the fabled cattle barons whose incalculable wealth in land and power is glimpsed in Owen Wister's *The Virginian.* (One ranch, among the largest, spanned nearly a million acres and covered parts of New Mexico, Colorado, and Arizona.)

And always, above all, there is the country: Big Sky, the Great Plains, the Rocky Mountains, the Grand Canyon. The young nation demanded of the frontier a literature that matched both its promise and its dimensions. Three novelists obliged, and created what is perhaps America's most durable myth—the Wild West.

EDWARD ZANE CARROL JUDSON arrived in Julesburg, Colorado, in 1869 on his first trip west. He expected great things from it.

Judson was merely his real name. He had fashioned a far more colorful—and lucrative—identity as Ned Buntline, the intrepid adventurer and inventor of the dime novel. By the time he reached the frontier, Buntline was America's most popular writer, having authored nearly 400 "penny dreadfuls." He was also its most highly paid, earning a reputed $20,000 a year. He had come in search of a new kind of story.

From the stage stop in the northeastern tip of Colorado, Buntline set out on horseback in search of Captain Frank North. A veteran cavalry officer, North and his troops had just routed the army of Chief Tall Bull at the sensational Battle of Summit Springs. Buntline knew a good plot when he heard one; he intended to make North the hero of his next book. But when the two men finally met at Fort Kearney, across the Nebraska border, North didn't conceal his contempt for the venture or for novelists in general, "If you want someone to write about," North told Buntline, "go write about *him*." The soldier was pointing to a twenty-three-year-old part-time Army scout who, at the moment, was asleep under a wagon.

Buntline tapped him for an interview, and the two spent the next few days riding on the plains and talking. The scout, Bill Cody, liked to talk about himself and found Buntline such a receptive listener that he allowed himself to embellish several already improbable tales. In short, he was Buntline's perfect subject.

Buntline himself never let facts stand in the way of a good story. "Once I strike a good title I consider a book about half-done," he once remarked. "After that I push ahead as fast as I can write, never making an alteration or correction."

That seems to have been his approach to life in general. During the Civil War, he was bounced out of the Union Army for drunkenness but later advertised himself as a colonel and Chief of Scouts for the Army of the Potomac. Buntline was covered with scars, each of which became the subject for an involved legend of adventure and brushes with death. (An inveterate duelist, Buntline said he was once "actually lynched" for shooting a town's favorite son, but was "rescued on the point of death" by comrades.)

The author's fertile imagination bloomed with Cody as subject. He transformed the scout into the hero of Summit Springs, although Cody didn't arrive at the scene until four hours after the fighting was over. The battle became a central event in "Buffalo Bill, King of the Border Men—The Wildest and Truest Story I Ever Wrote," which Buntline serialized in *Street and Smith's New York Weekly*. When the stories were released as a novel, the book became one of Buntline's all-time best sellers.

Buntline had invented an entirely new kind of story, the "Western," and the public was ravenous for more. Soon, yarns about Buffalo Bill, Buffalo Bob, Buffalo Ben, and every conceivable character of Western lore filled newsracks to overflowing. Buntline, though, remained "king of the Westerns" and looked on Cody as his own personal story mine. Under Buntline's pen, Buffalo Bill (Cody never applied the common nickname to himself until Buntline did) vanquished evil, displayed incredible frontier prowess, was killed and reborn in book after book. Buntline made the character a mouthpiece for many of his own prejudices, including strict temperance:

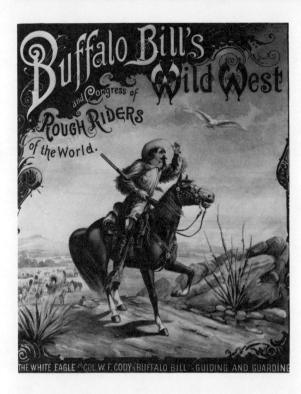

Bill said to his companion, "There is more fight, more headache—aye, more heartache in one rum-bottle than there is in all the water that ever sparkled in God's brilliant sunlight. And I, for the sake of my dear brothers and sisters, and for the sweet, trusting heart that throbs alone for me, intend to let the rum go where it belongs, and that is not down my throat."

Actually, Cody—who took to rum only when nothing stronger was handy—freely admitted that he enlisted in the Union Army as a scout when he was too drunk to know better. Later, when Buntline organized and promoted the legendary *Buffalo Bill's Wild West Show*, it was often a struggle to keep the headliner sober for a performance.

Still, under Buntline's pen, Cody became both a public fantasy and the symbol of the West:

A noble-looking white-haired man sits by a rough table, reading the Bible aloud. On stools by his feet sit two beautiful little girls—his twin daughters—not more than ten years of age, while a noble boy, twelve or thirteen,

stands by the back of the chair where sits the handsome,
yet matronly-looking mother....

He closes the holy book, and is about to kneel and ask
Heaven to bless and protect him and his dear ones.

Hark! The sound of horses galloping with mad speed
towards his house falls upon his ear....

After this opening—"drawn, to a very great extent, not from imagination
but from life itself," Buntline affirmed—to his 1886 *The Adventures of
Buffalo Bill,* the West simply was not allowed to produce literary heroes of
lesser character. (Buffalo Bill Cody's grave on Lookout Mountain, southwest of Denver, and the nearby cavalry museum are a steady attraction for
tourists seeking some kind of link with the "real" Wild West.)

The Adventures of Buffalo Bill was Buntline's last Cody tale. He died the
year it was published, and just one year after his successor—a sickly young
man equipped with sculpted moustaches and a Harvard music degree—
first arrived in Wyoming.

Owen Wister had been diagnosed by his Philadelphia family's physician
as "hysterical." He suffered from nightmares, depression, and violent
headaches. Something called the rest cure had come into fashion, and
Wister was packed off to Colonel Frank Woolcott's huge ranch in Wyoming. The visit had been arranged through mutual friends.

The pressures to achieve, heaped on him by his family, evaporated under
the prairie sun. The West had achieved nothing and, therefore, promised
everything. Wister could make up the difference in his imagination. He
had a habit of comparing his new land to a Wagnerian opera. "Its rise, its
hysterical and unreal prosperity...and its influence on the various sorts of
human character that have been subjected to it—have not been touched by
a single writer that I, at least, have heard of," he wrote to his family. "The
fact is, it is quite worthy of Tolstoi or George Eliot or Dickens. Thackeray
wouldn't do."

And, in more than 30 years of trying, Wister didn't quite do, either.

A patrician by birth and education, Wister felt a camaraderie with
Wyoming's landed gentry. He was refined, and a romantic, and the West's
commonplace harshness was repellant to him personally. An entry in his
journal relates:

On the way here [the Powder River in north central
Wyoming] yesterday, passed emigrants on their way from
the Black Hills to Oregon. A woman riding straddle...and
any amount of children. Three slow crawling wagons with
their long teams....A miserable population. These people,
it seems, have been moving in this way pretty much all
over the continent west of the Missouri, settling nowhere.

Wister's overly delicate sensibilities kept him from recognizing what Tolstoi or Dickens would have sensed: that the real story to be told of this vast wild land lay in its "miserable population" and not in the manor houses of his hosts.

Instead, he published his classic *The Virginian* in 1902, pieced together from his stories that had appeared in *Harper's* and other leading magazines over the previous decade. Rather than creating a genuine Western literature, says Bernard DeVoto, the region's leading historian, "*The Virginian* created Western fiction—the cowboy story, the horse-opera novel, the conventions, the clichés, the values, and the sun-god...the Hero."

Indeed, *The Virginian* now reads like a cliché because the book invented most of them, including that favorite phrase, "When you call me that, *smile!*" The nameless hero is "a slim young giant, more beautiful than pictures." He works as foreman on an enormous cattle ranch, patterned on Woolcott's. He does battle with rustlers and other forms of evil, improves his reading and spelling on his own time, kills his nemesis, the outlaw Trampas, in a "walkdown" on Main Street, marries the schoolmarm, buys a ranch, and himself rises from cow-puncher to wealthy landowner. The book was an international best seller and, for Wister, a literary failure.

It was well-written; even Henry James gave the novel favorable notice, except for the happy ending. But Wister had failed to create a real Western literature because he had failed to understand what the real West was all about.

The Virginian is set in Johnson County, Wyoming, scene of the vicious Johnson County War of 1892. For nearly a decade, the county's beef barons had seen scores of small ranchers and farmers move into the area and fence off a plot of ground for themselves. The open range that supported the sprawling cattle kingdoms was threatened. Finally, in 1892, the county's bigger landowners—ironically, led by Colonel Frank Woolcott—hired a small army of Texas gunslingers. When the small operators could not be bought or scared into selling their land, the hired guns took to shooting them outright. But the "squatters" fought back. Eventually, they won the war and stayed.

These small landowners are precisely the men whom Wister tags in his book as outlaws and rustlers and whom the Virginian is fighting and killing. Wister, the romantic aristocrat, was unable to see the demise of his class as a bitter necessity leading to a social reorganization of property and power. Instead, he viewed it as a tragic aberration. He continued to see the West as "a sprout of the Middle Ages," filled with knights errant:

> The cow-puncher's playground in those first glorious days
> of his prosperity included battle and murder and sudden
> death as every-day matters. From 1865 to 1878 in Texas he

fought his way with knife and gun, and any hour of the twenty-four might see him flattened behind rocks among the whiz of bullets and the flight of arrows, or dragged bloody and folded together from some adobe hovel. Seventy-five dollars a month and absolute health and strength were his wages; and when the news of all this excellence drifted from Texas eastward, they came in shoals...hither to the cattle country they flocked from forty kinds of home, each bringing a deadly weapon.

This passage from "The Evolution of the Cow-Puncher," published in *Harper's* in 1895, shows that even amid the danger of sudden death and murder, "all this excellence" seemed "a glorious playground" to the enchanted Easterner.

The essay quoted above was illustrated with several drawings by the Western artist Frederick Remington, and provides an example of the strong influence his collaboration with Wister had on the public imagination.

The two met in North's Inn near Soda Mountain in Yellowstone Park in the fall of 1893. Both took refuge from a snowstorm in front of the inn's

Frederick Remington was probably the preeminent illustrator of the cowboy's wild west, and the work he did with Owen Wister defined an entire myth of the West.
New York Public Library

fireplace and they began to chat. Each found his own goal—that of expressing the West as it really was—shared by the other. The pair was of complementary temperament: Wister delicate and articulate; Remington bluff and hearty, with an ironic and abrasive wit. The artist pushed the idea of their working together, but Wister wasn't sure. He decided to try the partnership on an upcoming *Harper's* story.

The illustrated story, "Balaam and Pedro," appeared just before Christmas. Wister happened to be carrying it on a train when a stranger asked him if he might have the latest issue of *Scribner's*. Wister offered *Harper's* in its place and his companion began to thumb through it, looking at the pictures. Wister remembers:

> When he came to Remington's, he stopped and looked at it three times as long as the others. Then…turning over some more leaves, finished all the illustrations the number contains. Then he returned and looked at Remington again. After that he found the beginning of the story and began to read it.

Adding that the traveler was "a matter of fact youth," Wister felt that "if such as this will read me, I am secure....I think I owe it to Remington's picture."

Indeed, the myth of the Wild West owes an incalculable debt to their union, which ended with Remington's death in 1909. Through their letters and collaboration, says author Wallace Stegner:

> We witness the triumphant ontology of the cowboy hero....The two men …create him before our eyes. They begin to mold him out of the observed realities of the brief, furious, passing empire of the cattlemen. Believing they record reality, they helplessly remake it larger than life until, when they are done, their creation rides off the page into the sunset of a thousand horse operas, the free, lonely, self-reliant, skilled, eternally ambiguous embodiment of a national, indeed a human, fantasy.

More than 50 of those thousand horse operas were written by a New York dentist who, as a schoolboy, read Buntline's dime novels tucked between the pages of oversize textbooks. He wrote a few fishing articles and boys' adventure tales, but until he discovered the West, Zane Grey was a flop as a professional author.

When Zane and Dolly Grey were married, she persuaded him to stop pulling teeth and to start pursuing his dream of becoming a novelist. Her grandfather's legacy supported them, and they lived in a tumbledown cabin in east Pennsylvania. Grey's first novel was *Betty Zane*, a romance about his illustrious pioneer family in the Ohio Valley. It didn't sell. Dolly used part of her inheritance to have it printed, and Grey put copies in bookstores. Sales were modest. His next effort was *The Spirit of the Border*, another family saga that met the same bleak reception from publishers. When a reprint house finally showed an interest, Grey let it be published "free," with no advance fee, simply grateful that this time it hadn't cost him anything. Then, at a 1907 meeting of the Campfire Club, a New York outdoor society, Grey met Buffalo Jones.

Jones was an old man, a former buffalo hunter and warden at Yellowstone Park, who had retired to a ranch on the north rim of the Grand Canyon. There, he was attempting to cross-breed buffalo and beef cattle to produce prime, yet range-hardy, stock. He had come east on a speaking tour to raise money to keep the ranch going.

Grey was perhaps the only member of the audience who took Jones seriously. He had been captivated by the Southwest when he and Dolly had stopped at the Grand Canyon 16 months earlier. (The newlyweds had ridden pack burros to the Canyon floor, a trip that left Dolly feeling that "Every bone in my body ached as if it were going to break.") Besides, Jones was a good storyteller and Grey was acutely aware of *The Virginian's* enduring popularity. The world, he decided, was waiting for another Western.

Grey suggested that he return with Jones to his ranch and write a book about him. He pointed out that publicity could mean money to Jones and his ranch. Jones was skeptical; was Grey a real writer? The ex-dentist produced a copy of *Betty Zane*. After Jones read it, he agreed to the proposition.

Although it took the last of her legacy, Dolly saw the trip with Jones as a vital step in Grey's career. He went reluctantly, but his financial worries disappeared in the desert. At Flagstaff, in central Arizona, Grey and Jones were met by the latter's neighbors. They were Mormons, the first Grey had met, and their quiet, sober self-sufficiency described to the author the characters who would later populate his best books.

The pack trip to the ranch was torture for Grey, who was in no condition to spend days in the saddle. But, in the weeks he spent with Jones, he became an avid rider. He absorbed the Western dialect of Jones and his hired men. He was gripped by the tales told around the evening campfire. He learned the names of every plant and bush and animal he saw. He took notes about everything.

As a climax, Grey killed a local legend, Old Tom. Tom was a cougar who had been feeding on the area's cattle for years. He had gone after Jones's precious cattalo and thereby had numbered his days.

A posse was formed and soon the hunting dogs had treed him. Jones, rope in hand, began to climb the tree to lasso the cat when it leapt—toward Grey. He swung his rifle and fired; Old Tom was dead. Grey went home hopelessly and irrevocably in love with the West.

The rugged land and purple sage mythologized by Zane Grey.
Colorado Department of Public Relations

His enthusiasm wasn't instantly shared. *The Last of the Plainsmen,* based on Grey's stay with Jones, went first to Ripley Hitchcock, the editor of Harper and Brothers. Grey had mentioned the trip to Hitchcock before he left, and the publisher had shown interest.

After reading the manuscript he called Grey into his office and told him, "I do not see anything in this to convince me that you can write either narrative or fiction." To most hopefuls, it would have been the voice of doom. But Grey, with Dolly in support, felt he had at last found his métier. He began work on another Western.

The latter proved him right. He nearly begged Hitchcock to read the new manuscript, *The Heritage of the Desert.* The editor relented, and a few days later called Grey to apologize for his earlier remark. Hitchcock called it "a fine novel" and offered him a contract. The same day, Street and Smith decided to serialize the story and wrote Grey a check for $1,000 on the spot. Here is a sample:

> Her clear sight intensified the purple sage-slope as it rolled before her. Low swells of prairie-like ground sloped up to the west. Dark, lonely cedar-trees, few and far between, stood out strikingly, and at long distances ruins of red rocks. Farther on, up the gradual slope, rose a broken wall,

a huge monument, looming dark purple and stretching its solitary, mystic way, a wavering line that faded in the north. Here to the westward was the light and color and beauty. Northward the slope descended to a dim line of canyons from which rose an up-flinging of the earth, not mountainous, but a vast heave of purple uplands, with ribbed and fan-shaped walls, castle-crowned cliffs, and gray escarpments. Over it all crept the lengthening, waning afternoon shadows.

The scene opens *Riders of the Purple Sage*, published in 1912 when Grey was forty-two. It was his third cowboy story. To date, it has sold over two million copies worldwide and vies with *The Virginian* when critics try to choose the best Western ever written. It was his first story after *Heritage*. Then, with *The Rainbow Trail* in 1915, Grey completed his best work.

Fans complain that fame and high fees enticed Zane Grey to double his output at the expense of his quality. He wrote so many books that new ones were still being published in 1964, a quarter of a century after his death. Many of the later ones read like poor imitations of his best. Still, readers could rely on Grey for thrilling action yarns of good versus evil, many set in the familiar landscape around his hunting cabin in the Arizona desert. As one 1920 critic remarked, "We turn to Grey not for insight into human nature and human problems, nor for refinement of art, but simply for crude epic stories, as we might to an old Norse skald, maker of sagas of the folk."

FOR ALMOST A CENTURY, WESTERN WRITERS—as opposed to writers of Westerns—have struggled to emerge from the cloud of public expectation and fantasy such sagas created. "A novel that is set in New York isn't called an 'Eastern,'" complained one Rocky Mountain publisher, "but the same story set in Santa Fe is labeled a 'Western' and, therefore, usually dismissed by readers and critics alike."

Paul Horgan's work has done much to rid Western fiction of its lightweight image. Of course, he may be the region's most widely-read contemporary author because he spent much of his life in the East.

Born in Buffalo, New York, in 1903, Horgan moved with his family to Albuquerque in 1915 for the sake of his father's health. The New Mexican desert was an exotic land that inflamed his delicate imagination. By 1919, when he enrolled in the New Mexico Military Institute at Roswell, he was already writing drama reviews and music and art criticism for a local newspaper.

Horgan's experiences in the Southwest were as diverse as his talents. His first novel, *The Fault of Angels*, in 1933, won that year's $10,000 Harper Prize. In 1955, he garnered the Pulitzer Prize in History and Columbia

University's Bancroft Prize for his *Great River: The Rio Grande in American History*. The Western Literature Association granted Horgan its Distinguished Achievement Award in 1973.

His themes include the subtle and complex tangle of human relationships, set against the backdrop of Santa Fe and smaller nearby towns. His *The Common Heart* and *Whitewater* are excellent novels; yet many readers insist his shorter fiction is his best. In that category, critics praise *Far From Cibola*, a novella scarcely 163 pages long.

The Seven Cities of Cibola, according to Spanish legend, were pueblos made of gold somewhere in the deserts north of Mexico. Modern Westerners have appropriated the name to describe popular attitudes toward the region as a promised land. The story, which has been called "the *Winesburg, Ohio* of the American Southwest," is set in Roswell during the Great Depression; and Horgan uses his title to remind his readers that the West is far different from Wister's popular notion of a "glorious playground":

> It was a land where men had to conquer trial and treachery always...the land of the Seven Golden Cities of Cibola, that had wooed the northward Spaniards long ago. The natural mystery of plains giving back to the sky a second sunlight and of mountains drawing the horizon up to blue pinnacles dazzled men through three hundred years, and led them up the dry beds of creeks and over the heat lakes to the Cities of Cibola, whose yellow gates they never found.... they were always far from Cibola; their hope had no strength in it but greed; and legend was only a powerful mockery. What wealth they ever found in that land was created by men with the earth, and toiled for in obedience to the seasons.

A DIFFERENT KIND OF MYTHIC STRUCTURE attracted D. H. Lawrence to New Mexico in 1922. The famed British novelist felt that humanity must recapture the primitive "blood-consciousness" of its ancient ancestors to free itself from the world of machines and materialism. He saw the American West as perhaps the last place where the attempt could be made.

Lawrence was lured to Taos, a village of artists and writers 70 miles north of Santa Fe, by Mabel Dodge Luhan. She was a resettled New York heiress who furnished her adopted town with interesting people. Lawrence, the most controversial writer of his time, was to be the prize in her collection of friends.

To be sure, Lawrence was intrigued by her: Mabel had forsaken New York, the citadel of modern society, moved to the desert, even taken an Indian as a husband. He hoped her story could become the parable of human wholeness he sought to write.

It didn't. Characteristically, Mabel adopted Lawrence as her personal pet. He found her shrewish and shallow, and began to hate her. It only increased Mabel's possessiveness. "He needs something new and different," she told Frieda, his wife. "He's done with you. You have mothered his books long enough. He needs a new mother. You are not the right woman for Lawrence." Always volatile, Frieda retorted, "Then try it yourself, living with a genius, see what it's like and how easy it is! Take him if you can!" The final verdict came from Lawrence himself: his novel about Mabel Dodge Luhan was scrapped after one chapter.

Even in her company, Lawrence enjoyed Taos. "It was the greatest experience of the outside world I ever had," he wrote. "The moment I saw the brilliant proud morning sunshine high up over the deserts of Santa Fe something stood still in my soul, and I started to attend."

The locale was one he had sought. Near town stood the Indian pueblo, an "apartment building" of adobe brick, occupied continuously since about 1200 A.D. It had been the second to the last stop on the old Santa Fe Trail freight road. Finally, it was "discovered" in 1900 by two painters on their way to Mexico in search of subjects. They wrote to their friends inviting them for visits. Mabel had arrived in 1917 and soon popularized the colony throughout the world.

"Taos in its way *is* rather thrilling," Lawrence said in a letter. "It is a tiny place 30 miles from the railway, high up—7,000 feet in the desert.... We have got a pretty adobe house with furniture made in the village and Mexican and Navajo rugs and some lovely pots. It stands just at the edge of the Indian reservation...."

Lawrence was keenly interested in the natives and their ceremonies. He became an adept horseman and took to wearing a 10-gallon hat that fell down over his ears. But he soon tired of Mabel, the curiosity-seekers, and of Taos's rampant "artiness." Afraid she might lose him completely, his hostess offered him use of a clay-chinked log cabin on an abandoned sheep ranch she owned, 20 miles into the mountains above town. Lawrence and Frieda settled in and soon bought the entire ranch. (Rumor still holds that it was paid for with the original handwritten manuscript of *Sons and Lovers*.)

Between frequent trips to Mexico, New York, and Europe, Lawrence lived on the ranch until 1926. He built furniture and fences, did chores, and even made an adobe oven to bake bread. Each morning he hiked into the woods to scribble notes, filling little blue bound notebooks with a small, careful hand.

Under the trees in the summer of 1924, he wrote three pieces of short fiction: *The Princess, St. Mawr,* and *The Woman Who Rode Away.* (In the latter, he took subtle revenge on Mabel by making the character based on her an Indian sacrifice.) Any one of the three stories would have been a good summer's work, but Lawrence saw them more as preliminary exercises. They were written to develop themes for an emerging novel; in each, a heroine sought to mesh herself with an omnipotent and possibly redeeming male "spirit of place" in Mexico and the Southwest. In *St. Mawr* Lawrence writes of a woman who fails at this task:

> And her love for her ranch turned sometimes into a certain repulsion. The underlying ratdirt, the everlasting bristling tussle of the wild life, with the tangle and the bones strewing. Bones of horses struck by lightning, bones of dead cattle, skulls of goats with little horns: bleached, unburied bones. Then the cruel electricity of the mountains. And then, most mysterious but worst of all, the animosity of the spirit of place: the crude, half-created spirit of place, like some serpent-bird forever attacking man, in a hatred of man's onward struggle towards further creation.

The question is left unresolved in his 1925 work, *The Plumed Serpent*, which Lawrence called "the most important of all my novels." The book is named for Quetzalcoatl, a religious symbol of Mexico's native culture. Its story revolves around Kate Leslie, a European visiting Mexico, who is at once intensely attracted and repelled by the Indian character she finds dominated and suppressed by European influences. In the end, perhaps, the Southwest had not been for Lawrence what he had hoped it would be.

Indeed, he soon moved to France, where he died in the town of Vence in 1930. Five years later, Frieda decided to settle on the Taos ranch and brought Lawrence's ashes with her. When she heard that Mabel, her old nemesis, was plotting to steal the remains, Frieda had the urn embedded in a cement slab and built a small chapel over it.

Frieda lived on the ranch until her death in 1956, willing it to the University of New Mexico. The school maintains the ranch as an occasional retreat for creative writers.

In July, 1980, actors and writers such as Julie Harris, Edward Albee, Stephen Spender, and Alan Bates gathered there for a D. H. Lawrence Festival. They gave public readings of his work and discussed his influence on today's literature. It was appropriate to convene the festival at the only real home, physical and spiritual, Lawrence had known.

D. H. AND FRIEDA LAWRENCE were the ones who persuaded Willa Cather to return to New Mexico after a 10-year absence. The pair was returning to the ranch in 1925 from Europe. Alfred Knopf, Cather's publisher, brought the three together for tea one afternoon. Cather remarked that she hadn't seen the Southwest since 1915 when she had visited her brother, a railroad brakeman, in Winslow, Arizona. The Lawrences invited her to visit their ranch. Happily for literature, she accepted.

During her stay with the Lawrences and Mabel Luhan, Cather conceived her classic *Death Comes for the Archbishop.* The region had echoed in her imagination since she camped and rode through parts of Colorado and New Mexico on horseback in 1912. Cather later said that she conceived of the story in a single evening at Santa Fe's La Fonda Hotel.

The book is a fictionalized biography of Father Jean Lamy, the French priest who came down from Lake Ontario in 1851 to bring Catholicism to the Southwest. Between 1925 and the novel's 1927 publication, Cather made several trips to New Mexico from her New York home. Although one critic complained that her knowledge of the Southwest was based on car trips between the Santa Fe railroad station and La Fonda, her research was far more extensive. She enlisted an old friend, Father James Connelly of Winslow, and traveled with him on his visits to remote parishes. The priest told her about the desert's history, legends, Mexicans, and Indians. Cather's biographer, E. K. Brown, says that in *Death Comes for the Archbishop,* "The persistence and diversity of references to the Southwest suggest—what is indeed the truth—that the discovery of this region was the principal emotional experience of Willa Cather's adult life."

The book seems almost ploddingly conventional on first reading, but it has also often been called one of the most unusual in all of American fiction. Cather rejected the traditional appeals of a novel—plot, powerful conflicts, social criticism. "Instead," says critic James Schroeter, "the author takes what may be the slightest resource at the author's command—simply what might be called 'scene,' the power of evoking with words the feel of a place—and elevates this to the unifying principle of the book. The Southwest is, so to speak, the canvas, and everything else—the character sketches, the stories and legends—are conceived of as elements to be subordinated to the background."

Here's a brief example:

> The bishop sat drinking his coffee out of the tin cup....
> The sun had set now, the yellow rocks were turning grey,
> down in the pueblo the light of the cook fires made red
> patches of the glassless windows, and the smell of pinion
> smoke came softly through the still air. The whole west-
> ern sky was the color of golden ashes....

The novel was an immediate success and had four times as many printings as any of her previous books. "There was a peculiar joyful happy mood about this one," she said. "It gave me so much pleasure day by day."

Lawrence Clark Powell, the Southwest's preeminent literary historian, agrees with those who call it Cather's most perfect book. *"Death Comes for the Archbishop* is full of murmurous overtones," Powell writes. "It goes on pulsing, glowing, and echoing after it is put back on the shelf."

THE MAGIC OF NEW MEXICO'S DESERT enticed scores of authors and painters to Taos and Santa Fe during the 1920s and 1930s. Undoubtedly, the most prominent was Oliver La Farge. His grandfather had been Oliver Hazard Perry, hero of the War of 1812; his father Grant La Farge, a famous illustrator; and his mother came from New York's social aristocracy. But La Farge's personal distinction stemmed from other sources.

He attended Harvard not to become a writer but an anthropologist. In the summer of 1924, La Farge was part of an Ivy League archaeological team sent to study Arizona's Navajo Indians. During the 200-mile pack trip across the state's central desert, the young man grew more and more comfortable with his native companions. He soon could differentiate among their dialects and even recognize their subtle jokes. He later said the Navajos' pantheistic faith "showed me the way out of despair."

This trip and subsequent visits planted the seed of his first novel, *Laughing Boy*, which won the 1929 Pulitzer Prize.

The story is about Laughing Boy, a young Navajo, and his love for Slim Girl. It is poetic prose, an idyll of youth and love in an enchanted land. Yet it touches as well the themes that were to occupy La Farge for the last 25 years of his life: the destruction of Indian culture by the encroaching white civilization. Slim Girl brings wealth to her family from periodic trysts with a white rancher who pays well for her favors. Even though the affair is kept secret, she is outcast by her people for mingling openly with whites. Finally, she is shot to death by a Navajo who seeks revenge on Laughing Boy for an imagined insult. La Farge set the novel in Winslow, Arizona, in 1915, "the year when the first automobile made it through Marsh Pass into Kayenta in the north Navajo country, an event that ... marked a turning point." In a foreword to a new edition of *Laughing Boy* in 1962, the year before his death, Oliver La Farge wrote:

> The Navajos liked the way they were living, they felt secure, they enjoyed life, they were wonderfully friendly. The beginning anthropologist who went among them could believe, as they did, that their general condition and mode of life, with all its hardships, simplicity, and riches, could continue indefinitely if only they were not inter-fered with....It was believed in the 1920's that there were 25,000 Navajos....There are now about 85,000, a powerful community equipped with a modern government and many other improvements, treated with great respect by the Senators and Congressmen....They are an unhappy people, sullen towards all others, unfriendly, harrassed by drunkenness, their leaders at once arrogant and touchy....
> In the space of thirty years...the wholeness is gone, the people described in *Laughing Boy*, complete to itself, is gone.

The Navajo have evolved a style of weaving that has become
synonymous with high quality.
New York Public Library

These ideas are more fully developed in La Farge's 1937 novel, *The Enemy Gods.* The plot concerns Myron Begay, and Indian child of six, who is orphaned and placed in a government boarding school. The boy grows up to become a spokesman for his race in the white world, detailing the humiliating tangle of federal bureaucracies the Navajos must cope with. The book is frankly polemical and so was less widely read. La Farge complained regularly about people who, he said, came to him exclaiming, " 'Oh, Mr. La Farge, I did so enjoy your *Laughing Boy!* When are you going to give us another book?' How do I explain that I've written three more since then?"

Unable and unwilling to maintain the New York lifestyle his family and social circle demanded, La Farge settled in Santa Fe in 1940. His small adobe home at 641 College Street became a meeting place for those seriously interested in Indian culture. La Farge himself became an authority, his fiction giving way to monographs on Indian history and phonetics. In the 1950s he assumed leadership of the Association for American Indian Affairs and spent the last years of his life traveling throughout the West, speaking, organizing, testifying before Congress. It wasn't until soon after his death that his relentless demands of justice for Indians even began to be met: In September, 1965, after fourteen years of courtroom battles, the Taos Pueblo Indians won payment for the confiscation of sacred tribal lands north of their village.

THE "MURMUROUS OVERTONES" of New Mexico do not extend east and south across its borders with Texas. Indeed, for many, Texas remains the quintessential Old West. In his 1962 *Travels With Charley*, Nobel Prize winner John Steinbeck—who had strong family ties to the Lone Star country—discovered:

> There is no physical or geographical unity in Texas. Its unity lies in the mind....The word Texas becomes a symbol to everyone in the world....
>
> The tradition of frontier cattleman is as carefully nurtured in Texas as is the hint of Norman blood in England ...all hold to the dream of the longhorn steer and the unfenced horizon. When a man makes his fortune in oil or...chemicals or wholesale groceries, his first act is to buy a ranch, the largest he can afford, and to run some cattle. A candidate for public office who does not own a ranch is said to have little chance of election....Businessmen wear heeled boots that never feel a stirrup, and men of great wealth who own houses in Paris...refer to themselves as little old country boys...in this way they try to keep their association with the strength and simplicity of the land.

The land—the broad, flat, sun-baked plains—has brought Texas its wealth: first cattle, then oil. It was this second boom that novelist Edna Ferber witnessed on her first train-trip to Texas in 1939. She found Texas "brash, overwhelming, hospitable, larger than life. No visitor, casual though he might be, could fail to feel the almost fierce vitality that rocked the whole vast region...here were arrogance and hard work, and almost stupefying riches spurting out of the earth in the form of oil, cattle, crops." Through her other fiction, through her years as a European correspondent during World War II, the author of *Dinner at Eight, Showboat,* and the Pulitzer Prize-winning *So Big* could not forget what she had seen: "the Texas experience...never ceased to prick my mind with sharp needles of interest, remembrance, and imagined scenes, characters, situations. Finally, vanquished, I gave up." The result was *Giant*, published in 1952.

Giant is an Easterner's attempt to cope with life on a Texas cattle ranch amid the oil boom—a life she finds "exhilarating, violent, charming, horrible, fascinating, shocking...."

Texans hated *Giant* in unison. They resented the crudeness, the tasteless ways in which Ferber's characters flaunted their wealth; they felt grossly misrepresented. It is easy to imagine how proud Texans must have shuddered on reading a speech such as Leslie Benedict's in *Giant:*

> "What's the opposite of lebensraum, Bick? That's what's the matter with them. They've got too much space. It gives

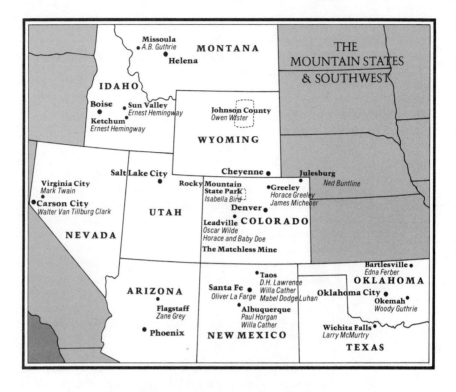

them delusions of grandeur. In the plane they kept yelling about it being the most wonderful place in the world—the most wonderful people in the world, the biggest cattle, fruit, flowers, vegetables, climate, horses. It isn't. They aren't. And what's so important about bigness, anyway? Bigness doesn't make a thing better."

When the movie, starring Rock Hudson, Elizabeth Taylor, and James Dean, was being filmed in Texas, the company was informed that if the picture was ever released in Texas the movie screen would be shot full of holes.

It wasn't Ferber's only brush with controversy. Twenty-two years before, she'd written *Cimmaron*, about the settling of Oklahoma, which had received a similar reception in its locale.

Ferber credited William Allen White, the famous author, statesman, and editor of the Emporia, Kansas, *Gazette* as *Cimmaron's* "legal father." Ferber explains:

> People had been known to travel from New York to California or from California to New York as an excuse to

stop over on the way to spend a day at Whites' house in Emporia. I was one of these.

It was the conversation. It was the stimulating, compassionate, constructive conversation that enriched the mind and heart of everyone who set foot within that house.

It was on one of those trips in the early spring of 1927...the talk was of the trip they had made...through Oklahoma.

Edna Ferber was captivated by White's stories of beaded and braided Indians being chauffeured about in Pierce Arrows, of millionaires living in wigwams. During the next two years she researched her way across the state, talking to old-timers, scouring libraries and yellowed newspapers. The book she finally wrote riled Oklahomans as much as *Giant* did Texans. She had uncovered some hard truths about the changes that the discovery of oil had wrought on Oklahoma life:

Cities like Osage were suave enough in a surface way. But what could a state do when oil was forever surging up in unexpected places...? At each newly discovered pool there followed the rush and scramble. Another Bret Harte town sprang up on the prairie; fields oozed slimy black; oil rigs clanked; false-front wooden shacks lined a one-street village. Dance halls. Brothels. Gunmen. Brawls. Heat. Flies. Dirt. Crime. The clank of machinery.... The human scum of each new oil town was like the scum of the Run, but harder, crueler, more wolfish and degraded.

After *Cimarron* was published, a Bartlesville, Oklahoma, newspaper reported:

Edna Ferber is best remembered in Bartlesville as an extremely offensive personality garnished with a profusion of hair dye and egotism. At a party one evening a gentleman of education and culture...volunteered some information that he thought she might use.

"Never mind giving me facts," she interrupted..."I'm a fiction writer and don't want facts.... I'll find some dumb publisher who will know as little about the state as I do...."

She fills her story with fantastic characters that could be fabricated only by a person as ignorant of the conditions of which she wrote as Miss Ferber and accepted for publication only by publishers as dumb-witted as she declared she would find.

A dust storm blowing up in the Panhandle.
Library of Congress Farm Security Administration

No doubt Ferber generated such enmity by deflating the powerful myth that Westerners wished to keep intact.

At the time *Cimarron* was published, Woody Guthrie was eighteen years old. America's greatest balladeer was born in Okemah in 1912, the son of a chronically unlucky land speculator. In 1914, the family moved into a six-room house in Okemah's best neighborhood. Two years later, the house burned down. The tragedy broke the Guthries, and Woody's parents never got over the sudden deprivation with which they were faced. The country's most eloquent advocate of economic security was born.

In 1925, Woody's father was seriously burned in another fire and was sent to his sister's wheat farm in Pampa, Texas, to recuperate. Guthrie quit school at 16, then bummed along the Gulf coast for a year before joining his father in the Texas panhandle. On the farm, Guthrie's uncle taught him to play the guitar. Soon the pair were performing at local rodeos and carnivals; and before long, the boy was beginning to make up new words for old tunes.

> There on the Texas plains right in the dead center of the dust bowl, with the [first] oil boom over...and the hard-working people just stumbling about, bothered with mortgages, debts, bills, sickness, worries of every blowing kind, I seen there was plenty to make up songs about.

Guthrie left Pampa in 1937, when the Depression eliminated his job as a sign painter. He wandered east, writing hundreds of songs including "This Land is Your Land," often called a national folk anthem, and "So Long, It's Been Good To Know You," which became the "Auld Lang Syne" of the Depression era. It was Guthrie, the poetic hobo in jeans and work boots, who became both pattern and symbol for the Beat, Hip, and Post-Hip generations that followed.

Guthrie and his successors seem to simultaneously seek and mourn the loss of some vague ideal. The same tone permeates the novels of Larry McMurtry, the West's preeminent contemporary novelist.

McMurtry, raised on his family's cattle ranch in Archer City, Texas, calls his work "elegiac.... The move off the land is now virtually completed and that was the great subject [the West] offered writers of my generation. The one basic subject it offers us now is loneliness."

The author deals with both in *Horseman, Pass By; Leaving Cheyenne;* and *The Last Picture Show.* In each, boys emerging into an uncertain manhood leave the confinement of ranches and little plains towns in search of something better. In *Horseman, Pass By,* which became the movie *Hud,* young Lonnie's grandfather is an old-school cattleman who keeps three longhorns in a corral to remind him of the good old days. Hud, Lonnie's older brother, has no interest in the ranch. Instead, he spends his time drinking and womanizing in town. Suddenly, the ranch's cattle are infected with hoof-and-mouth disease. The entire herd, hundreds of cattle, is gathered into pits and shot to death. The grandfather must kill the longhorns. Soon after, he drifts into senility and is run over by a truck while wandering at night along a highway. Hud shoots him to death, like the cattle, because:

> "He was bad off, Lonnie ... he got to spittin' blood and tryin'
> to get up, an' hurtin' himself. Tryin' to get to those
> goddamn dead people a his. I thought if he wanted to get to
> 'em so bad I'd just let him go. He always liked them better
> than us that was alive, anyhow."

The novel ends with Lonnie hitching a ride out of Thalia, his hometown, on a truck:

> We rode through the outskirts of Thalia. The sun was
> going into the great western canyons, the cattleland was
> growing dark. I saw the road and the big sky melt together
> in the north, above the rope of highway. I was tempted to
> do like Jesse once said: to lean back and let the truck take
> me as far as it was going.... I saw the lights of houses as we
> flashed by in the darkness, the little houses, the ranches
> and the farms I knew. Bobby Don hummed some old song

whose tune I had forgotten, and I sat thinking about
Thalia, making the rounds in my mind. At home it was
time for the train to go by, and nobody was sitting on the
porch....

After what McMurtry sees as the death of the traditional cattleman,
leaving a cynical pseudo-cowboy in his place, he came to feel that he could
"no longer deal creatively with the mental and emotional inarticulateness"
that was left in his home country. He made his own movement off the land
and now runs a bookstore in Washington, D.C.

THE SANTA FE TRAIL—from Independence, Missouri, across the Great
Plains—was primarily a trade route, carrying merchandise. The Oregon
Trail, which stretched 2,000 miles northeast from Independence, carried
people. In literature, this "miserable population" of migrants belongs to A.B.
Guthrie.

Guthrie's 1949 Pulitzer Prize-winning novel, *The Way West*, portrays
the great migration through ordinary people cast against a broad and
historically accurate panorama. "Along the beavered streams of Montana,"
Guthrie once wrote, "I hear the old shouts of the fur hunters. On the ridges I
can see the Blackfeet passing...the great backdrop of plains and mountains echo still to...the whine of dry axles, the boom of a cap and ball."

Guthrie was a newspaperman and a devout Montanan, not necessarily in
that order. His 20-year career as executive editor of the Lexington,
Kentucky, *Leader* ended in 1946 when he returned to his home state to
write *The Big Sky*, his acclaimed first novel of Indians and mountain men
on the northern frontier. Both *The Big Sky* and *The Way West* were good
history as well as popular successes. "We have enough creators of idols,"
Guthrie has remarked, "but not enough honest appraisers who recognize
that a part of all heroes is the clay common to all of us."

Guthrie is considered one of the nation's top experts on the West.
"Writers usually fail to express the real West. Reason: because they were
exploiting it or were applying Eastern standards of behavior and found the
West silly or incomprehensible."

Along with A. B. Guthrie, Idaho's Vardis Fisher is always cited as an
exception to that remark.

Fisher remains comparatively unknown, although he is often ranked as
one of the West's best serious writers. His *Children of God*, a 1939 novel
about the Mormon movement, won that year's Harper Prize and gave him
his only best seller. The work is historically accurate and action-packed,
both characteristics that define his other works of Americana: *Pemmican*,
about the traders who first settled the Northwest; *Tale of Valor*, celebrating
the Lewis and Clark expedition; *City of Illusion*, which portrayed the
West's early miners; and *Mountain Man*, which later became the popular

Robert Redford film, *Jeremiah Johnson*. Yet, these were written almost as potboilers, to support one of the most ambitious projects in the history of literature.

From 1943 to 1960, Fisher produced a twelve-novel series he called his *Testament of Man*. The books attempted nothing less than "presenting as imaginative experience the evolution of man's 'soul' from its first stirrings through the present day...."

A cosmic brooding suffused both Fisher's work and his life. He was born of strict Mormon parents in 1895 on the Idaho frontier. His father was a genuine pioneer; whites had settled in Idaho only 35 years earlier when 13 Mormon families built a small community, believing they were in Utah. When Fisher was a child, his father moved the family into a remote wilderness valley. They ate wild game and slept on beds of animal skins. Fisher did not leave the valley for five years. These experiences surface in his short tale "April: A Fable of Love":

> And mountains she loved, too, with their stupendous shoulders, with their backs to the stars where winds poured over and spilled. The sky also was a wonder of color and curve. The sun laid its burning path from east to west or clouds heaped their masses of wrath and spoke in thunder and flame. Or a deep blue veil would spread over all, a vast blue tenting all living things and coming down softly to the skyline; or a blue that was mellow with golden glows and mists; or a blue with the sun in its inverted bowl like a melon of fire.... And clouds, too, and winds: they were full of unpredictable mad designs. They could be politely cool or they could be cyclones of insanity and wrath. Sometimes a wind was full of moanings and prayer or sometimes it rolled across the sunlight in shimmering valleys of peace.

His mother, who despised the backwoods, schooled her two sons rigorously and thoroughly. At sixteen, Vardis took his younger brother Vivian into a nearby town to attend school. Unable to relate to people or to life in a community, the shy intellectual retreated more deeply into the familiar world of books and ideas. He attended the University of Utah and moved on to New York University, where he and Thomas Wolfe were English instructors and first novelists together. After Fisher returned to Idaho, Wolfe visited him there. Wolfe wrote to a mutual friend:

> What I saw...is the abomination of desolation: an enormous desert bounded by infinitely far-away mountains that you never get to, and little pitiful blistered towns huddled down in the most abject loneliness underneath the huge light and scale and weather and the astounding

brightness and dimensions of everything—all given a kind
of tremendousness and terror and majesty....what I've
seen today explains a lot about him.

Fisher's own sense of desolation increased after one publisher after
another dropped the *Testament* as each successive book failed to earn a
profit. (The series was finally completed by Alan Swallow, a well-known
small publisher of belles lettres in Denver.) But through all of his work
Fisher attempted to explore the conflicts between the individual and the
historical forces shaping society. It is that rich sense of the past that marks
Fisher as one of the West's finest authors.

Those same hills of Idaho also attracted a dying Ernest Hemingway who
took refuge from his own insanity.

Hemingway first went to the old mining town of Ketchum in 1939.
Averell Harriman and the Union Pacific Railroad had just built the new ski
resort of Sun Valley and, to promote it, were inviting celebrities. Hemingway took to the place at once. Staying in room 216 at the Sun Valley Lodge,
he worked on his new novel, *For Whom the Bell Tolls*, in the mornings and
hunted elk and grouse in the afternoons. Often he returned to Ketchum
when he needed to rest, and bought a house and 17 acres on the west bank
of Big Wood River a bit north of town.

Temporarily unable to write, obsessed with his health, Hemingway fled
to Ketchum in 1959. Finally, his motto *Il faut (d'abord) durer* ("One must
last") gave way to another: *Il faut (apres tout) mourir* ("One must die, after
all").

On July 2, 1961, in the foyer of the house in Ketchum, Hemingway
leaned his forehead against the muzzle of his favorite shotgun and tripped
both triggers.

Now a sculpture of the author rests on a simple pedestal near that house
in a small forest of alder, willow, and red birch overlooking Trail Creek. The
inscription is taken from a eulogy Hemingway wrote for an Idaho hunting
partner: "Best of all he loved the fall...the leaves yellow on the cottonwoods...leaves floating on the trout streams and above the high blue
windless skies...Now he will be part of them forever."

No SUCH FOREBODING HAD ACCOMPANIED SAM CLEMENS on his trip west
a hundred years before. "Fatigued by persistent retreating," he abandoned
the Confederate Army in the early days of the Civil War and accompanied
his brother, Orion, to the Nevada Territory. Orion had just been appointed
Secretary to the Territorial Governor. Sam appointed himself Secretary to
the Secretary. Since Orion had few official duties, Sam had none. So he set
out on what became six years of "variegated vagabonding" and, in its course,
transformed himself into Mark Twain.

Sam arrived in Nevada in the midst of the first silver strikes. "I would have been more or less than human," he wrote in *Roughing It*, "if I had not gone mad like the rest." The young tenderfoot threw in with three others on their way to the mineral camps. He later managed to turn his own naivete to comic use in a way that was typically Twain:

> I confess, without shame, that I expected to find masses of silver lying all about the ground. I expected to see it glittering in the sun on the mountain summits. I said nothing about this, for some instinct told me that I might possibly have an exaggerated idea of it, and so if I betrayed my thought I might bring derision upon myself. Yet I was perfectly satisfied...that I was going to gather up, in a day or two, or at furthest a week or two, silver enough to make me satisfactorily wealthy....

After several weeks of swinging an eight-pound sledge, tunneling through dirt, and shivering nights in a mountain shack of his own construction, Sam Clemens resigned. Returning to town, he found a letter for him from the Virginia City *Territorial Enterprise*, the chief newspaper of the region. He had written a few letters to the paper, satires from the mines, and signed them "Josh."

"My good opinion of the editors had steadily declined," he said, "for it seemed to me that they might have found something better than my literature to fill up with." When he opened the letter, his opinion must have plummeted still farther: he was offered the job of the *Enterprise's* city editor at $25 a week—"bloated luxury, a sinful and lavish waste of money." He took it.

Clemens's training in journalism was limited to some advice from an editor: "Never say, 'We learn' so-and-so, or 'It is reported'...but go to headquarters and get the absolute facts, and then speak out and say, 'It *is* so-and-so.' Otherwise, people will not put confidence in your news." He always had confidence, even if he didn't have all facts. Nobody minded:

> New claims were taken daily, and it was the friendly custom to run straight to the newspaper office, give the reporter forty or fifty "feet" [in the mine] and get him to go and examine the mine and publish notice of it. They did not care a fig what you said about the property so you said something....My salary was increased to forty dollars a week, but I seldom drew it.

When Sam Clemens began to be known as a humorist and practical joker as well as a reporter, he decided to separate his two vocations. Following common custom, he adopted a pen name for his hoaxes to protect his

reputation as a "serious" reporter. On February 2, 1863, he signed his first
Enterprise piece as Mark Twain.

Sam began to feel that he had at last found his "legitimate occupation"
and grew heady and restless in the boomtown. In the spring of 1864, he was
left in charge of the paper while the editor was away on business. Soon he
was exchanging printed insults with the editor of the rival *Virginia City
Union.* Finally, Sam challenged his adversary to a duel—duels having been
recently outlawed. He had not only committed a crime, but had committed
it in print. He quietly absconded to California to avoid jail, but he never
forgot his days in Nevada:

> From Virginia's airy situation one could look over a vast,
> far-reaching panorama of mountain ranges and deserts....
> Over your head Mount Davidson lifted its grey dome and
> before and below you a rugged canyon clove the battle-
> mented hills, making a somber gateway through which a
> soft-tinted desert was glimpsed, with the silver thread of a
> river winding through it, bordered with trees which many
> miles of distance diminished to a delicate fringe...far
> enough beyond a lake that burned in the desert like a
> fallen sun....

The same Nevada landscape which Sam Clemens described so haunt-
ingly serves as backdrop for the stories of Walter Van Tilburg Clark. His
novels *The Ox-Bow Incident* and *Track of the Cat,* as well as his short
fiction, have typed him as another "cowboy writer."

Clark used his home state as the stage for his own version of the modern
morality play. Just as the size of a room is emphasized by sparse furnishings,
the simple people who inhabit Clark's Nevada frontier make it ring with
cosmic overtones and hidden, overpowering forces.

The Ox-Bow Incident has been compared to the story of the Crucifixion.
A small-town mob forms when it is rumored that a local rancher has been
murdered. Davies, the voice of reason in the story, argues that the culprits
should be brought in for trial. A hothead, Winder, disagrees: "Yeah; and
then if your law lets them go?" Davies replies:

> "They probably ought to be let go. At least there'll be a
> bigger chance that they ought to be let go than that a
> lynch gang can decide whether they ought to hang." Then
> he said a lynch gang always acts in a panic, and has to get
> angry enough to overcome its panic before it can kill, so it
> doesn't ever really judge, but just acts on what it's already
> decided to do, each man afraid to disagree with the rest. He
> tried to prove to us that lynchers knew they were wrong;
> that their secrecy proved it, and their sense of guilt
> afterward.

"Did you ever know a lyncher who wasn't afraid to talk
about it afterward?" he asked us.

Driving on through the cold winds of the mountains, the posse finds three
men and lynches them for the crime, only to find the rancher has not been
murdered at all. The narrator, a cowboy named Art Croft, seems a kind of
Everyman. He follows the mob half-heartedly. After the lynching—again,
through careful understatement—Clark intimates the vague promise of
hope for the future.

Clark deepens his portrayal of the Western psyche in his 1949 novel, *The
Track of the Cat.* Here, the black panther becomes symbolic of uncon-
trollable forces. Three brothers on a turn-of-the-century Nevada ranch set
out to kill the cat. The first brother, a dreamer of sorts and ineffectual,
meets the cat and is killed by it. The second brother is cunning, earthy, an
animal not unlike the cat itself. He, too, is killed. The youngest brother
slays the beast. Through the trio, Clark seems to suggest that a new kind of
Westerner is emerging, one who is neither a simplistic visionary nor an
adversary of nature. His psychological exploration of Western myths and
symbols have, as one critic maintains, "laid forever to rest serious doubts
that great literature could come out of the West."

COLORADO LIES AT THE CENTER of the region and its literature. Its hills
have long proved an attraction for literary notables. The first to be lured
there was Horace Greeley, who took his own advice and went west in 1859.
On his way to Denver, the famed editor of the New York *Tribune* kept
track of the "descending order of civilization":

> May 12th, Chicago—Chocolate and morning journals last
> seen on the hotel breakfast table
> May 23rd, Leavenworth—Room-bells and bathtubs make
> their final appearance
> May 24th, Topeka—Beefsteaks and washbowls (other
> than tin) last visible. Barber, ditto.
> May 26th, Manhattan—Potatoes and eggs last recognized
> among the blessings which "brighten as they take their
> flight"—Chairs, ditto.
> May 27th, Junction City—Last visitation of a bootblack,
> with dissolving views of a board bedroom. Beds bid us
> goodbye.

When Greeley finally reached Denver, he found the six-month-old city
to consist of about "100 log buildings, each ten feet square or less," and any
number of tents. The town's only hotel was among the latter, and Greeley's
bed was separated from the hotel's bar by a single low partition. Each night,
he was roused by gunfire and laughter. Finally, he trudged to the bar and

mounted a chair. "Friends," he said, "I have been in pain and without sleep for almost a week. I am a guest at this hotel. I pay a high price for board and lodging, and I am entitled to rest during the night. But how can I get it with all this noise going on?" The revelers cheered their honored visitor and voted to close the bar every night at eleven until "Uncle Horace" was gone.

Actually, it was Greeley who saved the Colorado gold boom. Many prospectors couldn't find gold as fast as they thought they should. Several decided the reports of strikes must be a hoax. New arrivals began to leave; those not yet at the gold fields began to turn back. Local officials called on Greeley, who commanded international respect, to journey to the mines and verify the discoveries. He did; his report was printed on the front page of the *Rocky Mountain News*, and the Colorado gold rush continued unchecked.

Greeley was so impressed by the frontier that in 1869, 10 years later, he sponsored the Union Temperance Colony to found a community on the Colorado frontier. Memberships were sold for $15 each to teetotalling men of good character. Although it is no longer dry, the town of Greeley thrives today on the plains 50 miles north of Denver.

Greeley was one of the settlements that Isabella Bird visited on her solitary trek from California to St. Joseph, Missouri, in 1873. In a letter to her sister, Bird reported:

> The men of Greeley carry their crusade against drink even
> beyond their limits and have lately sacked three houses

A gambling room in the back of a saloon: a typical setting for the kind of mayhem Horace Greeley found in western bars.
New York Public Library

open for the sale of drink near their frontier.... As the men have no barrooms to sit in, I observed that Greeley is asleep at an hour when other places were beginning their revelries.

Bird's was a unique journey. To improve her health, she sailed to the Sandwich Islands (now Hawaii) and decided to return to her native Scotland by way of the United States. Her letters written from the frontier to her sister were published in *Leisure Hour*, an English weekly, in 1878. The following year, they appeared as a book titled *A Lady's Life in the Rocky Mountains*. The small volume still stands as a classic and uncompromising view of Western life in the American wild.

> One of the most painful things in the Western States and Territories is the extinction of childhood. I have never seen any children, only debased imitations of men and women, cankered by greed and selfishness, and asserting and gaining complete independence of their parents at ten years old. The atmosphere in which they are brought up is one of greed, godlessness, and frequently of profanity... this is a wretched existence. The poor crops have been destroyed by grasshoppers over and over again, and that talent deified here under the name "smartness" has taken advantage of [my host] in all bargains, leaving him with little except food for his children.

Her ultimate destination was "a most romantic place" called Estes Park. Now a tourist town at the entrance to Rocky Mountain National Park, in Bird's time Estes Park was a storybook valley where consumptives went to regain "robust and perfect health." When she arrived there, only three cabins dotted the hills. One she boarded in during the winter of 1873. Another belonged to "Mountain Jim" Nugent, an authentic mountain man who courted Isabella Bird during her stay in the mountains.

After returning to Scotland, Isabella Bird became an active missionary. She journeyed through Japan, Tibet, Korea, China, India, and Malaysia, founding many hospitals and training medical technicians. She was the first woman ever elected to the Royal Geographical Society, in 1891. Yet, it is her indelible picture of the wild Rocky Mountains for which she is best remembered. In the most recent edition of her letters, Daniel Boorstin says in his preface:

> Isabella Bird luxuriated in the paradoxes of this world: an English lady wearing Hawaiian riding dress, mounted on "Birdie," her borrowed pony, guided by the one-eyed desperado Mountain Jim, entertaining her with his recitations of poetry and cultivated conversation. Her Rocky

Leadville in Colorado during the late 19th century, one of the
big silver boom towns of the Southwest.
Colorado Historical Society

Mountain adventure symbolized the improbable combination of opposites which was the American West, and
which was perhaps the most American aspect of that
West.

At the time, America was a fashionable destination for Britons in search
of adventure without much risk. One who came was the poet Oscar Wilde,
barnstorming the country on a personal appearance tour in 1882.

One of his most successful stops was in the Colorado mining camp of
Leadville. At the time, it had the reputation of being the world's richest
city, and the roughest. "I was told that if I went there they would be sure to
shoot me," Wilde said. But he went, and found the miners "charming."

I read them passages from the autobiography of Benvenuto
Cellini and they seemed much delighted. I was reproved
by my hearers for not having brought him with me. I
explained that he had been dead for some little time,
which elicited the inquiry, "who shot him?"

After the performance, Wilde was a guest of the local saloon, where he saw "the only rational method of art criticism I have ever come across." A sign hanging above the piano said, "Please Do Not Shoot The Pianist. He Is Doing His Best."

Wilde's companions cheered him as he smoked a cigar, "quaffed a cocktail without flinching," and called him "a bully boy with no glass eye"—which the poet deemed "artless and spontaneous praise which touched me more than the pompous panegyrics of literary critics ever could or did."

In the 1880s, Leadville belonged to Horace Tabor. He built the hall in which Wilde appeared. He was the town's mayor and an owner of the Matchless Mine, the richest silver lode ever found in the Colorado mountains. His own tragic story forms the thread of the superb opera, *The Ballad of Baby Doe*, written in 1956 by Broadway veterans John Latouche and Douglas Moore.

In 1880, the fifty-year-old Tabor saw Elizabeth "Baby" Doe in a Leadville restaurant. The attraction was immediate. Baby Doe had just divorced her husband, a miner in close-by Central City, and had come to town to better her prospects.

She did so magnificently. What began as a simple flirtation deepened into an abiding love that scandalized the Rockies and became the celebrated story of Colorado's only opera.

Horace and Baby Doe were cast out of polite society when Tabor divorced his prim wife, Augusta, and married his new love in 1883. For years, the couple lived a solitary, but wealthy, life until silver was replaced by paper money in 1896. Tabor was ruined. Before he died, broken, three years later, he made Baby Doe promise to "hang onto the Matchless Mine." Ever faithful, she did. She lived, penniless, in a shack beside the pit for 36 years, until she froze to death there in the winter of 1935.

Colorado has received artistic notice also through its official poet laureate, Thomas Hornsby Ferril. Winner of *Poetry* magazine's 1937 Oscar Blumenthal Prize and many other citations, Ferril is widely regarded as the West's best living poet.

His work has been dismissed by some critics as too regional, and his extensive use of Colorado history as poetic material has tended to keep him from the mainstream of modern poetry. Ferril himself, in his 1946 essay *Writing in the Rockies*, describes the obstacle a Western writer must overcome.

Rocky Mountain literature is devitalized by a low-grade mysticism dictated by landscape. Mysticism is a nebulous word. I use it simply as a blanket concept covering a crude field of emotional response to magnificent landscape. The

imagination, transported by enormous mountains, deserts, and canyons, endeavors to answer landscape directly
and tends to disregard, or curiously modify, what might
otherwise be normal considerations of human experience.
...Indeed Oscar Wilde may have been talking sense when
he said our West could never produce literature because,
as in Switzerland, the mountains were to high.

Ferril published his first poem when only 10, and later became well-
known for his newspaper verse during his stint as a reporter on the old
Denver Times. He wrote verse and a regular column for the weekly *Rocky
Mountain Herald* for more than 30 years, while contributing poems and
essays to *Harper's* and other national magazines.

In 1957 his verse play, *And Perhaps Happiness,* about Colorado's gold
rush, won the *Denver Post*/Central City Prize of $10,000 for a dramatic
work based on Colorado's early history. Ferril's career was crowned three
years later when he was awarded the 1960 Robert Frost Award. Despite the
regional label Ferril remains an enduring figure in any consideration of
Western literature. During the final years of his life, Ferril became a
recluse.

Colorado and the West also served James Michener's novel, *Centennial.*
The author decided to pursue his long-time yen to write a story based in the
West, he said, after failing to inspire Congress to plan an appropriate
bicentennial celebration.

It was natural for Michener to turn to Colorado, the "Centennial State." In
1936, when he was 29, Michener appalled his academic colleagues by
announcing he had been appointed Director of Social Sciences at the
Colorado State College of Education (now Colorado State University) in
Greeley. He had a meteoric career at Harvard and St. Andrew's; a fellow
professor warned him, "The sands of the desert are white with the bones of
young men who went west and are trying to get back east."

Michener never regretted his decision. "At Greeley, I grew up spiritually,
emotionally, intellectually," he later wrote.

While there, Michener became friends with Floyd Merrill, Greeley's
newspaper editor. The pair made almost weekly ventures into the surrounding country. "At least three times a month, Merrill and I went on
excursions out of Greeley, sometimes to the intricate irrigation systems
that made our part of the desert into a garden of melons, sometimes to glens
far above timberline, from which we would look down into valleys crowded
with blue spruce and aspen, and quite often out onto the prairie east of
town where majestic buttes rose starkly from the barren waste."

Merrill also taught the young professor to use a camera. Michener
credits the photos he took in Colorado with keeping his images of the West
alive and vital long enough for *Centennial* to be conceived.

Michener returned to Colorado in May, 1970, determined to write an exhaustive story of the Western experience. He plumbed the natural and social history of the region. Based in an apartment near downtown Denver, he made constant forays into Texas, Mexico, Wyoming, Utah, Nebraska. He hired two assistants to retrace the route of the flatboats down the Ohio River to the Mississippi. Meanwhile, he corresponded with scores of area geologists, teachers, and historians: When was the first mammoth excavated in Nebraska? When was the first outbreak of cholera? How many sheep could fit into a boxcar in 1886? Between trips and interviews, he read through the shelves of the Denver Public Library's renowned Western History collection. In John Kings's book, *In Search of Centennial* (Random House, N.Y., 1978) Michener describes how he felt when he finally sat down to convert his research into a novel.

> In 1972, when I started the actual writing of *Centennial*, I had already lived with the Platte River for thirty-six years, and I wanted all men and women who read my account of its wandering across the plains to become as familiar with it as I was. The mountains had been my associates for three decades, and they would be characters in any story I elected to tell; especially the prairie, reaching to the horizon in all quarters, had been an object of love, and I intended to write of it in that way. These were the components of a tremendous universe, one that I wanted every reader to share. I wanted the west that I would be writing about to be real, and to achieve this, the reader had to follow the trails I had followed and see the land as I had seen it.

"Exhaustive" is almost too mild an adjective to describe *Centennial*. Michener opens the book with 80 pages of geological investigation into the forces that shaped the land and mountains on the patch of ground known as Colorado. He then populated it with insects, dinosaurs, more modern creatures, and finally, the migrating tribes and Arapaho Indians who settled there.

Michener's pioneers built their town of Centennial on the Platte River, which one character calls "the sorriest river in America." The story is one of struggle, success, failure, and, above all, endurance. Perhaps the closest thing to the fictional Centennial is the near-ghost town of Keota, Colorado, 40 miles northeast of Greeley. Michener returned to Keota more than a dozen times to absorb its dusty atmosphere and talk with postmaster Clyde Stanley.

Stanley had lived in Keota most of his 70 years. He had seen the farmers come, eager, only to be chased out by drought and dust storms. He watched the town dwindle from 129 people in 1929 to six in 1970. And he remembered it all. *Centennial's* land commissioner, Walter Bellamy, is modeled on him; Michener dedicated the book to Stanley, "who introduced me to the prairie."

The novel centers on a young college professor, who is reminiscent of Michener himself. The teacher is hired by a popular magazine as a consultant for a massive article: the publication is outlining the entire history of a section of America in celebration of the Bicentennial. The editor's choice: Centennial, Colorado. "If we can make [it] comprehensible to Americans," he explains, "we can inspire them with the meaning of this continent."

It is Michener's voice, there and in the final pages of the novel when Paul Garrett speaks. Garrett is the descendant of the Indians, Russians, English, Japanese, who made Centennial and populated Michener's story. Garrett explains to the professor that he continues to live and work in Centennial because "it could even be the best remainin' spot on earth."

For a variety of reasons, most Western writers would probably agree.

CALIFORNIA &
THE FAR WEST

BILL LOGAN

CONSIDER THE PLACE NAMES "New York" and "California." New York was formerly New Amsterdam; the name changed but the thought remained the same. Each wave of settlers—first the Dutch, then the English—chose a name for their new home that would define its (and their) position in relation to their forebears. California, on the other hand, takes its name from the 16th century Spanish romance *Las sergas de Esplandian:* "Now you are to hear the most extraordinary thing that was ever heard of in the writings or in the memory of man. . . . Know that on the right hand of the Indies, there is an island called California, very close to the Terrestrial Paradise." It took the Spaniards nearly 200 years to discover that California was not in fact an island, but the name they gave it seems nonetheless appropriate. California: from the start, a place of the imagination, a place quite near Paradise, a land on which some of the primal fertility and uncloudy days of Eden had apparently rubbed off.

IN JANUARY 1835 the brig *Pilgrim,* 150 days out of Boston, floated on the swells off Santa Barbara. In it rode ordinary seaman Richard Henry Dana, Jr., late of Harvard University, Cambridge, Mass. Measles had so weakened the young man's eyesight that he was temporarily unable to continue his studies, and so this son of a prominent Cambridge family traded Homer for the halyards of a sailing ship. His chronicle of the trip, *Two Years Before the Mast,* written in 1840 when he had returned to Harvard to study law, is remarkable not only for its accurate portrayal of pre-Gold Rush California but also as the first compelling record of an Easterner's attempt to come to terms with the Pacific coast.

Dana was in the first boat to go ashore:

I shall never forget the impression which our first landing on the beach of California made upon me. The sun had just gone down; it was getting dusky; the damp night-wind was beginning to blow, and the heavy swell of the Pacific was setting in, and breaking in loud and high "combers" upon the beach. We lay on our oars, just outside of the surf, waiting for a good chance to run in, when a boat, which had put off from the *Ayacucho*, came alongside of us, with a crew of dusky Sandwich-Islanders....

Never having landed in such a surf, the Yankees watch while the Hawaiians show them how:

We saw at once how the thing was to be done...We pulled strongly in, and as soon as we felt that the sea had got hold of us, and was carrying us in with the speed of a race horse, we threw the oars as far from the boat as we could, and took hold of the gunwales, ready to spring out and seize her when she struck, the officer using his utmost strength, with his steering oar, to keep her stern out. We were shot up upon the beach, and seizing the boat, ran her up high and dry....

Thus, Massachusetts came to the Pacific slope. Dana is well pleased with this feat of seamanship, less well so with California and its people. His

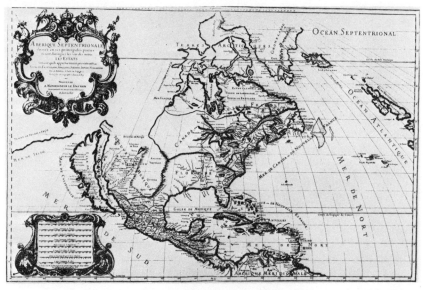

An early map of California by the French cartographer Sanson, portraying it as an island.
California Historical Society Library

Clipper cards like these advertised the new fast method of transportation between the Atlantic and Pacific coasts.
New York Historical Society

work—carrying stiff, tanned cowhides the size of bedsheets down to the shore and loading them in the long boats for the pull out to the mother ship—is exhausting and disagreeable, hardly befitting his newfound status as a seaman. The langor of the local populace, both Indian and European, piques him all the more for this.

> The Californians are an idle, thriftless people, and can make nothing for themselves. The country abounds in grapes, yet they buy, at a great price, bad wine made in Boston and brought round by us... Their hides, too, which they value at two dollars in money, they barter for something that costs seventy-five cents in Boston; and buy shoes (as like as not made of their own hides, which have been carried twice around Cape Horn) at three and four dollars....

What he says about "California fever"—his name for laziness—will be repeated by countless observers following him. But the foundation of his disgust with Californians is not simply their laziness but their idleness, with all the Puritan connotations that word carries. It's not that they are slothful; Dana is at pains to show the vigor of the festival called a fandango, and he notes with amusement a Californian love for swift horses that rivals their modern love for cars. The trouble is that they're not profitably employed. Dana is surprised above all by the Californians' lack of paper credit: "They have no credit system, no banks, and no way of investing money but in cattle. Besides silver, they have no circulating medium but hides, which the sailors call "California banknotes."

But a year and a half's cruising the coast gives Dana at least one happy memory:

> The rocks were as large as those of Nahant or Newport, but, to my eye, more grand and broken. Besides, there was a grandeur in everything around, which gave a solemnity to the scene, a silence and solitariness which affected every part! Not a human being but ourselves for miles, and no sound heard but the pulsations of the great Pacific! I separated myself from the rest, and sat down on a rock, just where the sea ran in and formed a fine spouting horn.

For a moment, the idler in Dana is set free.

> I experienced a glow of pleasure at finding that what of poetry and romance I ever had in me had not been entirely deadened by the laborious life, with its paltry, vulgar associations, which I had been leading. Nearly an hour did I sit, almost lost in the luxury of this entirely new scene....

But after that hour, his duty calls, and the moment's exclamation—a flirtation with the high style quite unusual for this practical man—trails away in the wake of the ship that carries him back to Boston.

Dana became a successful lawyer, but died before completing the treatise on international law that was to be his major work. Again and again towards the end of his life, he regretted that he had ever left the sea: "I believe I was made for the sea.... My life on shore is a mistake." Whatever he was made for, he made California a place in the American mind.

When the next great interpreter of California to the world came East for a triumphal lecture tour, it was none other than Richard Henry Dana who introduced him at his first speech. Like Dana, he had gone to California in early youth, though his starting point was Albany rather than Boston and he crossed the continent instead of rounding the Horn. Unlike Dana, he had stayed.

Bret Harte worked as everything from miner to law clerk to druggist's assistant in Gold Rush California before he landed a job on a northern

California newspaper in 1860. Run out of town for printing an editorial sympathetic to the local Indians, he went to work for the *Golden Era,* San Francisco's leading literary journal at the time. There, his local reputation as a sketch-writer and satirist grew until in 1868, at the age of thirty-two, he became editor of the *Overland Monthly.* Under his leadership, that periodical would publish such writers as Mark Twain, Ambrose Bierce, Clarence King, and Ina Coolbrith, but the main thing the *Monthly* did for Harte was to make his national reputation. His two finest stories, "The Luck of Roaring Camp" and "The Outcasts of Poker Flat," appeared within the first year of his editorship.

Even in these, the best of his stories, the characters are cardboard and the plots soggy with sentimentality. Worse, the "local color" for which he is famous reads today like slightly souped-up Longfellow. Why, then did West and East go wild for him? Why did the *Atlantic Monthly* offer him $10,000 for a one-year contract?

Because he was the first first-hand observer to embrace the life of the Western boomtowns that the Gold Rush had created. He found elemental drama, however inflated, in the plain people of the hills.

Placerville was one of the first boom mining towns to spring up during the Gold Rush.
California Historical Society Library

And there is something about the best stories which avoids being dressed-up Dumas, something elemental—natural violence. In neither of the stories mentioned above is the tragedy brought on by human conduct. A flood sweeps away Roaring Camp and its beloved child; relentless snow kills the outcasts of Poker Flat and the couple they befriend. In both cases, disaster comes out of a clear blue sky. Early readers of "The Outcasts of Poker Flat" must have been reminded of the fate of the Donner Party, a group of settlers who crossed the Sierra too late in the year and were caught by the snows and forced to spend the winter surviving on each other's flesh. When observing disaster, at least, Harte's sight is true. Look at the short paragraph that destroys Roaring Camp's idyll:

> The winter of 1851 will long be remembered in the foothills. The snow lay deep on the Sierras, and every mountain creek became a river, and every river a lake. Each gorge and gulch was transformed into a tumultuous watercourse that descended the hillsides, tearing down giant trees and scattering its drift and debris along the plain. Red Dog has already been twice under water, and Roaring Camp had been forewarned...And that night the North Fork suddenly leaped over its banks, and swept up the triangular valley of Roaring Camp.

If Dana hung suspiciously on the outskirts of old California, Harte went to the humming center of the new West, the American West of Boom and Bust. He set his stories where the lust for wealth was building and naming the ephemeral Red Dogs and Roaring Camps, towns that would last no longer than the veins of ore in their hills. And he had the instinct of a Californian when he set loose the destructive power of water and snow, not as some kind of vengeance of the gods on prideful man but as pure, inexplicable natural force.

The only story of mining life to rival "The Luck" and "The Outcasts" for permanent popularity is Mark Twain's "The Celebrated Jumping Frog of Calaveras County." No wonder. Though Twain was already known for his Nevada sketches when he reached San Francisco in 1863, it was Harte who, according to Twain, "trimmed and polished and schooled me patiently, until he changed me from an awkward utterer of coarse grotesqueness to a writer of paragraphs and chapters that have found a certain flavor." Harte was then on the verge of the national fame that would propel him eastward and eventually to exile in Europe, after he'd reneged on his *Atlantic* contract. He would play the same tune again and again for the rest of his days, but Twain was still 20 years from *Huckleberry Finn*. He may have honed a style thanks to Harte, but it is not through Harte that he found his own voice.

Dana's return was to duty; Twain's would be to a land he loved better, whose contours he would reimagine as lovingly as John Muir and Robinson Jeffers would the California landscape. In *Roughing It*, Twain's observation of California is shaped by contrast with what it is not. Pine trees bore him: he "tires of the endless tufts of needles and yearns for substantial, shapely leaves." He vehemently refuses to admit to California's beauty, because "no land with an unvarying climate can be very beautiful." Thunderstorms, maples, and Eastern winters are ever on his mind. Even Yosemite bores him. Refusing to join the mass of Yosemite rhapsodists, he comments, "I could give the reader a vivid description of the marvels of the Yosemite—but what has this reader done to me that I should persecute him?"

But his sight is no less sharp for the faraway look in his eyes. Indeed, his emotional distance let him outline, in a few brief sketches, as lively and accurate a picture of Gold Rush California as was ever written. No misty-eyed Harte could see the traces left by past mines, the "grassy slopes and levels torn and guttered and disfigured by the avaricious spoilers of 15 and 20 years ago." Nor could Harte have written about the destructive side of the mining fever. Reading Twain, not Harte, leads to an understanding of how men like Sutter and Marshall, the discoverers of gold in California, died broke. Twain's distance, however, keeps his moral sense from warping his pictures.

Finest of all the bits in *Roughing It* is Twain's account of "How I enjoyed my first earthquake" in San Francisco:

> The entire front of a four-story brick building in Third Street sprung outward like a door and fell sprawling across the street, raising a dust like a great volume of smoke! And here came the buggy—overboard went the man, and in less time than I can tell it the vehicle was distributed in small fragments along three hundred yards of the street. One woman who had been washing a naked child ran down the street holding it by the ankles as if it were a dressed turkey. Prominent citizens who were supposed to keep the Sabbath strictly rushed out of saloons in their shirtsleeves, with billiard cues in their hands ... A prominent editor flew downstairs, in the principal hotel, with nothing on but one brief undergarment—met a chambermaid and exclaimed:
> "Oh, what shall I do! Where shall I go!"
> She responded with naive serenity:
> "If you have no choice, you might try a clothing store!"

A moment of terrible violence exposes the manners of the whole town.

The third great figure of the San Francisco of the 1870s has proved the most elusive. Two things made him easy to dismiss: his naive self-promotion and his Godawful poetry. Unfortunately for Joaquin Miller's

Two panels from a seven-plate daguerrotype panorama of

reputation, like virtually every California poet before Robinson Jeffers, he was wedded to singsong forms archaic even in his own day, and his efforts to keep rhythm and rhyme made him squash the life out of his landscapes and situations. To his credit as a poet, however, he insisted on writing narratives about the adventures of California characters in their own landscape, and so prefigured Robinson Jeffers.

Why did he want to be a poet? Because it was the grandest thing to be for an Indiana boy whose parents had brought him West to Oregon at an early age, who by his own account had then run away to the gold mines, lived with the Indians, rode for the Pony Express, and was a teacher, an editor, and a judge. There is good reason to believe that his own account is considerably elaborated—indeed, critics are divided as to whether his great work was meant to be an autobiography or fiction. After all, this was a man who changed his name from Cincinnatus to Joaquin, because he admired the bandit Joaquin Murieta. Like Harte, he was a child of the still obscure West who thought the best way to achieve fame was to speak in the largest manner. Also like Harte, he was right.

America refused to pay attention, so he took his privately printed *Pacific Poems* and *Songs of the Sierras* to London. Suddenly, he was famous. Literary London fêted him, and the "Byron of Oregon" did his best to live up to his press by dressing in boots and chaps, strutting around London with

San Francisco Bay, taken in Spring 1851.   California Historical Society Library

hair down to his shoulders. But for all of this, some quality—perhaps it was sincerity—saved him where Harte was lost; and instead of living out his days an exile looking at the Alps and longing for the Sierras, as Harte did, Miller returned in triumph to the San Francisco Bay Area in the 1880s. There, at "The Hights", his estate in the hills above Oakland, his fantasy had free play. He built separate houses for his mother, his wife, his daughter, and himself, because he thought each being should be independent. He built monuments to Moses, Browning, and John C. Fremont, and constructed his own funeral pyre. He loved to compose in bed, and to inspire him he had a water spout made which would drip a rainlike patter of droplets on the roof above his bower. If Easterners have loved taunting Marin County faddists, think what fun they would have had with Joaquin Miller!

Distracted by his outrageous behavior and his gooey verse, everyone overlooked the fact the he had written the first great Far Western book, though it wasn't poetry at all. Though there are parts of *Life Amongst the Modocs* that are as bombastic as anything in Miller, at its best it is like a combination of Harte's embrace with Twain's pure sight:

> As lone as God, and white as a winter moon, Mount Shasta
> starts up sudden and solitary from the heart of the great

black forests of Northern California.

You would hardly call Mount Shasta a part of the Sierras; you would say rather that it is the great white tower of some ancient and eternal wall, with here and there the white walls overthrown.

It has no rival! There is not even a snow-crowned subject in sight of its dominion. A shining pyramid in mail of everlasting frosts and ice, the sailor sometimes, in a day of singular clearness, catches glimpses of it from the sea a hundred miles away to the west; and it may be seen from the dome of the capital 340 miles distant. The immigrant coming from the east beholds the snowy, solitary pillar from afar out on the arid sagebrush plains, and lifts his hands in silence as in answer to a sign.

The praise of the initiate sketches the lineaments of the land.

But the home is not uncomplicated, because in it the Pit River, Shasta, and Modoc Indians meet the miners. The book's hero lives among both miners and Indians, describing both without the rancor of either. He know local Indian cultures well enough to retell their creation myth—the mating of a bear and the gods' daughter near the gods' teepee, Mt. Shasta—and he describes his own mining techniques with equal ease. His deepest sympathies are clearly with the Indians but he is a miner himself, and in the battles that come he fights on both sides.

Both peoples have a direct connection to the land: the one by myth and heredity, the other by desire for gold. They thus embody different elemental attitudes—the constructive versus the expansive—and neither side can be said to wear the white hats. Their conflict is violent and inevitable and without easily identifiable villians.

The book presages the titanism and physical culture of Jack London, the sexual violence of Robinson Jeffers, the epic of the land in Frank Norris, the ecstatic nature visions of John Muir, the respect for local Indian cultures in Gary Snyder, even the loggers' individualism in Ken Kesey.

Joaquin Miller is the first full-fledged Pacific writer. Miller, Harte, and Twain represent the Argonaut generation. They witnessed the Gold Rush, wrote about it, and lived in and near the city it built, San Francisco. The next generation came to map and to settle, and it too produced three great figures: a surveyor, a rancher, and another rancher's wife.

THE SURVEYOR WAS YALE-EDUCATED GEOLOGIST CLARENCE KING. And though his 1872 book, *Mountaineering in the Sierra Nevada,* predates *Life Amongst the Modocs* by a full year, it belongs to the next generation.

King was one of the "best and brightest" of his day. He rode west at the age of twenty-one, intending to join the Whitney Survey of California; worked there with Whitney and Brewer; headed the famous Survey of the 40th Parallel; and finally became the first chief of the United States Geological Survey. Leaving government service to make his fortune in the stock market, he lost everything in the panic of 1893, and was thereafter incarcerated in an asylum. He died of tuberculosis in 1901, having sent his black wife, Ada, and their five children to Canada where, he hoped, they would not suffer the racial stigma that had forced him to keep their marriage a secret throughout his life.

As Richard Henry Dana loved the sea, so King loved the high mountains. Wildness gave each an opportunity to achieve the sublime, but neither cared much for Californians.

His lowland sketches satirize the "dull, unrelieved" farmers and the degenerated hog farmers "The Newtys of Pike." In his best sketches, he and a friend make a perilous ascent of Mount Tyndall, or he describes the geological and geometrical formation of Yosemite Valley. He hates the "army of literary travellers" who have waxed poetic over Yosemite, and so avoids the grandiosely scenic.

One of his most colorful characters is an eccentric landscape painter whom he makes to say: It's all Bierstadt and Bierstadt and Bierstadt nowadays! [Bierstadt was a landscape painter well-known for his grand scenes.] What has he done but twist and skew and distort and discolor and belittle and be-pretty this whole doggonned country? Why, his mountains are too high and slim; they'd blow over in one of our fall winds.

King has just the same limits as his painter: he knows what's wrong, but he can't quite do it right himself. When King wants to use the high style he's forced to resort to adjectives like "Dantesque" and "splendid". He's better off with "conoidal."

> But our grandest view was eastward, above the deep shel-
> tered valley and over the tops of those terrible granite
> walls, out upon rolling ridges of stone and wonderful
> granite domes. Nothing in the whole list of irruptive
> products, except volcanoes themselves, is so wonderful as
> these domed mountains. They are of every variety of
> conoidal form, having horizontal sections accurately el-
> liptical, ovoid or circular, and profiles varying from such
> semicircles as the cap behind the Sentinel to the graceful
> infinite curves of the North Dome. Above and beyond
> these stretch back long bare ridges connecting with sunny
> summit peaks.

It is his obsession with form that makes King's descriptive sketches worth reading.

If precision is what lifts King up, it is precision that keeps the Sierra's other great apologist from floating away into silliness. It's this second

Ansel Adams's famous photograph Winter Sunrise, From Lone Pine, Sierra Nevada
*(c.1944) captures with beautiful and breathtaking precision John Muir's vision of
"The Range of Light."*
Courtesy of Ansel Adams

comer who, though a less fluent writer than King, did by direct attack what
King and his painter friend could not.

John Muir reached the Sierra Nevada in 1868, via his native Scotland and
a boyhood in Wisconsin. He had come to San Francisco by boat, walking
over the Coast Range and across the valley to the Sierras. In *The Mountains
of California*, he describes what he saw from a Coast Range pass:

> At your feet lies the great Central Valley glowing golden in
> the sunshine, extending north and south farther than the
> eye can reach, one smooth, flowery, lake-like bed of fertile
> soil. Along its eastern margin rises the mighty Sierra,
> miles in height, reposing like a smooth cumulus cloud in
> the sunny sky, and so gloriously colored and so luminous,
> it seems not to be clothed with light, but wholly composed
> of it, like the wall of some celestial city. Along the top, and
> extending a good way down, you see a pale, pearl-gray belt
> of snow; and below it a belt of blue and dark purple,
> marking the extension of the forests; and along the base of
> the range a broad belt of rose-purple and yellow, where lie

the miner's goldfields and the foothill gardens. All these colored belts blending smoothly make a wall of light ineffably fine, and as beautiful as a rainbow, yet firm as adamant.

When I first enjoyed this superb view, one glowing April day, from the summit of the Pacheco Pass, the Central Valley, but little trampled and plowed as yet, was one furred, rich sheet of golden compositae, and the luminous wall of the mountains shone in all its glory. Then it seemed to me the Sierra should be called not the Nevada, or Snowy Range, but the Range of Light.

This paean is almost embarrassing in its directness. Elsewhere in the book when he tries for similar effects of grandeur, he trails off in ineffectual strings of qualifiers like "glorious" and "in the most striking manner." Why does this particular description work? Why has everyone from Ansel Adams to governors of California seen fit to quote it? Because it is absolutely accurate, from the botanist's "compositae" to the four-tiered ecosystem of valley, foothills, forest belt, alpine zone. A natural history could be based on this division. Light not only freezes the whole scene for viewing, but also exalts it. Light spiritualizes the view, but does not distort it.

It's easy to have this very big feeling, but quite hard to describe it. King was afraid of being laughed at as a "literary traveller," so he rarely tried. Muir fails repeatedly, but when he hits there's nothing like it. King was content to show what things were made of; Muir celebrated the way things worked. The power of a Muir explanation sometimes takes a few readings to catch. Here, he is describing the formation of great airborne "banners" of blowing snow that he has seen the wind lift up off the mountain faces:

No perfect banner is ever hung on the Sierra peaks by a south wind. Had the gale that day blown from the south, leaving other conditions unchanged, only a dull, confused fog-like drift would have been produced; for the snow, instead of spouting up over the tops of the peaks in concentrated currents to be drawn out as streamers, would have been shed off around the sides, and piled down into the glacier wombs. The cause of the concentrated action of the north wind is found in the peculiar form of the north sides of the peaks, where the amphitheaters of the residual glaciers are.... In general, the south sides are convex and irregular, while the north sides are concave both in their vertical and horizontal direction. This difference in form between the north and the south sides of the peaks was almost wholly produced by the difference in the kind and quality of the glaciation to which they had been subjected, the north sides having been hollowed by residual shadow-glaciers of a form that never existed on the sun-beaten sides.

It appears, therefore, that shadows in great part determine not only the forms of lofty icy mountains, but also those of the snow-banners that the wild winds hang on them.

Instead of waxing rhapsodic over these streams of snow, Muir outlines a capsule history of the mountain range to explain them. And his history has a mythic quality: note that the whole cosmological apparatus again hinges on the effect of light—light that left the shadows, that left the glaciers, that carved the mountains, that upsweep the wind, that catches the snow, that makes the banners. But this cosmology is not fantasy. It was, scientifically speaking, ahead of its own time. Whitney and King had thought such great Sierra features as Yosemite were the result of some violent cataclysm; the botanist and, later, fruit rancher, John Muir, suggested that glaciers had in fact been responsible. Muir was right.

John Muir met Mary Austin at Carmel's turn-of-the-century bohemian colony, where Austin lived for a time. But, he also knew the land of little rain she wrote the best of her many works about. It lies right in the shadow of the Sierras, where Muir saw it from the peak of Mt. Ritter:

> Eastward the whole region seems a land of desolation covered with beautiful light. The torrid volcanic basin of Mono, with its one bare lake fourteen miles long; Owen's Valley and the broad lava table-land at its head, dotted with craters, and the massive Inyo Range, rivaling even the Sierras in height; these are spread, map-like, beneath you....

The group of sketches collected as *The Land of Little Rain* narrate what Austin saw. What makes the book remarkable—and makes Austin a writer of the Pacific West and not the interior West—is that it puts all creatures on the same plane of life. While her passion is nowhere near as intense as Muir's, her sense of interconnectedness of all things is just as strong. Writers of the mountain West were busy with gunslingers and vast, hostile places when Mary Austin anatomized the very edge of their country where it ran up against California. Cactus flower, mesquite, rabbit, pocket miner, Shoshone Indian; none of these escapes her mention or, if it can talk, her conversation.

"Water Trails of the Carrizo" is a good example. Mice, rats, squirrels, and coyotes are folk looking for water, but we have even other signs, the Shoshone Indians, too, have clear markers of their own, both on the rocks and in the sand, to show the way to water. The imperatives of desert life reinforce the direct connection between man and nature that Muir so palpably feels.

Austin didn't stay long in "the brown house under the willow tree at the end of the village street" where she promises in her preface to greet the traveler who may come to the region. Her marriage broke up and the growing city of Los Angeles began to rob the precious water of the Owens River. She went to Carmel, then New York, then Santa Fe, New Mexico. She wrote 35 books, becoming the most famous woman writer of her time, but her first, *The Land of Little Rain*, is the only one remembered today.

WITH THE NEXT GENERATION, the city enters the literature of the Far West, and the drama of the country becomes as much a social as an elemental one. Immigrants, workers, ranchers, and the railroads are the characters of the new writing, replacing the Indians, the miners, and the unpeopled, apotheosized land of the old.

Before he died at the age of thirty, Frank Norris had introduced the West and the world to the new city of San Francisco and the new country of the great Central Valley. Born in Chicago but brought up in San Francisco, he had studied art in Paris, Rome, and Florence, and letters at Berkeley and Harvard. He fell simultaneously under the influence of the grim, naturalistic novels of Zola and the turn-of-the-century enthusiasm for Darwinian evolution.

McTeague, pointedly subtitled "A Story of San Francisco," suffers from Norris's education. He penned it for a writing class at Harvard, and it's easy to imagine him going over his notes from Joseph LeConte's Social-Darwinist evolution classes at Berkeley before sitting down to write. The hero, McTeague, an unlicensed dentist on Polk Street, doesn't even get to speak before his author has described him: "His head was square-cut, angular; the jaw salient, like that of the carnivora." McTeague, it is quickly made apparent, is slow and stupid and carries the weight of "hereditary evil." So much for the dentist and all the other lowlifes he encounters: like dinosaurs, they are doomed to extinction but are too witless to do anything about it.

What makes the book worth reading then? Possibly Norris's nostalgia. The young man must have sat through the cold Cambridge winter using his writing to bring before his eyes the city he'd left behind him. The plot's programmatic nastiness is undercut repeatedly by portraits of people and places which, though lower class, do not seem bestial. Polk Street was then a working class neighborhood, but only a block from the rich section of town:

> It was one of those cross streets peculiar to Western cities,
> situated in the heart of the residence quarter, but occupied

by small tradespeople who lived in the rooms above their shops. There were corner drugstores with huge jars of red, yellow, and green liquids in their windows, very brave and gay; stationers' stores where illustrated weeklies were tacked upon bulletin boards; barber shops with cigar stands in their vestibules; sad-looking plumbers' offices; cheap restaurants in whose windows one saw piles of unopened oysters weighted down by cubes of ice, and china pigs and cows knee-deep in layers of white beans. At one end of the street McTeague could see the huge power-house of the cable line. Immediately opposite him was a great market; while farther on, over the chimney stacks of the intervening houses, the glass roof of some huge public baths glittered like crystal in the afternoon sun....

Once this neighborhood has been introduced, McTeague's habits lose their grossness. He has been situated in a real place and struggles against his type-casting for a good 75 pages before his author's intentions overwhelm him.

McTeague is a beginner's work, and its main supports are raw talent and memory. Norris ranges farther from home in his titanic valley novel, *The Octopus*, but he is closer to the heart of Far Western writing. A new figure watches on the edge of the struggle between the ranchers and the railroads: Presley the poet. Presley is Norris's attempt to come to terms with himself, though the character was modeled on Edwin Markham, the San Francisco poet who that same year had published his one great poem, "The Man with the Hoe," in the *San Francisco Examiner*. Presley, like Norris rather than Markham, had graduated "with high honors from an Eastern college," and come home to write the epic of the West, "the world's frontier of Romance, where a new race, a new people—hardy, brave, and passionate—were building an empire." The course of the novel forces Presley to come to terms with the brutality of that empire.

Established agrarian capital, the ranchers, come up against expansive urban capital, the railroad, in a battle that had actually taken place in the Central Valley some 20 years before. Presley lives with the ranchers, and since they live on the land, his sympathies are with them. The railroad owners make money simply so they can make more money; the ranchers support a way of life in concert with the land. Land grabs, manipulated sales, and political and journalistic maneuvering threaten to rob the ranchers of their holdings. They band together to resist politically, and in the end, by direct confrontation. The climactic scene in the book recreates the 1880 incident at Mussell Slough, where the ranchers and the railroad men fought hand to hand. Just before that battle, however, comes the novel's strangest scene, the running of the jack rabbits across the thousands of harvested acres:

From out of the ground apparently, some twenty yards
distant, a great jack sprang into view, bounding away with
tremendous leaps, his black-tipped ears erect. He disappeared, his grey body losing itself against the grey of the
ground....

From off the surface of the ground, at first apparently
empty of all life, and seemingly unable to afford a hiding-
place for so much as a field-mouse, jack-rabbits started up
at every moment as the line went forward. At first, they
appeared singly and at long intervals; then in twos and
threes, as the drive continued to advance....

By noon the number of rabbits discernible by Annixter's
field glasses on ahead was far into the thousands. What
seemed to be ground resolved itself, when seen through
the glasses, into a maze of small moving bodies, leaping,
ducking, doubling—running back and forth—a wilderness of agitated ears, white tails and twinkling legs....

Then the strange scene defined itself. It was no longer a
herd covering the earth. It was a sea, whipped into confusion, tossing incessantly, leaping, falling, agitated by un-
seen forces....

This scene far outweighs the fight between the ranchers and railroad,
though the latter is central to the plot. Both Presley and the narrator try to
dismiss the scene as a simple manifestation of the great, primal energies of
the People. Here, as elsewhere, when they resort to the power of the People
or the Wheat to defuse the tragic carnage of animals or of men, the book
stands in danger of becoming ludicrous. Fortunately for Norris, his own
descriptive abilities carry him beyond his or Presley's desire to find a
motive that makes the killing all right. After all, his big ranchers and their
vassals are hardly honest representations of the People. The remarkable
thing that Norris managed to do was to show the direct conflict of two
kinds of capital and the explosions their energies produced. Like Joaquin
Miller, he succeeds in standing between two competing urges.

Where Norris, the son of a wealthy jeweler and an art-loving mother, had
to reach down and away from home for his power, his contemporary Jack
London had to reach up towards the literate bourgeosie from an illegiti-
mate birth and a hoodlum youth. Both were infected with the social
Darwinist passion of their time; both knew the work of Joseph LeConte at
Berkeley. Martin Eden, the autobiographical character in London's 1909
novel of the same name, is talking pure LeConte when in arguing with a
professor he says:

Oh, I know there is an elaborate evolution of the various
arts laid down, but it seems to me to be too mechanical.
The human itself is left out. The evolution of the tool, of

> the harp, of music and song and dance, are all beautifully
> elaborated; but how about the evolution of the human
> itself, the development of the basic and intrinsic parts that
> were in him before he made his first tool or gibbered his
> first chant? It is that which you do not consider, and which
> I call biology. It is biology in its largest aspects.

But where the comfortable Norris could sit back and observe the giant forces of human evolution clashing, London himself crossed from one class to another, and so embodied the dynamic power that Norris only watched.

Two books bracket London's career: *The Call of the Wild* (1909) and *The Valley of the Moon* (1913). In the first, he, like Mary Austin, managed to double back on the device of personification. Instead of making animals into little people, he looked for the common denominator between animal and human traits. His dog hero is stolen away from its lovely California home and brutalized in the Yukon North; by calling up the savage instincts buried under his domestic habits, Buck throws off his servitude and becomes the leader of a wolf pack. Given London's evolutionary ideas, only this notion of primal, instinctive force can account for a man like himself. *The Valley of the Moon*, superficially the most Californian of his books, is a human-dress version of the same story, but with a love plot and domestic fantasy thrown in. Billy and his wife Saxon, the one a teamster and the other a laundress, leave the Oakland home where they had been jailed and beaten for their socialist sympathies, fleeing to the pastoral Valley of the Moon in Sonoma County. There, they set up as successful farmers and live happily ever after. London was trying to work out his own fate, on a grander scale, in just that way. In 1909, he had bought his own ranch in the Valley of the Moon.

But *The Valley of the Moon* is just as much a fantasy for its optimism as is *McTeague* for its pessimism. The class barrier is crossed by an aggressive act—by leading the wolfpack—not by retiring to yeoman simplicity. The falseness of *The Valley of the Moon* and the flaw in *The Call of the Wild* show clearly in London's autobiographical classic, *Martin Eden*.

Turn-of-the-century San Francisco was busily piling Greek statuettes on the counting room floor without having bothered to remove the corpses. London became the novelist of that moment in *Martin Eden;* he bridged the gap between poor Polk Street and rich Van Ness Avenue in a way Norris could not.

Martin Eden wants to trade his brutish sailor's life for the world of art and beauty, personified for him in the ethereal, educated girl he meets through her brother. The process by which he reaches that goal makes the book's most memorable scenes. His work in a resort laundry where he and his partner struggle heroically against the "fancy starch," the rich women's silk undergarments, each worth a full week of their wages, is as terrifying as anything in *McTeague*'s underworld. But where McTeague is foredoomed by heredity, Eden is doomed to success. His writing finally sells; he becomes famous overnight. The girl he wanted, who abandoned him over his failure to observe drawing-room proprieties and his refusal to love art but study business, comes back to him only then. He rejects her: she wants him only when he has made himself into a commodity.

The only character Martin Eden unequivocally admires is Russ Brissenden: "He was not long in assuming that Brissenden knew everything, and in deciding that here was the second intellectual man he'd met. But he noted that Brissenden had what Professor Caldwell lacked—namely, the fire, the flashing insight and perception, the flaming uncontrol of genius..." This same genius advises him to forget success and live for beauty. The man the character was modeled on was the poet George Sterling, head of the original bohemian colony at Carmel. Sterling was, in the long run, a mediocre poet. Whatever repute he had was swept away before the tide of the poetry renaissance that carried, among others, Ezra Pound and T.S. Eliot. But his friendship, his generosity, and his wit are what London and others who knew him most remember him for. During the seven years he ruled the roost at Carmel (1905–12), at that time an isolated spot on the Monterey Bay, it attracted writers as diverse as Mary Austin, John Muir, Upton Sinclair, and Jack London himself. A love of the local landscape and the quality of life held the group together. Rare was the artist who could get any work done at Carmel, but the talks and the walks and the beach parties were wonderful. The one lasting product of the Carmel experience was the joint composition, "The Abalone Song." Its basis was a simple quatrain with a simple point. Here's one example:

*The young Jack London,
already a success and
romantically portrayed*
New York Public Library

> Some stick to biz, some flirt with Liz
> Down on the sands of Coney,
> But we, by hell, stay in Carmel,
> And whang the abalone.

This bit of doggerel notwithstanding, Sterling was a successful poet and, as London characterized him in *Martin Eden*, was probably not overanxious for fame. Indeed, when both he and Carmel suddenly became famous as the result of a poem he published in *Cosmopolitan* in 1907, Sterling suspected William Randolph Hearst of spreading his notoriety in order to sell magazines. Outraged at the torrent of visitors descending on Carmel, he remarked, "It's as though he had launched a drove of swine into my big sitting room." Failure didn't kill George Sterling; the good life did. As he grew older and his body fell away from his control, he at last took the cyanide he'd been keeping in an envelope marked "peace."

One of Sterling's firmest friendships was with a reclusive poet who moved with his wife to Big Sur, a few miles south of Carmel, in 1914, and stayed the rest of his life. Robinson Jeffers lived near Sterling's former haunt, but he was as far in temperament from its hedonism as though he'd been on the other side of the world. Still, it was Jeffers who wrote Sterling's elegy, called "Winter Sundown," whose ending fuses the two men to a particular landscape focus.

> The gray mothers of rain sail and glide over,
> The rain has fallen, the deep-wombed earth is renewed;
> Under the greening of the hills
> Gulls flock in the back furrows.

> And how shall one believe he will not return
> To be our guest in the house, not wander with me
> Again by the Carmel river,
> Nor on the reef at Soberanes?

Opinion is divided as to whether this and other Jeffers poems are great or lousy. Though none dispute the sentiment. The two leading members of the post-World War II San Francisco Renaissance, William Everson and Kenneth Rexroth, who have enormous respect for each other, diverge on this point. Everson cites the whole poem reverently in his *Archetype West* and goes on to assign Jeffers first place among the writers of the Pacific Coast. Rexroth, on the other hand, declared about Jeffers, "In my opinion, the verse is shoddy and pretentious and the philosophizing is nothing but posturing."

When Jeffers is good, however, as he is in that elegy and in narrative poems like "The Roan Stallion" and "Tamar," he achieves a rare symbiosis of character and landscape. He explains his discovery of the Monterey Coast in his Introduction to the 1938 *Selected Poems*.

I could see people living—amid magnificent scenery—
essentially as they did in the Idyls or the Sagas, or in
Homer's Ithica. Here was life purged of its ephemeral
accretions. Men were riding after cattle, or plowing the
headland, hovered by white sea gulls, as they have done for
thousands of years, and will for thousands of years to
come. Here was contemporary life that was also permanent life; and not shut from the modern world but conscious of it and related to it; capable of expressing its spirit,
but unencumbered by the mass of poetically irrelevant
details and complexities that make a civilization.

Where rhyme helped Joaquin Miller and Sterling himself fade away in
airy platitudes, freedom from rhyme lets Jeffers complicate his plots, his
rhythms, and his landscapes. For all that Jeffers may stick to hardy motifs of
classical tragedy.

Half-way between sea and sky, beaten on by both,
Burning with light; wakening she found she had
    tumbled
The bed-clothes to the floor and torn her night-gown
To rags, and was alone in the room, and blinded
By the great glare of the sun in the western windows.

Tamar has seduced her brother; later, she'll be raped by the spirits on the
coast at night; the whole family will die when their house burns. Why is
this not ludicrous to read? "Naturally, when a man lives virtually alone for
so long, he'll start to see rapes in the sky and families dying in burning
houses. Just bring him back among his fellows and he'll be all right." That's
the therapeutic answer to Jeffers; but he also reveals in these narratives an
isolation not merely his own but fundamental to the West Coast. There
seems to be some way in which, under that terrible white light that
transfixes Tamar, every Californian has a relationship first to his or her
own strong shadow, and only then to the rest of the human race.

BETWEEN JEFFERS'S COUNTRY ON THE COAST and the great Central Valley
lies the Salinas Valley, and accordioned up even closer to the Coast Range
is the little subvalley of the Jolon. Here, the family of John Steinbeck's *The
Red Pony* lives in an isolation nearly as complete as Jeffers's. Jody, the child
of the family, looks at the mountains to the west and imagines the
mysteries beyond his sight:

He thought often of the miles of ridge after ridge until at
last there was the sea. When the peaks were pink in the
morning they invited him among them; and when the sun
had gone over the edge in the evening and the mountains

were a purple-like despair, then Jody was afraid of them; then they were so impersonal and aloof that their very imperturbability was a threat.

Now he turned his head towards the mountains of the east, the Gabilans, and they were jolly mountains, with hill ranches in their creases, and with pine trees growing on the crests. People lived there, and battles had been fought against the Mexicans on the slopes. He looked back for an instant at the Great Ones and shivered a little at the contrast. The foothill cup of the home ranch below him was sunny and safe. The house gleamed with white light and the barn was brown and warm. The red cows on the farther hill ate their way slowly toward the north. Even the dark cypress tree by the bunkhouse was usual and safe. The chickens scratched about in the dust of the farmyard with quick waltzing steps.

The young Steinbeck clears a small space for himself to write about, sandwiched between the epics of the Valley and the tragedies of the Coast. Even in this space, however, innocence is only one step away from terror— nature is unpredictable. On the way from school, Jody fills his lunchbox with "two more horny toads, four little grass lizards, a blue snake, sixteen yellow-winged grasshoppers and a brown damp newt from under a rock." His mother is understandably surprised. His father buys him a red pony which he lovingly cares for and trains. After spending a day in a cold rain, it begins to die. Jody sleeps out in the stable with it; the night wind blows open the barn door, and the horse goes out. At dawn, the boy wakes and chases it:

The wet ground muffled his steps and the brush hid him. When he arrived, it was all over. The first buzzard sat on the pony's head and its beak had just risen dripping with dark eye fluid. Jody plunged into the circle like a cat. The black brotherhood arose in a cloud, but the big one on the pony's head was too late. As it hopped to take off, Jody caught its wing tip and pulled it down. It was nearly as big as he was. The free wing crashed into his face with the force of a club, but he hung on. The claws fastened on his leg and the wing elbows battered his head on either side. Jody groped blindly with his free hand. His fingers found the neck of the struggling bird. The red eyes looked into his face.... He held the neck to the ground with one hand while the other found a piece of sharp white quartz. The first blow broke the beak sideways and black blood spurted from the twisted, leathery mouth corners.... He was still beating the dead bird when Billy Buck pulled him off and held him tightly to calm his shaking.

This is as strong and harsh a moment as anything in Steinbeck. Too often, even in his best known books, *Tortilla Flat* and *The Grapes of Wrath*, Steinbeck lets homespun philosophies stand between his characters and their feelings.

The Grapes of Wrath is an epical book, and there's no doubt that it bulked heavy in the minds of the judges who awarded John Steinbeck the Nobel Prize in 1962. It tells the story of the Okies who were driven West during the Depression and ended up migrant laborers in California's Central Valley. The book is much more honestly the story of a people's struggle than is Frank Norris's *The Octopus*, but its characters seem equally foredoomed. The relentless brutality practiced by bank agents, sheriffs, and farmers against the Okie immigrants takes over the rhythm of the book.

Steinbeck says goodbye to the California of *The Red Pony* in *The Grapes of Wrath*. In the latter book, the state has become the prime example of how in America the rich rob the poor:

> Once California belonged to Mexico and its land to Mexicans; and a horde of tattered, feverish Americans poured in. And such was their hunger for land that they took the land—stole Sutter's land, Guerrero's land, took the grants and broke them up and growled and quarrelled over them, those frantic hungry men; and they guarded with guns the land they had stolen. They put up houses and barns, they turned the earth and planted crops. And these things were possession, and possession was ownership.

Etcetera. Steinbeck moved from California to New York in 1939 and never returned but to visit. He used the California landscape in later books, but never again would he get as near the region's life as he had before *The Grapes* except perhaps in parts of *East of Eden*, which, again, begins as a book about a boy.

If Steinbeck was at his best when he used boys as narrators, his contemporary from the Central Valley, William Saroyan, seems to some never to have left off being a boy. Saroyan himself admits there's truth to this assertion. In his Preface to the First Edition of *The Daring Young Man on the Flying Trapeze*, the Fresno-born Saroyan outlines in brief his rules for writing:

> I wrote rule Number One when I was eleven and had just been sent home from the fourth grade for having talked out of turn and meant it. Do not pay attention to the rules other people make, I wrote. They make them for their own protection, and the hell with them. (I was pretty sore that day.)

But doing exactly what he likes is a very difficult thing for Saroyan. It is just as willful as Jeffers's bringing Greek plots to the Big Sur coast. Saroyan's sketches and stories are so short and well-integrated that they seem like spontaneous utterance. It must take enormous concentration on the writer's part just to maintain this quite real spontaneity, to prevent the invasion of cliché.

Whether he's writing the children's tales found in *My Name is Aram* or the Depression sketches of *The Daring Young Man on the Flying Trapeze*, he delights with an optimism that is always turning to pessimism, then back to optimism again.

> In order not to be a fool, you must believe that as much as death is inevitable, life is inevitable. That is, the earth is inevitable and people and other living things on it are inevitable, but no man can remain on the earth very long.... If you will remember that living people are as good as dead, you will be able to perceive much that is very funny in their conduct that you might perhaps never have thought of perceiving if you did not perceive that they were as good as dead.

The other new element in Saroyan in California literature, it should be said here, is unassimilated racial diversity. For a change the primacy of the Anglo-Saxon is set aside. A Yale-educated grocer questions Aram and his friends in "The Three Swimmers and the Educated Grocer":

> Well, I'll be gathered into a pile and burned, the grocer said. Now, boys, tell me—of what race are you? Californians or foreigners?
> We're all Californians, Joe said. I was born on G Street in Fresno. Mourad here was born on Walnut Avenue or someplace on the other side of the Southern Pacific tracks, I guess, and his cousin somewhere in that neighborhood, too.
> Well, I'll be irrigated. Now, tell me, boys, what sort of educations have you got?
> We ain't educated, Joe said.
> Well, I'll be picked off a tree and thrown into a box. Now, tell me, boys, what foreign languages do you speak?
> I speak Portugese, Joe said.
> *You* ain't educated? I have a degree from Yale, my boy, and I can't speak Portugese. And you, son, how about you?
> I speak Armenian, my cousin Mourad said.
> Well, I'll be cut off a vine and eaten grape by grape by a girl in her teens. I can't speak a word of Armenian and I'm a

college graduate, class of 1892. Now, tell me, son, what's
your name?
 Aram Garoghlanian....
 And what strange foreign language do *you* speak?
 I speak Armenian, too. That's my cousin, *Mourad*
Garoghlanian.

Saroyan is as gregarious as Jeffers is solitary, but both raise their own
interior life (and that of their characters) to the surface of the narrative. The
obvious question about assimilation that this sketch raises is answered by
Saroyan not in a discussion of the problem but in a sketch called "70,000
Assyrians." Once again, a California writer refuses to analyze an event, but
instead lets it stand and create its own wealth of meaning. An Assyrian
barber in San Francisco complains to Saroyan about the certainty of the
destruction of his people, regarding it as already accomplished. "Now we
are a topic in ancient history," he says. Saroyan goes home and thinks of
those 70,000 remaining Assyrians, "a great race," one by one.

COMPARED WITH THE LOVING DETAIL that these writers lavished on their
West Coast locales, it would seem, at first, that Dashiell Hammett is no San
Franciscan at all. Illness brought him to the West in the first place, and he
spent only the years 1921 to 1929 in San Francisco. The San Francisco of the
Continental Op stories as well as of Sam Spade and *The Maltese Falcon* is a
town of addresses rather than descriptions. Nonetheless, like Richard
Henry Dana long before him and Allen Ginsburg a quarter-century after
him, Hammett would find his voice on the Pacific. In return, he put San
Francisco on the map as an American city, as capable of roaring as the
Chicago or New York of the 1920s, but with an air of fantasy all its own.
 Hammett had worked for the Pinkertons in the East; when he was
released from a California tuberculosis sanatarium in 1921, he took a job
with the San Francisco branch of the same detective agency, and moved
there with his new wife. Neither his job nor his marriage lasted through the
year. He took a room and wrote advertising copy and detective stories. He
began to publish the latter in 1922, placing them chiefly with the pulp
magazine *Black Mask*. Between that date and 1930, Hammett and *Black
Mask* were synonymous with the so-called hard-boiled school of detective
writing. If this school had had any motto at all, it would have been "Out of
the drawing room and onto the street." It shifted the focus off the detective's brilliant mind and onto the ambiance of crime. Some Eastern literary
men, like Edmund Wilson, preferred the older kind of detective story
precisely because of its emphasis on analysis. The hard-boiled story had too
much action, too little reflection, for his taste. Though this group later

developed a national following, Dashiell Hammett in his San Francisco stories of the Continental Operative was its first great practitioner. This regional base for the tough-guy school might seem coincidental were it not for the fact that all three of its great writers—Hammett, Raymond Chandler, and Ross Macdonald—were Californians.

The pace of Hammett's *Continental Op* stories leaves no time for leisurely descriptions of the City by the Bay, but the story-by-story buildup of addresses and briefly sketched settings fills in a map of Prohibition San Francisco for the reader. The Continental detective agency's ace operative is following a suspicious character in "The Whosis Kid":

> He was alone. It was the simplest sort of shadowing. The streets were filled with departing fight fans. The Kid walked down to Fillmore Street, took on a stack of wheat cakes, bacon and coffee at a lunch room, and caught a No. 22 car.
>
> He—and likewise I—transferred to a No. 5 car at McAllister Street, dropped off at Polk, walked north one block, turned back west for a block and a fraction, and went up the front stairs of a dingy light-housekeeping room establishment that occupied the second and third floors over a repair shop on the south side of Golden Gate Avenue, between Van Ness and Franklin.

With the same economy, Hammett's tales can journey to posh Russian Hill or down the coast to the roadhouses of Half Moon Bay. "The Girl with the Silver Eyes"—probably the best "black widow" detective story ever written —follows exactly this trajectory.

The poet Pangborn has lost his girl. He's the perfect rich bohemian; he is supported by his brother-in-law, a mining magnate. When the detective asks for a precise description of the missing beloved, the poet blurts out, "She's beautiful! The most beautiful woman in the world!" "That would look nice on a reward circular," thinks the Op. He gets down to specifics: "What color eyes?" Pangborn rhapsodizes, "You've seen shadows on polished silver when...." "I wrote down *gray eyes* and hurried on with the interrogation." Pangborn is a kind of degenerated George Sterling.

The story ends in Half Moon Bay, where the poet dies, far from his home seraglio. Actually, Half Moon Bay is only 20 miles down the coast from the city, but it's as long as 30 years between bohemian and prohibition San Francisco. The finale comes at a roadhouse called the White Shack which is "a relay station for the booze that comes through Half Moon Bay for points beyond." San Francisco loses its half-finished look in Hammett. It becomes an urban place, replete with store-bought illusions and the guns to back them up or blow them down.

IF SAN FRANCISCO GOT A HEADSTART on Los Angeles as an urban place, it didn't take the city of Los Angeles long to catch up. Richard Henry Dana landed on the coast near what is now Long Beach and found it a "desolate-looking place," noting only its fame as a cattle-producing region and the reputed existence of the large Pueblo de Los Angeles 30 miles inland. By the time Joan Didion began to write about it in the 1960s, it had expanded in one direction to the sea and in the other to the slopes of the mountain range behind, not a traditional city but a string of suburbs. The Los Angeles boom had begun in the 1880s, when ranchers first subdivided their land, but settlers didn't flood in until the Southern Pacific Railroad reached Los Angeles. In 1887, the Santa Fe Railroad followed the Southern Pacific into the area, and a fare war ensued. At one point, you could travel from Kansas City to Los Angeles for $1.00! Lured by the low rates and the promise of a healthy climate, settlers flocked to L.A. Fully a quarter of the residents at the turn of the century had come for their health.

The intense physicality of Los Angeles culture, then, predated the emergence of "Hollywood Babylon." The English poet W. H. Auden, observing from his New York perch, claimed that Americans went to California to die; on the contrary, they went to find prolonged and pleasant life. The motion picture industry was itself attracted West by the mild, dry climate of the area and the availability of every type of natural scenery within a radius of 50 miles. It was also attracted by the large pool of non-unionized workers—all those recent arrivals—who would work for rates typically half those demanded in New York. Hollywood meant two things to the largely fundamentalist and Midwestern population that had occupied LA before the movies came: sin and jobs.

The first Hollywood novel to achieve a lasting reputation—*The Day of the Locust* (1939), by the screenwriter Nathaniel West—is built on just this model. Its writer, the son of a well-to-do New York building operator, was close enough to the Hollywood community to describe it well. His moral distance, however, often makes him confuse the merely grotesque with the truly horrible. The crush at a Hollywood premiere and the lowlife extras like West's dwarf and the cowboy are less frightening Hollywood facts than is the relentless ease with which reality bends at the touch of a monied hand.

What makes the book fine reading is the accuracy of the character portraits elaborated in the interstices of an otherwise predictable plot. Faye Greener and her father, for instance, are drawn far beyond the necessary type. A scene in which the father, a vaudeville clown turned salesman, tries to sell his silver polish to a recent immigrant from Iowa, blurs the distinction between the actor and the man. Not even his daughter can tell clearly if he's having a heart attack or just elaborating on his sales pitch. The daughter, an unknown aspiring to stardom who generally measures men by wealth, influence, and good looks, comes close to breaking the

The movie poster for The Day of The Locust.
Paramount Pictures

book's cynicism in one scene. Tod, who wants to sleep with Faye, sits up with her, talking, while her father is sick. She tells him what she does with her idle days:

> She would get some music on the radio, then lie down on her bed and shut her eyes. She had a large assortment of stories to choose from. After getting herself in the right mood, she would go over them in her mind, as though they were a pack of cards, discarding one after another until she found the one that suited. On some days, she would run through the whole pack without making a choice. When that happened, she would either go to Vine Street for an ice cream soda or, if she was broke, thumb over the pack again and force herself to choose.
>
> While she admitted that her method was too mechanical for the best results and that it was better to slip into a dream naturally, she said that any dream was better than no dream and beggars couldn't be choosers.

The deadpan tone of this passage adds to its effect, but Tod carefully keeps himself free of the complications that might result from raising his voice.

Nathaniel West was a mediocre screenwriter. He came with no reputation, started at the bottom of the pay scale, and worked himself into a decent living. The Hollywood of the 1930s would, however, pay an established writer handsomely to write screenplays. Such literary notables as F. Scott Fitzgerald, William Faulkner, Aldous Huxley, S. J. Perelman, and James Agee were lured to Hollywood. While Faulkner's work with Howard Hawks and Agee's with John Huston are remembered in film history, Fitzgerald's and Huxley's permanent contributions to Hollywood are in the novels it gave them the material to write. Fitzgerald died before he could finish *The Last Tycoon*, though as much as he had completed was published in 1941. The roughness of the book betrays the fact that it was no more than a part of a first draft. It might have told a Hollywood story from the point of view of an insider, showing the connections of Eastern capital and Western production facilities. Huxley's California books, *After Many a Summer Dies the Swan* and *Ape and Essence*, are, for the most part, like West's novel, the work of an outside observer.

Huxley, the Englishman, stands at an even greater psychic distance from southern California than does West. So, like the man who lives 50 miles from the slum instead of right next door, he is more willing than the New Yorker to give Los Angeles the benefit of the doubt. Jeremy Pordage, his English scholar narrator in *After Many a Summer*, is impressed by, for example, Beverly Hills architecture: "elegant and witty pastiches of Lutyens manor houses, of little Trianons, of Monticellos; light-hearted parodies of Le Corbusier's machines-for-living-in; fantastic adaptations of Mexican haciendas and New England farms." Pordage's unfamiliarity with the culture makes him a wonderfully wide-eyed observer, and the ride into Los Angeles at the opening of the book is, as observed by Pordage, one of the great pieces of reportage about the city.

> The first thing to present itself was a slum of Africans and Filipinos, Japanese and Mexicans. And what permutations and combinations of black, yellow and brown! What complex bastardies! And the girls—how beautiful in their artificial silk! "And Negro ladies in white muslin gowns." His favorite line in *The Prelude*. He smiled to himself. And meanwhile the slum had given way to the tall buildings of a business district. The population took on a more Caucasian tinge. At every corner there was a drug-store. The newspaper boys were selling headlines about Franco's drive on Barcelona. Most of the girls as they walked alone, seemed to be absorbed in silent prayer; but he supposed, on second thought, it was only gum that they were incessantly ruminating. Gum, not God. Then suddenly the car

plunged into a tunnel and emerged into another world, a vast, untidy suburban world of filling stations and billboards, of low houses in gardens, of vacant lots and waste paper, of occasional shops and office buildings and churches—primitive Methodist churches built, surprisingly enough, in the style of the Cartuja at Granada, Catholic churches like Canterbury Cathedral, synagogues disguised as Hagia Sophia, Christian Science churches with pillars and pedestals like banks....

Los Angeles is a city stretched out along a roadway, from slum to suburb to center to cemetery to the great exurban palace of the magnate Stoyte. Pordage's description of the mansion, which he refers to as "the Object," is almost as fine as a guided tour of Hearst Castle, the monument on which it's based. His anatomy of the cemetery, modeled on Forest Lawn with its replica of Shakespeare's tomb, its Perpetual Wurlitzer organ music, its marble Vestibule of Ashes, and its garden full of the statues of nubile naked girls is quite as delightful as Evelyn Waugh's in *The Loved One*, a book wholly devoted to the subject.

But as an outsider, Huxley necessarily has to cast all this as some kind of problem. The problem is mortality. Stoyte—with his lively cemetery, his statuesque mistress, his Dr. Obispo experimenting with youth potions, and his castle which tries to convert time into space by anthologizing all the world's treasures within its precincts—is simply trying to prove what he once blurts out: "God is love. There is no death." The narrator constructs a lasting quote, which is supposed to have been the Puritan motto on which Stoyte was raised: "It is a terrible thing to fall into the hands of the living God." Stoyte's life is thus an effort to forget his childhood's model and substitute its contrary.

After Many a Summer is as good a Los Angeles book as the more well-known *Day of the Locust*, but both are books about ideas rather than things or people. Huxley's *Ape and Essence* starts out as though it were going to be a book in which its narrator participated rather than observed. The novel opens in a somber, post-war world on the day of Gandhi's assassination. The narrator spends the first five pages demolishing the character of the screenwriter, Bob, a limp and whining lecher. The story is as tough as anything by Joan Didion. In final justification of his refusal to budge on Bob's salary, the producer Lublin exclaims, "In this studio, at this time, not even Jesus Christ himself could get a raise." After this promising opening, however, Bob and the narrator discover a rejected script thrown from a truck on its way to the incinerator. The rest of the novel consists of the script, a post-apocalyptic story about explorers from New Zealand returning to Los Angeles many years after the Bomb has destroyed western civilization. Again, the idea jumps out ahead of the action. The screenplay shows only that in order to write science fiction about Los Angeles, it has to be blown up first. Anything less, and science fiction would quickly have been subsumed by reality.

It was Raymond Chandler who turned Los Angeles from a literary plaything into a city where people work and die. Lawrence Clark Powell, himself an Angeleno and the writer of the authoritative *California Classics*, describes Chandler's achievement:

> In those four miraculous novels, *The Big Sleep, Farewell, My Lovely, The High Window*, and *The Lady in the Lake*, Chandler stopped the Los Angeles kaleidoscope; he arrested its spinning, so confusing to most writers who have tried to see the city clearly; and then he fixed in prose of poetic intensity the brilliant bits and pieces, until he found in his "Big Four" a glittering mosaic of greater Los Angeles from San Bernardino to the sea.

The "Big Four" were written between 1939 and 1943 by a middle-aged former oilman. Driven out of the oil business by the Depression in 1933, Chandler sold his first story to *Black Mask* for $180 and "never looked back." He, too, turned briefly to screenwriting after the fever of his four creative years had passed, writing the script for James M. Cain's *Double Indemnity* as well as the original screenplay of *The Blue Dahlia*. Of the novels he wrote after that, only one, *The Long Goodbye*, comes up to the level of his earlier work.

It is difficult to abstract any one quote from Chandler because he covered so much of the varied Los Angeles scene: his office with the automatic doorbell and the secretary-less waiting room; the homes of the rich, the lousy hotels and jail cells; the smell of pepper trees; the hot dry Santa Ana winds that blow in October from the South; the clapboard spas hidden in the hills just outside town; the fog-shrouded beach roads that make the world a "wet emptiness." Over the course of books, he even shows the change in places. The "Idle Valley" that is a rich people's hideaway blessed by sea winds even in midsummer in *The Long Goodbye* was the same locale used as the home of fancy speakeasies in *The High Window*; before that even, it was the home of respectable estates. A place can go from being the devil's den to paradise by the provident application of the right kinds of money.

The third of the great hard-boiled detectives is Ross Macdonald's Lew Archer, and if he represents one place less securely than does Chandler's Marlowe, he shows a whole way of life more surely. Though Archer started as a tough guy in postwar Los Angeles, he soon divorced his wife and went into therapy. He has a soft spot in his heart for mad people and his clients' children. Lew Archer is the detective of the suburban middle class. Where the Santa Barbara of Chandler's novels is a haven for the wealthy, by Macdonald's time it has come to serve the same function for the upper middle class. These people have enough money to cover the tracks of their mistakes, but not enough to provoke a scandal if they fail.

Archer is as mobile as the highways of postwar California can make him, but whether his clients live near San Diego, San Francisco, or in the hills above Santa Theresa (his version of Santa Barbara), their homes look something like this:

> I drove up to the house on a private road that widened at the summit into a parking apron. When I got out of my car I could look back over the city and see the towers of the mission and the courthouse half submerged in smog. The channel lay on the other side of the ridge, partly enclosed by its broken girdle of islands.
>
> The only sound I could hear, apart from the hum of the freeway that I had just left, was the noise of a tennis ball being hit back and forth. The court was at the side of the house, enclosed by high wire mesh. A thick-bodied man in shorts and a linen hat was playing against an agile blond woman. Something about the trapped intensity of their game reminded me of prisoners in an exercise yard....
>
> The house was a sprawling pile of white stucco and red tile, set on the highest point in Santa Theresa. The only things higher were the mountains standing behind the city and a red-tailed hawk circling in the bright October sky.

Santa Barbara is the apogee of California bourgeois culture, and this house is the archetypal residence of the nouveau riche, designed to be seen, not lived in, "It was more like a public building than a house—the kind of place where you go to pay your taxes or get a divorce." Predictably, the Biemeyers' problem in The Blue Hammer is not a murder, but the loss of a valued painting. The painting implies a half-hidden adulturous affair and ultimately leads to a neglected daughter who had everything money could buy.

In most of the Lew Archer novels the problem is the same. Parents living the California dream have deprived their children of the past. They hope that their offspring will be able to leap to even greater heights than they have by avoiding any of the gritty knowledge of their origins. In Macdonald's work, the origins are more often grisly, and it is only by fully understanding their past that the children are able to escape the shadows of their parents' lies.

THE BEST SOURCE FOR AN INTRODUCTION to the still-active postwar generation in San Francisco is Kenneth Rexroth's "The Second Post-War, The Second Interbellum," which appears in his 1970 volume of essays entitled *The Alternative Society*. Allen Ginsberg and Jack Kerouac, the first names usually associated with the group, were only a moment in a general trend. They came from the East, were energized in San Francisco, and went away again. Before them came William Everson (also known as Brother Antoninus during his years as a Dominican lay brother), Robert Duncan, and Kenneth Rexroth himself. Slightly younger than these, but still wedded to the San Francisco scene, are Lawrence Ferlinghetti and Michael McClure. These two are quintessential oral poets, Ferlinghetti reading many of his poems to jazz accompaniments and McClure writing a

City Lights Bookstore, home to the San Francisco Beats, provided a forum for both their readings and their books.
The Bancroft Library University of California, Berkeley

"beast language" which requires oral performance for its full energy. McClure's 1964 *Ghost Tantras* are a kind of pre-human shouting, but their validation is the pleasure they are for anyone (not just the whacked-out poet) to perform. Number 1 begins "GOOOOOOR! GOOOOOOOOOO!/ GOOOOOOOOOR!/GRAHHH! GRAHH! GRAHH!..."

Slightly after McClure and Ferlinghetti, the real younger generation of the San Francisco Renaissance arrived: Gary Snyder and Philip Whalen, both Northwestern natives who had attended Reed College in Oregon.

That this group of poets is associated chiefly with Allen Ginsberg's book *Howl* is due to several coincidences. Ginsberg, Gregory Corso, and Jack Kerouac had but recently arrived in San Francisco in 1955 when Kenneth Rexroth invited Ginsberg and Corso to participate in a reading at the Six Gallery. Also reading were Duncan, Brother Antoninus, Lamantia, Ferlinghetti, McClure, Snyder, and Whalen. Ginsberg read *Howl* there for the first time, and it brought down the house. Articles in *Life* magazine, together with the obscenity trial of *Howl*, brought the reading and the so-called Beats to national attention. Kerouac's novel *The Dharma Bums* was a *roman a clef* which, though it gave prominent place to Japhy Ryder (that is, Gary Snyder), so sensationalized both him and the rest of the group as to justify every *Life*-inspired notion of the poets as wild men and hedonists. That *Howl* is one of the most important poems of its time is true—Everson compares its impact to that of Edwin Markham's "The Man with the Hoe" at the turn of the century—but it is barely a part of the San Francisco Renaissance at all.

The real members of that group, according to Rexroth, came largely out of San Francisco's radical 1930s and were influenced by pacifists who'd served in the Northwest's conscientious-objectors' camps during the war. They held in common a profound distrust of government. They admired, for example, Simone Weil's 1934 essay, "The Next World War." In it, she had said, "War in the last analysis appears as a struggle led by all the State apparatuses and general staffs against all men old enough and able to bear arms."

The general solution of the San Franciscans was, again in Rexroth's terms, "disengagement" from the existing social pattern and meditation on reasonable alternatives. This is far from wild-eyed hedonism. A measure of just how far is the realization that the three main figures of the Renaissance —Rexroth, Everson, and Snyder—are all quite as cogent essayists as they are startling poets. No reader should neglect Rexroth's three collections of essays (*Assays* and *Bird in the Bush*, besides the one already mentioned), Everson's *Archetype West*, or Snyder's *The Old Ways*. None of these poets accepts the traditional literary notion of a great line of poets filiating throughout western history. On the contrary, each seeks such predecessors as will lead him to the essential facts about the present condition on the West Coast as it relates to the whole world.

This is much what Jeffers wanted to find—a modern world but cleansed of all extraneous accretions—and indeed Everson looks to Jeffers as his predecessor not for that poet's skill at fables but for the direct, high style that will let him confront the principle of plenitude with the facts of corruption. These are not new themes, but where his Eastern counterparts represent the difficulty, Everson enacts it. Everson, like Jeffers or Muir, is frequently embarrassing in his repeated grand invocations, but he is seldom simply posing. From his youth poems about the Central Valley, to his war poems, to his sex poems, and his Catholic poems, he "cries out for another future," never forgetting the look of life around him.

Rexroth reaches to anything from Greek poets, to Japanese and Chinese poets, to a landscape, to his lost wife, looking for the essence in existence. In his great long poem, "The Phoenix and the Tortoise" (1940–44), he spends the night on a Calfornia beach, unable to sleep, wondering what he or anybody else is doing there in the middle of a senseless war:

> And I,
> walking by the viscid, menacing
> Water, turn with my heavy heart
> In my baffled brain, Plutarch's page—
> the falling light of the Spartan
> Heroes in the late Hellenic dusk—
> Agis, Cleomenes—this poem
> Of the phoenix and the tortoise—
> of what survives and what perishes.
> And how, of the fall of history
> And waste of fact—on the crumbling
> Edge of a ruined polity
> That washed away in an ocean
> Whose shores are all washing into death.

The poem is spent in contemplative agony; only the dawn and his naked wife can break the spell. Where Everson is ecstatic, Rexroth is contemplative. Everson takes less than 40 lines to dismiss Churchill and his war as terrible but irrelevant in "The Unkillable Knowledge"; Rexroth takes hundreds to weigh basically the same question.

Snyder comes from leftist, pacifist roots, but he is not of the war generation. He looks back in a direct and uncomplicated way to northwest Indian lore and the people like Jaime de Angulo (author of the neglected classic Indian Tales) who helped transmit it. He is also a true Zen monk (as distinguished from the faddish Zen of a Kerouac), conversant with the Japanese, Chinese, and Sanskrit languages. His first and as yet best book of poetry is called Myths and Texts. His poems are deceptively easy to imitate; anyone who can wax outdoorsy and mention particulars like pine bark, bearshit, berries, girls' tits, the names of mountains, can sound like

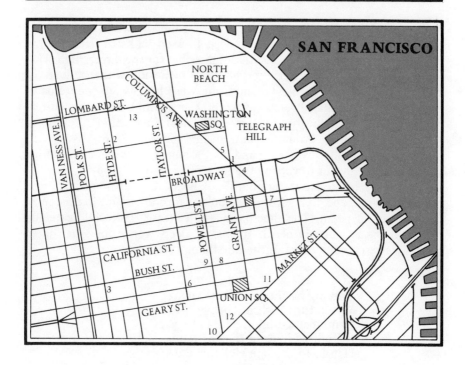

1   *City Lights Bookstore*
    261 Columbus Ave.

2   *Jack Kerouac*
    29 Russell St.

3   *Wentley Apartments*
    1214 Polk St.
    Allen Ginsberg wrote *Howl* here.

4   *Vesuvio's*
    255 Columbus Ave.
    Adjacent to City Lights, a hangout for
    the Beats.

5   *Cafe Trieste*
    601 Vallejo St.
    A popular Beat generation coffee
    house.

6   *Bohemian Club*
    Post and Taylor St.
    A private club started by journalists
    but occupied today chiefly by the
    wealthy.

7   *Trans America Pyramid*
    Built on the site of the Duncan Nicols
    Bank Exchange Salon, a literary bar.
    Part of the bar is preserved.

8   *Robert Louis Stevenson*
    608 Bush St.

9   *Dashiell Hammett*
    20 Monroe St.
    Where Hammett wrote *The Maltese
    Falcon.*

10 *Flood Building*
    San Francisco office of the Pinkerton
    Detective Agency where Hammett
    worked.

11 *Hearst Building*
    Offices of the San Francisco Examiner,
    whose contributors included Ambrose
    Bierce, Edwin Markham, and Joaquin
    Miller.

12 *John's Grill*
    63 Ellis St.
    Mentioned in *The Maltese Falcon.*

13 *Russian Hill*
    Home to many San Francisco writers.

Snyder. Kerouac made a whole book trying. Snyder's synthetic reach is huge not because he is irresponsible, but because he believes western civilization has reached the end of its "40,000 year loop," and that now everyone must concentrate on reinhabiting the earth as an ecosystem, learning to respect it and live with it, instead of using it up. Snyder's poetry reaches far beyond its region, but its basic gesture is the effort to recover the kind of relationship to other beings that is revealed in the Indian texts of the northwest. His own poems borrow freely from such sources.

> I hold it
> I tell of it, standing
> I look here
> I look there
> Standing
> > great limp mouth
> > hanging loose in the air
> > quivers, turns in upon itself,
> > gone
> > with a diabolical laugh
> The night bat
> Rising flies, I tell it
> I sing it
>
> "Jesus was a great doctor, I guess he was
> the best gambler in the United States"
> at Hawwinyava
> Imagine a dark house
> Blue

The key to a good Snyder poem is the engagement of rhythm in a text that moves easily back and forth between pure narrative and shamanistic chant.

THE PRESENT-DAY LITERARY MAP of the Pacific states looks something like an exclamation point. The upper body stretches from around Santa Barbara north into Oregon and Washington. The dot extends as far in any direction as Los Angeles needs to look for water, living space, a new airport, or a shooting locale. But like the parts of the exclamation point, they need each other to mean what they do.

Three notable novelists of the last 20 years—Joan Didion, Ken Kesey, and Ursula K. Le Guin—seem at first glance to be strangers to each other's sensibilities: Kesey the masculine, Didion the neurotic, LeGuin the anthropologist's daughter writing sci-fi. A closer look finds that Jeffers's blood runs strong in all of them, and fuels the will to see reality purged of its civilized accretions. One thing that holds them all together is their radical distrust of psychotherapy, "the talking cure." Kesey's *One Flew Over the* distrust of psychotherapy, "the talking cure." Kesey's *One Flew Over the Cuckoo's Nest*, Didion's *Play It As It Lays*, her book of essays, *The White Album*, and LeGuin's *The Lathe of Heaven* all involve characters who eventually rise in revolt against manipulation by psychotherapy. For all three, it is the therapist who has the most fascinating and terrible delusions. The therapist, Haber, in LeGuin's *Lathe of Heaven* burns himself up with a furious will to power disguised as the desire to help people, but the most effective portrait of the type is not fiction at all. Didion's essay "James Pike, American" in her collection *The White Album* shows how a do-gooder's life is founded in exhibitionism, and makes him forgetful of his friends and of his past, and capable of taking a young wife with it into the desert with nothing but a bottle of Coke and delusions of grandeur to sustain them.

"What makes Iago evil? Some people ask. I never ask," says Maria at the beginning of Joan Didion's *Play It As It Lays*. The simple fact is sufficient for her, like the fact that sometimes a snake bites you and you die. Maria is in a psychiatric asylum. She is not violent or schizoid but disconnected; her husband complains about what psychiatrists call "inappropriate affect". She is there because, though she did not approve of it, she did not try to prevent a miserable man from committing suicide.

Play It As It Lays is the perfect Hollywood novel, succeeding where all of them have failed. It is both a frightening exposé and an accurate portrayal, because Maria, around whom all else revolves, is both the central character of the drama and herself the drama's observer. Maria's absolute free agency, coupled with the scene in which she floats, makes her an even freer observer of Los Angeles than Chandler's Marlowe. Like Hammett rather than Chandler, though, her vision of the region is visceral and shows itself in action rather than in set pieces:

> Once she was on a freeway and had maneuvered her way to a fast lane she turned on the radio at high volume and she drove. She drove the San Diego to the Harbor, the Harbor up to the Hollywood, the Hollywood to the Golden State, the Santa Monica, the Santa Ana, the Pasadena, the Ventura. She drove it as a riverman runs a river, every day more attuned to its currents, its deceptions, and just as a riverman feels the pull of the rapids in the lull between sleeping and waking, so Maria lay at night and saw the great signs soar overhead at seventy miles an hour, *Normandie ¼ Vermont ¾ Harbor Fwy 1.*

This kind of relentless factuality takes us from freeway to Hollywood parties to location shooting in the desert. It is abetted by a style which, though it is frequently praised for resembling cinematic cutting, serves largely to erase rather than suggest connecting generalities. Chapters are short, single scenes. Even negative abstractions are undercut. Towards the end, Maria writes off the people who have patronized her. "Never discuss," she says. "Cut. In that way I resemble the only man in Los Angeles County who does clean work." Earlier in the novel, the man who "does clean work" is the doctor who performs an abortion on Maria.

Whether or not Maria is crazy, she is accurate, and the only desire she herself expresses—to live a quiet life with her daughter and "do some canning"—is so sane compared with the lives of her compatriots it's frightening. Maria is by no means a self-portrait of Joan Didion, but they share the same passion for facts. Her books of essays, *Slouching Towards Bethlehem* and *The White Album*, never ask what good or evil is. The most common complaint about her writing is its slipperiness, its apparently *ad hoc* morality. One minute she is sniffing at the vulgarity of the house former Governor Ronald Reagan built in Sacramento, the next she is longing to run the machines that pump water all over California. Her essays are organized just the same way the novel is: short evocations of individual events or experiences. She seems to want to become the pure voice of her experience, because she believes there is nothing else worth her effort. She is the apotheosis of honesty.

Didion takes the kaleidoscope world of Huxley, West, and Chandler, cuts it up, and lists the pieces. Ken Kesey pushes the class-struggle novel north from the Central Valley, north even from Joaquin Miller's Mt. Shasta area, to an Oregon logging settlement, in his *Sometimes A Great Notion* (1963). Kesey was born in Colorado and educated in both Oregon and northern California. His great Western book is not a California or a Colorado book but an Oregon book. Like the emigrants who have fled north from a California too densely populated, Kesey gets to the primitive life on the land that California once had by leaving it for Oregon. His book follows the class-struggle novels of Norris and Steinbeck, but it claims a new literary geography and adds a new twist.

> Along the western slopes of the Oregon Coastal Range...
> come look: the hysterical crashing of tributaries as they
> merge into the Wakonda Auga River....
> The first little waves flashing like rushing winds
> through sheep sorrel and clover, ghost fern and nettle,
> sheering, cutting...forming branches. Then, through
> bearberry and salmonberry, blueberry and blackberry, the
> branches crashing into creeks, into streams. Finally, in the
> foothills, through tamarack and sugar pine, shittim bark
> and silver spruce—and the green blue mosaic of Douglas
> fir—the actual river falls five hundred feet...and look;
> opens out upon the fields. Metallic at first, seen from the
> highway down through the trees, like an aluminum rain-
> bow, like a slice of allow moon. Closer, becoming organic,

a very smile of water with broken and rotting pilings
jagged along both gums, foam clinging to the lips. Closer
still, it flattens into a river, flat as a street, cement-gray
with a texture of rain.

Rain and river are the two basic natural facts of Kesey's Oregon. The
labor organizer from California can't stand either one:

This will be the last of the Stamper business, the last of
this whole Northwest business for a good long time,
knock wood. After today, he can get back down south and
let some of that good old California Vitamin D dry up this
blasted skin rash. Always get skin rash up here. And
athlete's foot all the way to the ankle. The moisture. It's
certainly no wonder that this area has two or three natives
a month take that one-way dip—it's either drown your
blasted self or rot.

Notice that in the previous quote the river was compared to aluminum
and that this labor organizer sounds more like a bored bureaucrat than a
committed friend of the working man. Kesey's is a "second Interbellum"
world. The relationship of people to the land is regulated not only by
ownership but also by union rules. One measure of Kesey's committment
to a West Coast worldview is reflected in the union's status in this book: it
is not the friend but the enemy of the Stampers, the independent family of
loggers whose drama is the subject of the book.

The Stampers are marginal and proud to be so. Their way of life is as
conservative as the one Didion's Maria dreams of. Maria wants to just live
with her daughter and put up fruit for the winter. The Stampers live as a
clan, want their women in the kitchen, and respect resourcefulness before
a problem more than witty conversation. Theirs, and Kesey's, is a belliger-
ent conservatism, based on pride in a family's traditions. The strongest
scenes pit the Stampers against the river: this is where their qualities are
most admirable. There is no scene as frightening in the literature of the
Coast as that in which Hank Stamper tries to rescue his brother who is
trapped beneath a log on the water's edge from the river's rising tide. Hank
resorts to mouth-to-mouth resuscitation before he must finally let his
brother drown.

Ursula K. LeGuin, like Kesey, spent time in California before going
north. The daughter of the California anthropologist A. L. Kroeber, she has
written six volumes of science fiction and a book of poetry. Her poems are
influenced by Robinson Jeffers, and one of the sci-fi books, The Lathe of
Heaven, is an important book for the Pacific States. Huxley had to wipe out
Los Angeles in order to write science fiction about it. Le Guin works a
series of ecosystem mutations on a future Portland, Oregon.

> Rain was an old Portland tradition, but the warmth—70° F on the second of March—was modern, a result of air pollution. Urban and industrial effluvia had not been controlled soon enough to reverse the cumulative trends at work in the mid-Twentieth Century; it would take several centuries for the CO_2 to clear out of the air, if it ever did....
>
> It had always rained in western Oregon, but now it rained ceaselessly, steadily, tepidly. It was like living in a downpour of warm soup, forever.

This passage is a Sierra Club prophecy come true, but the book is not a Pacific novel for that alone. Its basic conflict is between the kind of social redeemer who would get rid of this and all other pollutions and ordinary man. George Orr happens to have dreams that change reality. He wants to be rid of them. Haber, the psychologist, who treats him, would like to use the "effective dreams" to make a perfect rule. The aborted futures that Haber's manipulations produce—plagues that reduce overpopulation by decimating the world, peace on earth brought about by an invasion from space—are warnings to the meliorism of the "helping professions" and their social-policy superiors. George Orr—like Didion's Maria and Kesey's Stampers—wants only to live an ordinary life. LeGuin chooses epigraphs for each chapter, mainly from the Taoists Lao Tse and Chuang Tse. The best aphorism for the whole book is this: "When the great way is lost, we get benevolence and righteousness." Still, in 1971, West Coast literature continues to be more interested in examples of life than of talking about it. Just before Haber, who has programmed the brain function that allows Orr to dream "effectively" so that he himself can experience it, destroys himself, Orr proposes to him an alternative theory of dreams. It sounds like Gary Snyder out of Robinson Jeffers:

> Everything dreams. The play of form, of being, is the dreaming of substance. Rocks have their dreams, and the earth changes.... But when the mind becomes conscious, when the rate of evolution speeds up, then you have to be careful. Careful of the world. You must learn the way. You must learn the skills, the arts, the limits. A conscious mind must be part of the whole, intentionally and carefully—as the rock is part of the whole unconsciously.

Taking her cue from Chinese philosophy, LeGuin promotes dream into the very fabric of reality. Like the first explorers of California and like all those who have gone there since, LeGuin does not attempt to explain dream, but sees it as part of the continuing interplay of fact and fiction. The mirror image of Joan Didion, where that writer "cuts," LeGuin weaves. But neither would wonder "what makes Iago evil."

BIBLIOGRAPHY

NEW YORK & ENVIRONS

Atherton, Gertrude. *Black Oxen.* New York: Boni and Liveright, 1923.

Brace, Charles Loring. *The Dangerous Classes of New York.* New York: Wynkoop and Hallenbeck, 1872.

Brooks, Van Wyck. *The Times of Melville and Whitman.* New York: Dutton, 1947.

—— *The World of Washington Irving.* New York: Dutton, 1944.

Cahan, Abraham. *The Rise of David Levinsky.* New York: Harper and Bros., 1917.

—— *Yekl, A Tale of the New York Ghetto.* New York: Appleton, 1896.

Cheever, John. "Moving Out." *Esquire: The Best of Forty Years.* New York: McKay, 1973.

Churchill, Allen. *The Improper Bohemians.* New York: Dutton, 1959.

Cooper, James Fenimore. *The Pioneers.* New York: John Wiley, 1823.

—— *Satanstoe.* New York: Stringer and Townsend, 1852.

Corso, Gregory. *Long Live Man.* New York: New Directions, 1962.

Crane, Hart. *Complete poems and selected letters and prose.* New York: Liveright, 1966.

Crane, Stephen. *Maggie: A Girl of the Streets.* New York: Appleton, 1896.

Cullen, Countee. *Color.* New York: Harper and Bros., 1925.

Davenport, Marcia. *East Side, West Side.* New York: Scribner's, 1947.

Dos Passos, John. *Manhattan Transfer.* New York: Harper, 1925.

Dreiser, Theodore. *A Book About Myself.* New York: Boni and Liveright, 1922.

—— *The Color of a Great City.* New York: Boni and Liveright, 1923.

Drennan, Robert E. (ed.) The *Algonquin Wits.* Secaucus, NJ: Citadel, 1968.

Ferguson, Blanche E. *Countee Cullen and the Negro Renaissance.* New York: Dodd, Mead, 1966.

Ginsberg, Allen. *Howl.* San Francisco: City Lights Books, 1963.

Goodman, Nathan (ed.). *A Benjamin Franklin Reader.* New York: Crowell, 1971.

Gruen, John. *The New Bohemia.* New York: Grosset and Dunlap, 1966.

Huggins, Nathan I. *Harlem Renaissance.* New York: Oxford, 1971.

Hughes, Langston. *The Weary Blues.* New York: Alfred A. Knopf, 1926.

Irving, Washington. "Sleepy Hollow", in *The Collected Works of....* New York: Greystone Press, 1940.

Irving, Washington. *Letters of Jonathan Oldstyle, Gent.* New York: Wilson, 1824.

Irving, Washington, William Irving, and J.K. Paulding. *Salmagundi.* New York: Longworth, 1807-8.

—— *The Sketch Book.* New York: Van Winkle, 1819-20.

James, Henry. *Notes of a Son and Brother.* New York: Scribner's, 1914.

—— *A Small Boy and Others.* New York: Scribner's, 1913.

—— *Washington Square.* New York: Harper and Bros., 1881.

Kaplan, Justin. *Lincoln Steffens: A Biography.* New York: Simon & Schuster, 1974.

Locke, Alain (ed.). *The New Negro.* New York: Boni and Liveright, 1925.

Mailer, Norman. *Advertisements for Myself.* New York: Putnam's, 1959.

—— *The Naked and the Dead.* New York: Rinehart, 1948.

McKay, Claude. *Harlem Shadows.* New York: Harcourt, Brace, 1922.

—— *Home to Harlem.* New York: Harper and Bros., 1928.

Mencken, H.L. *Happy Days 1880-1892.* New York: Alfred A. Knopf, 1940.

Millay, Edna St. Vincent. *Collected Poems.* New York: Harper & Row, 1956.

O'Hara, Frank. *Collected Poems of....* New York: Knopf, 1965.

O'Hara, John. *The Farmer's Hotel.* New York: Random House, 1951.

—— *A Rage to Live.* New York: Random House, 1949.

Poe, Edgar Allen. *The Collected Works of....* Cambridge: Harvard University Press, 1978.

Porter, William Sydney (O. Henry). *The Four Million.* New York: McClure, Phillips, & Co., 1906.

Reed, John. *The Day in Bohemia.* New York: Hillacre, 1913.

Riis, Jacob. *How the Other Half Lives.* New York: Dover, 1971.

Roth, Henry. *Call It Sleep.* New York: Ballou, 1934.

Roth, Philip. *Goodbye, Columbus.* New York: Houghton, Mifflin, 1959.

Wharton, Edith. *The Age of Innocence.* New York: Scribner's, 1920.

——*The House of Mirth.* New York: Scribner's, 1905.

——*New Year's Day.* New York: Appleton, 1924.

Whitman, Walt. *The Complete Poems.* New York: Penguin, 1975.

Williams, William Carlos. *Paterson.* New York: New Directions, 1958.

NEW ENGLAND

Alcott, Bronson. *Concord Days.* Boston: Roberts Brothers, 1888.

Alther, Lisa. *Kinflicks.* New York: Alfred A. Knopf, 1976.

Botkin, B.A. *A Treasury of New England Folklore.* New York: Crown, 1947.

Bowen, Catherine Drinker. *Yankee From Olympus.* Boston: Little, Brown & Co., 1944.

Brooks, Van Wyck. *New England Indian Summer: 1865–1915.* New York: E.P. Dutton
    & Co., 1940.

——*A New England Reader.* New York: Atheneum, 1962.

——*A Chilmark Miscellany.* New York: E.P. Dutton, 1948.

——*Howells.* New York: Dutton, 1959.

——*Essays On America.* New York: E.P. Dutton & Co., 1970.

——*The Flowering of New England.* New York: E.P. Dutton & Co., 1952.

——*The Writer in America.* New York: Avon Books, 1953.

Chase, Mary Ellen. *A Goodly Heritage.* New York: MacMillan, 1939.

——*The White Gate.* New York: Norton, 1954.

——*A Goodly Fellowship.* New York: MacMillan, 1939.

Cheever, John. *The Stories of John Cheever.* New York: Knopf, 1979.

De Luna, Alice and Reik, Cynthia. *On Common Ground: A Selection of Hartford Writers.*
    Conn.: The Stowe-Day Foundation, 1975.

Dickinson, Emily. "Apparently with no surprise", in *The Complete Poems of....* (Thomas H.
    Johnson, ed.). Boston: Little Brown, 1960.

Edel, Leon. *Henry Thoreau.* Minneapolis: University of Minnesota Press, 1970.

Emerson, Ralph Waldo. *Selected Prose.* Boston: Houghton Mifflin, 1960.

Hale, Nancy, *The New England Discovery.* New York: Coward-McCann, Inc., 1963.

Hawthorne, Nathaniel. *The Marble Faun.* Boston: Houghton Mifflin, 1891.

——*The Blithedale Romance.* New York: Norton, 1978.

Howard, Leon. *The Connecticut Wits.* Chicago: University of Chicago Press, 1943.

Jewett, Sarah Orne. *Letters of Sarah Orne Jewett.* Houghton Mifflin Co., 1911.

——*The Country of the Pointed Firs.* Jonathan Caps, 1927.

Jones, Howard Mumford. *The Many Voices of Boston.* Boston: Little Brown, 1975.

Lowell, James Russell. "The Bigelow Papers", in *The Complete Writings of....* Boston:
    Houghton, Mifflin and Co., 1904.

Melville, Herman. *Moby Dick.* New York: Signet, 1963.

Miller, Perry, ed. *The American Puritans.* New York: MacMillan Co., 1956.

Morse, Samuel French. *Wallace Stevens.* New York: Pegasus, 1970.

Nutting, Wallace. *Connecticut Beautiful.* Framington, Mass.: Old America Co., 1923.

Schorer, Mark. *The Story.* New Jersey: Prentice-Hall, Inc., 1950.

Swift, Lindsay. *Brook Farm.* New York: National Studies in American Letters, 1904.

Thoreau, Henry David. *Walden and Civil Disobedience.* New York: Modern Library, 1937.

Warren, Austin. *The New England Conscience.* Ann Arbor: University of Michigan Press,
    1966.

Wharton, Edith. *Ethan Frome.* New York: Scribner Sons, 1911.

Whittier, John Greenleaf. "Snow-Bound," in *The Complete Poetical Works of....* Boston and
    New York: Houghton, Mifflin and Co., 1894.

THE MIDWEST

Anderson, Sherwood. *The Portable Sherwood Anderson:* ed. Horace Gregory; Hammonds-
    worth; Penguin, 1977.

Bennett, Arnold. "Books and Persons", in *The Evening Standard Years.* London: Chatto and
    Windus, 1974.

Bly, Robert. *Silence in the Snowy Fields.* Middletown, CT: Wesleyan University Press, 1953.

Bourjaily, Vance. *Now Playing at Canterbury*. New York: Ballantine Books, 1964.

Carter, William. *Middle West Country*. New York: Viking Press, 1976.

Cather, Willa. *O Pioneers!*. Boston: Houghton Mifflin, 1913.

Dell, Floyd. *Homecoming*. New York: Farrar and Rinehart, Inc., 1933.

——*Moon Calf*. New York: Sagamore Press, 1957.

Dickens, Charles. *The Works of....* New York: Crowell, 1904.

Dorn, Edward. *Selected Poems*. ed. Donald Allen. Bolinas, CA: Grey Fox Press, 1965.

Dreiser, Theodore. *Sister Carrie*. New York: Bantam, 1958.

——*The Titan*. New York: John Lane Co., 1914.

Eggleston, Edward. *The Hoosier Schoolmaster*. New York: Grosset and Dunlap, 1913.

Garland, Hamlin. *Main-Travelled Roads*. New York: Harper & Row, 1899.

——*Rose of Dutcher's Coolly*. Lincoln: University of Nebraska Press, 1969.

Gildner, Gary. *Nails*. Pittsburgh: University of Pittsburgh Press, 1975.

Grossman, Richard. *Tycoon Boy*. Santa Cruz, CA: Kayak, 1977.

Iowa: A Guide to the Hawkeye State: American Guide Series. New York: Hastings House, 1949.

LeSueur, Meridel. *North Star Country*. New York: Duell, Sloan and Pearce, 1945.

Lewis, Sinclair. *Main Street*. New York: Harcourt, Brace and World, 1920.

Lindsay, Vachel. *Earth Man and Star Thrower: Vachel Lindsay, His Adventures, Rhymes and Designs*. New York: Eakins Press, 1968.

——*Selected Poems of Vachel Lindsay*. Edited with an introduction by Mark Harris. New York: The McMillan Co., 1963.

Martineau, Harriet. *Autobiography of...*, edited by Maria Weston Chapman. Boston: J.R. Osgood & Co., 1877.

Masters, Edgar Lee. *Spoon River Anthology*. New York: Crowell-Collier Co., 1962.

McGrath, Thomas. *New and Selected Poems*, in *Heartland: Poets of the Midwest*, ed. Lucien Stryk. DeKalb: Northern Illinois University Press, 1967.

Morrison, Toni. *Sula*. New York: Knopf, 1973.

The Ohio Guide. Federal Writers Project. New York: Oxford University Press, 1940.

Reigelman, Milton. *The Midland: A Venture in Literary Regionalism*. Iowa City: University of Iowa Press, 1975.

Rexroth, Kenneth. *American Poetry in the Twentieth Century*. New York: Herder and Herder, 1971.

Sandburg, Carl. *Always the Young Strangers*. New York: Harcourt, Brace, 1952.

Strong, Phil. *Hawkeyes: A Biography of the State of Iowa*. New York: Dodd, Mead, 1940.

Sklar, Morty, ed. *The Actualist Anthology*. Iowa City: The Spirit That Moves Us Press, 1977.

Wood, Grant. *Revolt Against the City*. Iowa City: Whirling World, 1935.

Wright, James. *Shall We Gather at the River*. Middletown, CT: Wesleyan University Press, 1968.

——*The Branch Will Not Break*. Middletown, CT: Wesleyan University Press, 1963.

THE SOUTH & BORDER STATES

Agee, James. *A Death in the Family*. New York: Bantam, 1972.

Agee, James and Walker Evans. *Let Us Now Praise Famous Men*. New York: Ballantine Books, Inc., 1966.

Byrd, William. "History of the Dividing Line", in *The London Diary*. New York: Oxford University Press, 1958.

Caldwell, Erskine. *Tobacco Road*. New York: Little, Brown and Co., 1932.

Chesnutt, Charles. "The House Behind the Cedars", in *The Works of....* Boston: Houghton, Mifflin and Co., 1899.

Crane, Stephen. *The Open Boat*. New York, New American Library, 19

Dickey, James. *Poems 1957-1967*. Middletown, CT: Wesleyan University Press, 1967.

Dunbar, Paul Lawrence. "An Antebellum Sermon", in *The Complete Poems of....* New York: Dodd Mead, 1970.

Faulkner, William. *Collected Stories of....* New York: Random House, 1950.

Heyward, Dubose. *Porgy and Bess* in *Twenty-Five Best Plays of the Modern American Theatre: Early Series*, ed. John Gassner. New York: Crown, 1949.

Johnson, James Weldon. *God's Trombone*. New York: George Allen and Unwin, 1929.

Lanier, Sydney. *Marshes of Glynn*. Darien, GA: Ashantilly Press, 1963.

Lee, Harper. *To Kill a Mockingbird*. New York: Popular Library, 1960.

Longfellow, Henry Wadsworth. *The Slave in the Dismal Swamp*. Boston: Houghton, Mifflin and Co., 1904.

McCullers, Carson. *The Heart is a Lonely Hunter*. New York: Houghton Mifflin, 1967.

Stowe, Harriet Beecher. *Uncle Tom's Cabin*. Boston: J.P. Jewett & Co., 1852.

Warren, Robert Penn. *All the King's Men*. New York: Random House, 1953.

Welty, Eudora. *A Curtain of Green*. New York: Doubleday, Doran & Co., 1941.

Wolfe, Thomas. *Of Time and the River*. New York: Charles Scribner's Sons, 1935.

Wright, Richard. *Black Boy*. New York: World Publishing Co., 1945.

MOUNTAIN STATES & THE SOUTHWEST

Arnold, Lloyd. *High on the Wild with Hemingway*. Caldwell, Idaho: Caxton Printers, 1969.

Baker, Carlos. *Ernest Hemingway: A Life Story*. New York: Charles Scribner's Sons, 1969.

Bird, Isabella. *A Lady's Life in the Rocky Mountains*. Norman, OK: University of Oklahoma Press, 1960.

Brown, E.K. *Willa Cather: A Critical Biography*. New York: Alfred Knopf, 1953.

Cather, Willa. *Death Comes for the Archbishop*. New York: Alfred Knopf, 1927.

Clark, Walter Van Tilburg. *The Ox-Box Incident*. New York: Random House, 1940.

——*The Track of the Cat*. New York: Random House, 1949.

Clemens, Samuel L. *Roughing It*. New York: Harper & Brothers, 1871.

Day, A. Grove. *James A. Michener*. New York: Twayne Publishers, 1977.

Duncan, Charles, ed. *Horace Greeley: An Overland Journey from New York to San Francisco in the Summer of 1859*. New York: Alfred Knopf, 1964.

Ferber, Edna. *Cimarron*. New York: Doubleday, 1930.

——*Giant*. New York: Doubleday, 1952.

Ferril, Thomas Hornsby. *New and Selected Poems*. New York: Harper & Brothers, 1952.

Flora, Joseph. *Vardis Fisher*. New York: Twayne Publishers, 1965.

Foster, Joseph. *D.H. Lawrence in Taos*. Albuquerque: University of New Mexico Press, 1972.

Gilbert, Julie Goldsmith. *Ferber: A Biography*. New York: Doubleday, 1978.

Grey, Zane. *Riders of the Purple Sage*. New York: Harper & Brothers, 1912.

Gruber, Frank. *Zane Grey: A Biography*. New York: World Publishing Co., 1970.

Guthrie, A.B. *The Big Sky*. New York: Sloane and Associates, 1947.

——*The Way West*. New York: Sloane and Associates, 1949.

Guthrie, Woodrow Wilson. *Bound for Glory*. New York: E.P. Dutton, 1943.

Haslan, Gerald, ed. *Western Writing*. Albuquerque: University of New Mexico Press, 1974.

Hemingway, Ernest. *The Short Stories of Ernest Hemingway*. New York: Charles Scribner's Sons, 1955.

Herzberg, Max J. *The Reader's Encyclopedia of American Literature*. New York: Thomas Y. Crowell, 1962.

Holland, Vyvyan. *Oscar Wilde and his World*. New York: Charles Scribner's Sons, 1960.

Horgan, Paul. *Far from Cibola*. New York: Harper & Brothers, 1936.

Kings, John. *In Search of Centennial*. New York: Random House, 1975.

Kronenberger, Louis. *Oscar Wilde*. Boston: Little, Brown, 1976.

La Farge, Oliver. *Laughing Boy*. New York: Houghton, 1929.

——*The Enemy Gods*. Albuquerque: University of New Mexico Press, 1975.

Lawrence, D.H. *The Plumed Serpent*. New York: Alfred Knopf, 1926.

McMurtry, Larry. *Horseman, Pass By*. New York: Harper & Brothers, 1961.

Michener, James. *Centennial*. New York: Random House, 1974.

Monoghan, James, *The Great Rascal: The Life and Adventures of Ned Buntline*. Boston: Little, Brown, 1952.

Moore, Harry T. *The Priest of Love: A Life of D.H. Lawrence*. New York: Farrar, Strauss & Giroux, 1974.

Pearce, T. M. *Oliver La Farge*. New York: Twayne Publishers, 1972.

Peavy, Charles. *Larry McMurtry*. New York: Twayne Publishers, 1977.

Trusky, A. *Thomas Hornsby Ferril.* Boise, ID: Boise State College Press, 1973.
Vorpahl, Ben, ed. *My Dear Wister: THE FREDERICK REMINGTON-OWEN WISTER LETTERS.* Palo Alto, CA: American West Publishing, 1972.
Westbrook, Max. *Walter Van Tilburg Clark.* New York: Twayne Publishers, 1969.

CALIFORNIA & THE FAR WEST

Austin, Mary. *The Land of Little Rain.* New York: Houghton, Mifflin and Co., 1904.
Chandler, Raymond. *Raymond Chandler Omnibus.* New York: Knopf, 1964.
——*The Long Goodbye.* New York: Ballantine, 1977.
Clemens, Samuel. *Roughing It.* New York: New American Library, 1962.
Dana, Richard Henry. *Two Years Before the Mast.* New York: Dutton, 1969.
de Angulo, Jaime. *Indian Tales.* New York: Hill and Wang, 1962.
Didion, Joan. *Play It As It Lays.* New York: Farrar, Strauss and Giroux, 1970.
——*Slouching Towards Bethlehem.* New York: Farrar, Strauss and Giroux, 1968.
——*The White Album.* New York: Simon and Schuster, 1979.
Everson, William. *Archetype West.* Berkeley: Oyez, 1976.
——*Man-Fate.* New York: New Direction, 1974.
——*The Masks of Drought.* Santa Barbara, Calif: Black Sparrow, 1980.
——*The Residual Years. New York: New Directions, 1968.*
——*River Root.* Berkeley: Oyez, 1976.
——*The Veritable Years.* Santa Barbara, Calif: Black Sparrow, 1978.
Hammett, Dashiell. *The Continental Op.* New York: Random House, 1975.
Harte, Bret. *Outcasts of Poker Flat.* New York: New American Library, 1961.
Huxley, Aldous. *After Many a Summer Dies the Swan.* New York: Harper and Row, 1965.
——*Ape and Essence.* New York: Harper and Row, 1972.
Jeffers, Robinson. *Selected Poems.* New York: Random House, 1938.
——*Roan Stallion, Tamar, and Other Poems.* New York: Random House, 1925.
Kerouac, Jack. *The Dharma Bums.* New York: New American Library, 1959.
Kesey, Ken. *One Flew Over the Cuckoo's Nest.* New York: Penguin, 1976.
——*Sometimes a Great Notion.* New York: Penguin, 1977.
King, Clarence. *Mountaineering in the Sierra Nevada.* Lincoln, Neb: University of Nebraska Press, 1970.
LeGuin, Ursula K. *The Lathe of Heaven.* New York: Avon, 1973.
London, Jack. *The Call of the Wild.* New York: Penguin, 1980.
——*Martin Eden.* New York: Macmillan, 1957.
——*The Valley of the Moon.* Layton, Utah: Peregrine Smith, 1978.
Macdonald, Ross. *The Blue Hammer.* New York: Knopf, 1976.
——*The Galton Case.* New York: Bantam, 1959.
McClure, Michael. *Ghost Tantras.* Bolinas, Calif: Four Seasons Foundation, 1969.
Miller, Joaquin. *Unwritten History: Life Among the Modocs.* Eugene, Oregon, Urion Press, 1972. (variant title: *Life Amongst the Modocs.*)
Muir, John. *The Mountains of California.* New York: The Century Co., 1911.
Norris, Frank. *McTeague.* New York: New American Library, 1964.
——*The Octopus.* New York: New American Library, 1964.
Powell, Lawrence Clark. *California Classics.* Los Angeles: Ward Ritchie Press, 1971.
Rexroth, Kenneth. *The Alternative Society.* New York: Herder and Herder, 1970.
——*Assays.* New York: New Directions, 1961.
——*Bird in the Bush.* New York: New Directions, 1959.
——*The Collected Longer Poems.* New York: New Directions, 1968.
Saroyan, William. *The Daring Young Man on the Flying Trapeze.* New York: Random House, 1934.
——*My Name Is Aram.* New York: Dell, 1966.

Snyder, Gary. *Myths and Texts*. New York: New Directions, 1978.
—— *The Old Ways*. San Francisco: City Lights, 1977.
Steinbeck, John. *The Grapes of Wrath*. New York: Penguin, 1972.
—— *East of Eden*. New York: Penguin, 1979.
—— *The Red Pony*. New York: Viking, 1959.
—— *Tortilla Flat*. New York: Penguin, 1977.
Weil, Simone. "The Next World War", *International Review*, III, 1, 1938.
West, Nathaniel. *The Day of the Locust*. New York: New Directions, 1962.

FURTHER SUGGESTED READING

Deedy, John. *Literary Places: A Guided Pilgrimage*. Kansas City: Sheed Andrews and McNeal, Inc., 1978.
Edmiston, Susan and Linda Cirino. *Literary New York*. Boston: Houghton Mifflin, 1976.
Harting, Emile C. *A Literary Tour Guide to the United States: Northeast*. New York: William Morrow and Company, Inc., 1978.
Scherman, David E. and Rosemarie Redlich. *Literary America*. New York: Dodd, Mead & Company, 1952.
Stein, Rita. *A Literary Tour Guide to the United States: South and Southwest*. New York: William Morrow and Company, Inc., 1979.
—— *A Literary Tour Guide to the United States: West and Midwest*. New York: William Morrow and Company, Inc., 1979.
Thum, Marcella. *Exploring Literary America*. New York: Atheneum, 1979.

ACKNOWLEDGEMENTS

Lisa Alther, *Kinflicks*, pp. 280, 281. Copyright © 1976 by Alfred A. Knopf, Inc.

Abraham Cahan, *The Rise of David Levinsky*, p. 147. Copyright © 1917 by Harper & Row Publishers Inc.

Sherwood Anderson, *Poor White*. Reprinted by permission of Harold Ober Associates Inc. Copyright © 1920 by Eleanor Copenhaver Anderson. Renewed.

Erskine Caldwell, *Tobacco Road*, pp. 71, 72. Copyright © 1932, 1940 by Erskine Caldwell. Copyright renewed, effective 1959, © by Erskine Caldwell. Reprinted by permission of McIntosh and Otis, Inc.

Willa Cather, *O Pioneers!* Copyright © 1913 by Houghton Mifflin Co.

Excerpted from "what if a much of a which of a wind" from COMPLETE POEMS 1913-1962 by E.E. Cummings by permission of Harcourt Brace Jovanovich, Inc. Copyright © 1944 by E.E. Cummings: renewed 1972 by Nancy T. Andrews.

Joan Didion, *Play It As It Lays*, pp. 13, 14. Copyright © 1970 by Farrar, Straus & Giroux, Inc.

Theodore Dreiser, *The Titan*. Copyright © 1925 by Theodore Dreiser. Reprinted by permission of THE DREISER TRUST.

William Faulkner, *Collected Stories of William Faulkner*, pp. 119, 120. Copyright © 1950 by Random House.

Hamlin Garland, *Main-Travelled Roads*. Copyright © 1962 by The New American Library.

Hamlin Garland, *Rose of Dutcher's Coolly*. Copyright © 1969 by University of Nebraska Press, Bison Book.

Allen Ginsberg, *Howl*, p. 17. Copyright © 1956, 1959 by Allen Ginsberg. Reprinted by permission of CITY LIGHTS BOOKS.

Allen Ginsberg, *Reality Sandwiches*, p. 77. Copyright © 1963, 1966 by Allen Ginsberg. Reprinted by permission of CITY LIGHTS BOOKS.

From "The Whosis Kid" and "The Girl with the Silver Eyes" from *The Continental Op* by Dashiell Hammett. Copyright © 1925, 1924 by Dashiell Hammett. Copyright renewed 1953, 1952 by Dashiell Hammett. Reprinted by permission of the Harold Matson Company, Inc.

Langston Hughes, *The Big Sea*, p. 247. Alfred A. Knopf, Publishers. Reprinted by permission of Harold Ober Associates Inc. Copyright © 1940, 1963 by Langston Hughes.

Langston Hughes, *The Weary Blues*, p. 23, 32, 39. 103. Copyright © 1926 by Alfred A. Knopf, Inc.

From *After A Summer Dies Many A Swan* by Aldous Huxley. By permission of Mrs. Laura Huxley and Chatto and Windus Ltd.

From *Roan Stallion, Tamar and Other Poems* by Robinson Jeffers. New York: Random House 1925.

From *Sometimes A Great Notion* by Ken Kesey. Copyright © 1963, 1964 by Ken Kesey. Reprinted by permission of Viking Penguin Inc.

From *To Kill A Mockingbird* by Harper Lee (J.B. Lippincott). Copyright © Harper Lee.

Ursula K. LeGuin, *The Lathe of Heaven*, pp. 26, 167. Copyright © 1971 by Charles Scribner's Sons.

From *Main Street* by Sinclair Lewis, copyright © 1920 by Harcourt Brace Jovanovich, Inc.; copyright © 1948 by Sinclair Lewis. Reprinted by permission of the publisher.

Edgar Lee Masters, "Lucius Atherton", "Dorcas Gustine", "Fiddler Jones", from *Spoon River Anthology*. Macmillan Publishers. Reprinted by permission of Ellen C. Masters. Copyright © 1962 by Ellen C. Masters.

From *The Blue Hammer* by Ross Macdonald. New York: Alfred A. Knopf, 1976.

Michael McClure, *Ghost Tantras*. Four Seasons Foundation. Reprinted by permission of Michael McClure. Copyright © 1969 by Michael McClure.

Carson McCullers, *The Heart Is a Lonely Hunter*, p. 5. Copyright © 1967 by Houghton Mifflin Co.

Thomas McGrath, "Ah...to the Villages!" in *Heartland: Poets of the Midwest*, ed. Lucien Stryk, p. 128 © 1967. Reprinted by permission of Northern Illinois University Press.

H.L. Mencken, *Happy Days 1880-1892*, pp. 8, 9. Copyright © 1940 by Alfred A. Knopf, Inc.

Toni Morrison, *Sula*, p. 3. Copyright © 1973 by Alfred A. Knopf, Inc.

Quarto would like to thank Julie Guibord (picture research); Donna Sturm (map research); Randall Lieu (map illustration); and Eileen Friedman (bibliographic research).

INDEX

A

Adams, Ansel, *204*, 205
Adams, Franklin P. (F.P.A.), 36–37, *37*, 40, 41
After Many a Summer Dies the Swan
  (Huxley), 221–222
Agee, James, 156–158, 221
Age of Innocence, The (Wharton), 10
Alabama, 148
Alcott, Bronson, 67, 68, 74, 76–77
Alcott, Louisa May, 74, 76–77
Aldrich, Thomas Bailey, 58–59
All the King's Men (Warren), 155–156
Alther, Lisa, 60
Amherst, MA, 63
Anderson, Sherwood, 26, 50, 59, 87, 89, 98,
  105, 109, 116, *117*, 118, 119, 122, 151
Ape and Essence (Huxley), 221, 222
Appeal (Walker), 134
Asheville, NC, 136–137
Austin, Mary, 206–207, 211
Autobiography (Franklin), 47–48
Autobiography of an Ex-Colored Man, The
  (Johnson), 28, 147

B

Babbitt (Lewis), 87
Baltimore, MD, 49–50
Barlow, Joel, 84–85
Bayou Folk (Chopin), 153
Benchley, Robert, 36, 37, 38, 39, 41
Benton's Row (Yerby), 146
Berkshire Mountains (MA), 60–61
Bigelow Papers (Lowell), 65–66
Bird, Isabella, 186–188
Black Boy (Wright), 150–151
Boston, MA, 78–81
Bound East for Cardiff (O'Neill), 22
Bowery, The, *24*
"Bridge, The" (Crane), 26
Bronx, The, NY, 4–5
Brooklyn, NY, 6
Broun, Heywood, 18, 36, 67, 41
Bryant, William Cullen, 60, 62, 65
Buffalo Bill. *See* Cody, Bill
Buntline, Ned. *See* Judson, Edward Zane
  Carrol
Burroughs, William, 43, 45
Byrd, William, 135–136

C

Cahan, Abraham, 14, 16
Caldwell, Erskine, 124, 144–145
California, 193–202
  map of, *194*

California Gold Rush, 196–197, 199
Call It Sleep (Roth), 14–15
Call of the Wild, The (London), 210
Cambridge, MA, 64–71
Cane (Toomer), 144
Captains Courageous (Kipling), 72–73
Carmel, CA, 206, 211–212
Cather, Willa, 46, 80, 89, 102, 106–107, 123,
  171–172
Centennial (Michener), 190–192
Chandler, Raymond, 218, 223, 231, 232
Charleston (SC) School, 137–138, 140
Charleston, SC, 137–141, *138*
Cheever, John, 41, 81
Chesnutt, Charles, 136
Chicago, IL, 102–105, *103*
Chicago Renaissance, 105–107, 122
Chopin, Kate, 153
Cimmaron (Ferber), 176–177, 178
Cincinnati, OH, 93–98, *94*, 97, 108
Clark, Walter Van Tilburg, 184–185
Clemens, Samuel, 12, 83, 98, 182–184,
  198–199, 201, 202
Cody, Bill, 160–162, *161*
Colorado, 185–192
Color of a Great City, The (Dreiser), 25
Concord, MA, 74–78, 117
  map of, *75*
Confessions of Nat Turner (Styron), 134
Conjure Woman, The (Chesnutt), 136
Continental Op (Hammett), 217, 218
Connecticut, 83–86
Connelly, Marc, 37, 38, 40
Cooper, James Fenimore, 3–4
Corso, Gregory, 43, 44, 226
Country of Pointed Firs, A (Jewett), 58
Couples (Updike), 73
Crane, Hart, 25, 26–27
Crane, Stephen, 12–13, 147
Crockett, Davy, 153–154, *154*
Cummings, E.E., 65, 70

D

Dana, Richard Henry, 65, 80, 193–196, 198,
  203, 217, 219
Daring Young Man on the Flying Trapeze,
  The (Saroyan), 215–216
Davenport, IA, 106, 107–108, 110
Davenport, Marcia, 41–42
Day of the Locust, The (West), 219–221, *220*
"Dead Village, The" (Robinson), 55–57
Death Comes for the Archbishop (Cather),
  172
Death in the Family, A (Agee), 157–158
Deliverance (Dickey), 140

Dell, Floyd, 18, 19, 21, 22, 30, 105–108, 113–114, 120
Denver, CO, 185–186
Diary (Sewall), 80
Dickey, James, 140–141
Dickinson, Emily, 63–64
Dickinson, Jonathan, 146
Didion, Joan, 219, 229–230, 231–232, 233
Dismal Swamp, VA, 134, *135*
Dodge, Mabel. *See* Luhan, Mabel Dodge
Domestic Manners of the Americans (Trollope), 85–96
Dos Passos, John, 25–26, 42
Dred (Stowe), 134
Dreiser, Theodore, 23–25, 49, 50, 98, 103–105, 120
Du Bois, W.E.B., 27–28, 32
Dunbar, Paul Lawrence, 132–133
Duncan, Robert, 225–226

E

Eastman, Max, 18, 19, 30
East Side, West Side (Davenport), 41–42
Eggleston, Edward, 98–99, 100
Emerson, Ralph Waldo, 54, 60, 65, 67, 68, 69–70, 74, 77, 78, 80
Evangeline (Longfellow), 153
Evans, Walker, 156–157
Everson, William, 225, 226

F

Far From Cibola (Horgan), 169
Faulkner, William, 59, 151–152, 221
Ferber, Edna, 36, 37, 40, 41, 175–178
Ferlinghetti, Lawrence, 225, 226
Ferril, Thomas Hornsby, 189–190
Few Figs from Thistles, A (Millay), 21
Fisher, Vardis, 180–182
Fitzgerald, F. Scott, 221
Florida, 146–147
Four Million, The (Porter), 13
Franklin, Benjamin, 47–48, *47*, 79
Frost, Robert, 59–60, 65
Fuller, Margaret, 67–68, 74

G

Garland, Hamlin, 12, 13, 87, 89, 100–103, 109–110, 122, 125
Georgia, 141–146
Giant (Ferber), 175–176
Ginsberg, Allen, 42, 43, 44–45, 217, 225, 226
Glaspell, Susan, 21, 22, 81
Gloucester, MA, 72–73
God's Protecting Providence (J. Dickinson), 146
Gone with the Wind (Mitchell), 131–132, 145

Goodbye, Columbus (Roth), 45
"Good Man is Hard to Find, A" (O'Connor), 143–144
Grapes of Wrath, The (Steinbeck), 215
Greeley, Horace, 11, 185–186
Greenwich Village, NY, 5, 7, 17, 18, 19, 21, 25, 30
map of, *20*
Grey, Zane, 165–168
Guthrie, A.B., 180
Guthrie, Woody, 178–179

H

Hammett, Dashiell, 217–218, 231
Harlem, NY, 27–35
Harlem Renaissance, 27–35
Harlem Shadows (McKay), 29–30
Harris, Joel Chandler, 145
Harte, Bret, 74, 196–198, 199, 200, 201, 202
Hartford, CT, 84–86
Harvard University, 64–65, *65*
Hasty Pudding (Barlow), 84–85
Haverhill, MA, 73–74
Hawthorne, Nathaniel, 51–53, 55, 60–61, 68, 74, 77–78, 80–81, 153
Heart is a Lonely Hunter, The (McCullers), 141–143
Hemingway, Ernest, 182
Henry, O. *See* Porter, William Sydney
Heritage of the Desert, The (Grey), 167
Heyward, DuBose, 138–139
Heywood, Big Bill, 17, 18, 88
History of the Dividing Line (Byrd), 135–136
History of New York (Irving), 2

J

James, Henry, 7–9, 13–14, 17, 26, 60, 65, 74, 79, 82
Jamestown, VA, 133
Jeffers, Robinson, 200, 202, 212–213, 216, 227, 233
Jefferson, Thomas, 1, 10, 133
Jesuit Relations (Nicollet), 89–91
Jewett, Sarah Orne, 58, 80
Johnson, James Weldon, 28, 147
Judson, Edward Zane Carrol, 159–162

K

Kaufman, George S., 36, 37, *37*, 38, 40, 41
Kerouac, Jack, 42, 43, 44, 45, 225, 226, 229
Kesey, Ken, 229–230, 232, 233
Ketchum, Idaho, 182
Kinflicks (Alther), 60
King, Clarence, 202–204, 205
Kipling, Rudyard, 72–73

L

Lady's Life in the Rocky Mountains, A
  (Bird), 186–187
La Farge, Oliver, 173–174
Land of Little Rain (Austin), 206–207
Last Tycoon, The (Fitzgerald), 221
Late George Apley, The (Marquand), 79
Lathe of Heaven, The (LeGuin), 230,
  232–233
Laughing Boy (La Farge), 173–174
Lawrence, D.H., 169–171
Lawrence, Frieda, 170–171
Leadville, CO, 188–189
Lee, Harper, 148
LeGuin, Ursula K., 229–230, 232–233
LeSueur, Meridel, 92, 121, 123
Let Us Now Praise Famous Men (Agee),
  156–157
Lewis, Sinclair, 50, 87, 106, 109–110, 116,
  117, 122, 125
Life Amongst the Modocs (Miller), 201–202
Lindsay, Vachel, 98, 105, 106, 109, 114–116,
  117, 120, 122, 128
London, Jack, 202, 209–211
Longfellow, Henry Wadsworth, 64, 65, 67,
  82–83, 134, 153
Look Homeward, Angel (Wolfe), 136–137
Los Angeles, CA, 219–224
Louisiana, 90
Lowell, James Russell, 65–66, 67, 80
Lower East Side, NY, 10, 13, 14–15, 43
"Luck of Roaring Camp, The" (Harte), 197,
  198
Luhan, Mabel, Dodge, 17, 18, 19, 169–171

M

Macdonald, Ross, 218, 223–224
Maggie: A Girl of the Streets (Crane), 13
Mailer, Norman, 42–43
Main Street (Lewis), 87, 109, 116
Main-Travelled Roads (Garland), 87,
  101–102, 126
Manhattan Transfer (Dos Passos), 25–26
Marquand, J.P., 65, 79
Marquette, Jacques, 90–92
Martin Eden (London), 209–211, 212
Masses, The (journal), 18, 19, 30
Masters, Edgar Lee, 87, 105, 109, 110,
  112–113, 116, 117, 122, 126
McClure, Michael, 225–226
McCullers, Carson, 141–143
McKay, Claude, 28–30
McMurtry, Larry, 179–180
McTeague (Norris), 207–208, 210, 211
Melville, Herman, 5–6, 5, 51, 52, 53–54,
  60–61, 81, 82

Mencken, H.L., 49–50
Michener, James, 190–192
Midwest
  map of, 111
Millay, Edna St. Vincent, 21, 22, 55
Miller, Joaquin, 199–202, 213, 232
Mississippi, 149–152
Mississippi River, 90–92
Mitchell, Margaret, 131–132
Moby Dick (Melville), 52, 53–54, 61, 82
Montana, 180
Morrison, Toni, 127–128
Mosses from an Old Manse (Hawthorne), 77
Mountain States
  map of, 176
Mountaineering in the Sierra Nevada
  (King), 202
Mountains of California, The (Muir),
  204–205
Muir, John, 202, 204–206, 204, 211, 227
My Name is Aram (Saroyan), 216–217

N

Nevada, 182–185
Newark, NJ, 45, 46
New Mexico, 168–174
New Orleans, LA, 152–153
Newport, RI, 82–83
New Yorker, The, 39–40, 41
Nicollet, Jean, 89–91
Norris, Frank, 12, 17, 23–24, 65, 202,
  207–209, 210
North Carolina, 135–137
North Star Country (Le Sueur), 92, 121, 124

O

O'Connor, Flannery, 143–144, 152
Octopus, The (Norris), 208–209
Of Time and the River (Wolfe), 137
O'Hara, Frank, 44, 45
O'Hara, John, 48
Ohio River, 93–94, 99
Oklahoma, 178
One Flew Over the Cuckoo's Nest (Kesey),
  230
O'Neill, Eugene, 22–23, 79, 81, 83–84
On the Road (Kerouac), 44
"Open Boat, The" (Crane), 147
Oregon, 230, 232–233
"Outcasts of Poker Flat, The" (Harte),
  197–198
Ox-Bow Incident, The (Clark), 184–185
Oxford, MS, 151

P

Parker, Dorothy, 36, 37, 38–39, 40–41
Paterson (Williams), 46

Paterson, NJ, 46, 117
"Paul's Case" (Cather), 46
Philadelphia, PA, 47–48
Pittsburgh, PA, 49
Placerville, CA, 197
Play It As It Lays (Didion), 230, 231
Plumed Serpent, The (Lawrence), 171
Poe, Edgar Allan, 4–5, 79, 141
Poor Richard's Almanack (Franklin), 48
Porgy (Heyward), 138–139
Porter, William Sydney, 13–14
Portland, OR, 232–233
Portnoy's Complaint (Roth), 45–46
Provincetown, MA, 81, 83
Provincetown Players, 21–23
Puritanism, 51–52, 63, 64

R

Red Pony, The (Steinbeck), 213–215
Reed, John, 17–19, 21, 22, 23, 30
Remington, Frederick, 164–165
Rexroth, Kenneth, 93, 225, 226–227
Rhode Island, 82
Riis, Jacob, 11–12, *14*, 16, 25
Rise of Silas Lapham, The (Howells), 12, 79
Robinson, Edward Arlington, 55–57
"Rose for Emily, A" (Faulkner), 152
Ross, Harold, 39–40, 41
Roswell, NM, 168, 169
Roth, Henry, 14–15
Roth, Philip, 45–46
Roughing It (Clemens), 183, 199
Round Table, the, 36, 37, 38–39, 40–41

S

Salem, MA, 71–72
Salinas Valley, CA, 213
Salmagundi (Irving), 2
Sandburg, Carl, 105, 108–109, 112, 114, 120, 122, 136
San Francisco, CA, 17, 198–201, 200–201, 217–218
    map of, *228*
San Francisco Renaissance, 226–229
Santa Barbara, CA, 224
Santa Fe, NM, 169, 170, 173, 174
Saroyan, William, 215–217
Scarlet Letter, The (Hawthorne), 71–72, 80
Serpent Mound of the Adena, the, 88, 88–89
Sewall, Samuel, 80
"Sheep Child, The" (Dickey), 140–141
Sherwood, Robert E., 36, 37, 38, 40, 41
Sinclair, Upton, 79–80, 211
Sister Carrie (Dreiser), 23–25
Small Boy and Others, A (James), 7–8
Smith, John, 133

Snyder, Gary, 226, 227–229, 233
Sometimes a Great Notion (Kesey), 232
South, the
    map of, *142*
South Carolina, 137–141
Spoon River Anthology (Masters), 87, 112–113
Steffens, Lincoln, 16–18, 19, 25
Steinbeck, John, 175, 213–215
Sterling, George, 211–212, 213
Stevens, Wallace, 65, 83, 85–86
St. Mawr (Lawrence), 171
Story of a Bad Boy, The (Aldrich), 59
Stowe, Harriet Beecher, 57–58, 83, 130–131, 134, 146
Styron, William, 134
Sula (Morrison), 127–128

T

Tales of Uncle Remus (Harris), 145
Taos, NM, 169, 173
Taylor, Edward, 62–63, 64
Ten Days That Shook the World (Reed), 19
Tennessee, 153–158
Testament of Man (Fisher), 181–182
Texas, 175–176
Thoreau, Henry David, 54–55, 60, 65, 74–76, 117
Titan, The (Dreiser), 103–105
Tobacco Road (Caldwell), 144–145
To Kill a Mockingbird (Lee), 148
Toomer, Jean, 144
Track of the Cat, The (Clark), 184, 185
Trollope, Frances, 95–96
Twain, Mark. *See* Clemens, Samuel
Two Years Before the Mast (Dana), 193–196

U

Uncle Tom's Cabin (Stowe), 57, 130–131
"Under the Lion's Paw" (Garland), 100–101
Updike, John, 48–49, 73, 81

V

Valley of the Moon, The (London), 210–211
Vermont, 60
Virginia, 133–135
Virginian, The (Wister), 159, 163, 166, 168

W

Walden (Thoreau), 54–55, 60, 74–76
Walker, David, 134
Warren, Robert Penn, 152, 155–156
Washington, Booker T., 27, 132
Washington Square (James), 8–9
Weary Blues, The (Hughes), 33
Welty, Eudora, 149–150
Wescott, Glenway, 87, 109

West, Nathaniel, 219–221, 232
Wharton, Edith, 9–10, 17, 60
Whitman, Walt, 6–7, 6, 30, 43, 74
White Album, The (Didion), 230, 231
White, William Allen, 176–177
Whittier, John Greenleaf, 65, 73–74
Wilde, Oscar, 188–189
Williams, Tennessee, 149
Williams, William Carlos, 43, 46, 117
Winesburg, Ohio (Anderson), 87
Winslow, AZ, 173
Wister, Owen, 159, 162–165
Wolfe, Thomas, 65, 136–137, 181
Woollcott, Alexander, 35–36, 37, 40–41
Wright, James, 98, 125
Wright, Richard, 35, 150–151

Y

Yerby, Frank, 146
Young Goodman Brown (Hawthorne),
  52–53